WALKING ON MALTA

by Paddy Dillon

2 POLICE SQUARE, MILNTHORPE, CUMBRIA LA7 7PY
www.cicerone.co.uk

Third edition 2016
ISBN-13:978 1 85284 822 4

First edition 2007
ISBN-10: 1 85284 422 1
ISBN-13: 978 1 85284 422 6
Second edition 2012
ISBN-13: 978 1 85284 719 7

Printed in China on behalf of Latitude Press Ltd
A catalogue record for this book is available from the British Library.
All photographs are by the author unless otherwise stated.

The maps in this guide are based on the 1:25,000 Maltese Government maps, and have been reproduced with the permission of the Ministry for Resources and Infrastructure, Malta.

While eve … cy of
guidebook … etime
of an editi … n the
Cicerone … check
before pla … about
such thing … hts of
way can b … about
any discre … , sent
by email t … uare,
Milnthorp

Front cover: Marsaxlokk harbour and traditional fishing boats (Walk 3)

CONTENTS

Emergency Assistance

Malta has adopted the standard European emergency number of **112**. Use this to call for the police, ambulance or fire service. There are also two other numbers for specific rescue requests, handled by the Armed Forces of Malta: to call for a rescue **patrol boat**, tel 2123 8797, and to call for a rescue **helicopter**, tel 2124 4371. Whatever the nature of the emergency, be ready to give full details of the incident and stay in contact to await further instructions. Mobile phone coverage is generally excellent around Malta and Gozo, but signals can be blocked near cliffs or in deep valleys. Check with your network provider about roaming and charges.

There are both public and private hospitals and health centres, as well as abundant pharmacies. Malta has a reciprocal health agreement with the United Kingdom, which is useful to know if hospitalisation is required. However, it's wise to take out appropriate insurance and to carry a European Health Insurance Card, as not all treatments or medication may be provided free of charge.

Map Key

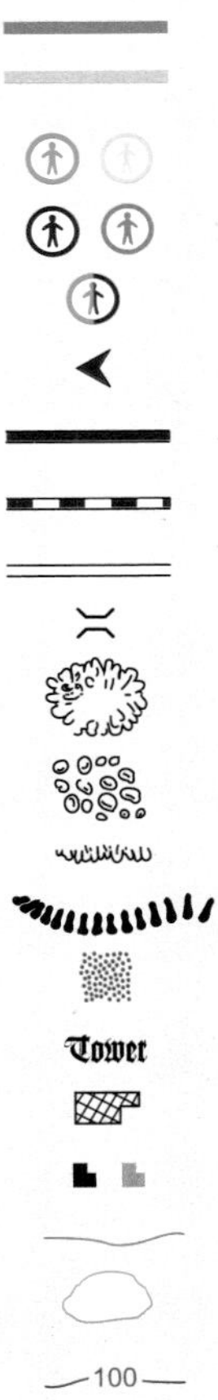

	route
	alternative route
	start/alternative point
	finish/alternative finish point
	start/finish point
	route direction
	main road
	secondary road
	minor road and car park
	bridge
	quarry
	boulder rocks
	cliff
	steep slope
	sand and mud
Tower	antiquity
	factory
	named building, other building
	river
	pond
100	contour (25ft)

Route map scale: 1:25,000

GPX files

GPX files for all routes can be downloaded for free at www.cicerone.co.uk/822/GPX

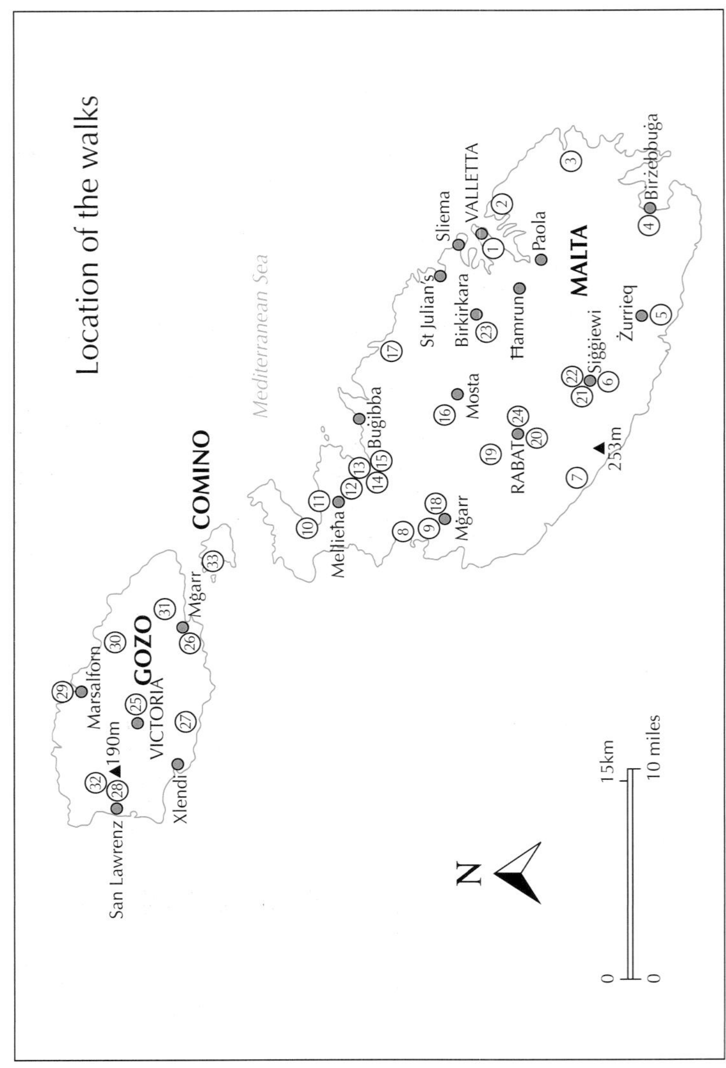
Location of the walks
Mediterranean Sea
GOZO
COMINO
MALTA
San Lawrenz
Xlendi
VICTORIA
190m
Marsalforn
Mġarr
Mellieħa
Mġarr
Buġibba
RABAT
253m
Mosta
St Julian's
Sliema
VALLETTA
Birkirkara
Ħamrun
Paola
Siġġiewi
Żurrieq
Birżebbuġa
1
2
3
4
5
6
7
8
9
10
11
12
13
14
15
16
17
18
19
20
21
22
23
24
25
26
27
28
29
30
31
32
33
N
0
15km
0
10 miles

INTRODUCTION

The shattered headland of Għemieri with Gozo seen far beyond (Walk 33)

The Maltese islands of Malta, Gozo and Comino bask in sunshine at the heart of the Mediterranean, between Europe and Africa, the Christian and Muslim world, on busy shipping lanes running north, south, east and west. Sicily is Malta's nearest neighbour, followed by Tunisia and Libya. History has ensured that the islands have been colonised time and time again in the name of trade, warfare, politics and religion, leaving them with a colourful and complex history and heritage, and defended by all kinds of fortifications. It is reputedly the most bombed country in the world. The islanders take a fierce pride in the independence won just over 50 years ago in 1964, and summertime seems to be an endless round of festivals and fireworks. The Maltese islands are a popular tourist destination. They offer plenty of historic walks, stunningly beautiful and dramatic architecture, and a surprising amount of excellent scenery away from the urban sprawl, especially around their cliff coastlines.

LOCATION AND POPULATION

The islands of Malta, Gozo and Comino lie between 14°12' to 14°25'E and 35°48' to 36°05'N, approximately 95km (60 miles) south of Sicily and 290km (180 miles) from Tunisia and Libya. The combined area

Looking along the rough and rocky coast from near Għar Lapsi (Walk 5)

of the islands is only around 315km^2 (122 square miles) – about the same size as the Isle of Wight – but the population is around 400,000, compared with around 30,000 for the Isle of Wight. In fact, Malta is one of the most densely populated micro-states in the world, and there are over a million visiting tourists per year, mostly from sun-starved northern Europe!

GEOLOGY AND LANDSCAPE

In simple terms, the Maltese islands are part of the floor of the Mediterranean that crumpled upwards as the continental plates carrying Africa and Europe slowly crushed together. The forces unleashed are evident further north around the hot-spot Sicilian and Italian volcanoes of Etna and Vesuvius, as well as in the occasional earthquakes that shake the area. These forces have buckled and broken the Maltese bedrock so that it is severed by a number of fault lines. However, the basic geology is fairly simple, and the rocks seen on the island date only from the past 30 million years.

There are five main layers of rock which make up these islands and they always occur in the same order, or succession. The bottom layer is a thick, hard bed of **Lower Coralline Limestone**. This is the most stable rock in the entire succession. On top of it lies a thick layer of softer **Globigerina Limestone**, which is reasonably durable but crumbles easily when exposed to the weather. This rock can be cut to any shape and is found in buildings throughout the islands. Next up is a thick layer of **Blue Clay**, which crumbles easily wherever it is exposed, breaking down to form a particularly fertile soil. A thin layer of **Greensand** lies on top of the clay, which is often so easily weathered that it forms a pronounced undercut notch on steep slopes. The top layer of rock on the islands is the **Upper Coralline Limestone**. This is a tough rock, but it can be very unstable where the lower layers of Greensand and Blue Clay are crumbling, so that huge boulders break off the cliff edges, and the cliffs themselves often feature deep and slowly widening fissures.

The underlying geology has a profound effect on the landscape of the Maltese islands. Most of the sea cliffs of Malta are Lower Coralline Limestone, but much of the inland parts of eastern and central Malta are Globigerina Limestone. The higher western and northern parts of Malta are Upper Coralline Limestone. The sea cliffs around the north and west feature crumbling slopes of Blue Clay, so that the overlying Upper Coralline Limestone is often dramatically fissured and drops heaps of huge boulders onto seaward slopes. Due to faulting, the island of Comino sits lower than Malta and Gozo, so that only the Upper Coralline Limestone is exposed.

Gozo's sea cliffs are mostly Lower Coralline Limestone, but large parts of the interior are Globigerina

Limestone. However, a series of hills are dotted all over the island, and these are all capped by Upper Coralline Limestone supported by crumbling slopes of Blue Clay. If you bear in mind the basic succession of five rock types, you will quickly come to expect certain types of landscape while exploring the islands on foot.

Perhaps the best way to understand more about the geology of the islands is to visit the 'Limestone Heritage' site on the outskirts of Siġġiewi. This is located in an old Globigerina Limestone quarry, and the site includes notes about the succession of rock types around the Maltese islands. The Globigerina Limestone is also termed 'softstone' (or *zonqor* in Maltese). The Upper and Lower Coralline Limestones are known as 'hardstone' (or *franka* in Maltese).

The predominance of limestone around the Maltese islands is quite evident on the surface – the landscape is criss-crossed with rubble walls; active and inactive quarries can be seen; limestone pavements abound; and with diligent searches all kinds of caves can be discovered. Many of the caves have been used for burials and as dwellings over the centuries. Some have been enlarged, and occasionally new caves are discovered during construction work.

DISCOVERY AND HISTORY

Malta's long and convoluted history could easily fill several volumes and still leave much unsaid. The political wranglings of the past two or three thousand years of Maltese history are open to various interpretations. Serious students of Maltese history could devote their lives to the subject, while casual visitors to the islands will be happy to accept a condensed version. The key events in Malta's history are listed in Appendix C for easy reference.

The earliest settlement of the islands is shrouded in doubt, but by 5200BC Neolithic people were living there as subsistence farmers. Remains of temples and defensive settlements are evidence of later complex societies on the islands. In 800BC Malta came under Phoenician rule. The islands were then conquered by the Carthaginians and later by the Romans, then became part of the Byzantine Empire before they were once again invaded and came under Arab rule in AD870.

During the Medieval period the islands were ruled successively by the

The 'Eye of Osiris' has a Phoenician origin and is painted on Maltese boats

Maltese temples may be the world's oldest freestanding stone structures

Monument to Malta's independence – 21 September 1964

Red postboxes are one of the legacies of British rule in Malta

Normans, Swabians and Angevins; then, after a period under the kings of Aragon, Malta came under Spanish rule in 1479. The Knights of St John came to the islands in 1530 and exercised considerable authority until they were expelled by Napoleon at the end of the 18th century. The French were in turn ousted in 1800 by the British, who ruled Malta until the island gained its independence in 1964. More recently, Malta joined the European Union in 2003 and adopted the Euro as its currency in 2008.

The historical background to some events is given in the route descriptions, and more information may be available at museums or visitor centres. A handy pocket-sized digest of Maltese history is *The Story of Malta* by Brian Blouet, published by Progress Press.

Maltese bookshops are treasure-troves of history books if you wish to immerse yourself in the subject.

WEATHER

Although the Maltese islands are often envisaged as enjoying everlasting Mediterranean sun, the truth is that it is sometimes cold and sometimes wet. The islands do have an enviable number of sunshine hours, but there are occasional days when you might prefer to stay indoors. The winter months can be wet and even chilly in exposed locations. Snow cover is virtually unknown, but there can be the odd shower of hail or ferocious downpour of rain. The winter rains are essential for the islands' agriculture and ensure a flower-filled spring.

Spring is an ideal time to visit Malta, and certainly the most colourful time. Flowers pop up everywhere in riotous colours, but as the days lengthen and the sun shines full-strength, everything soon starts to look rather parched. Indeed, by mid-April the colours are more muted, and by mid-May the islands turn golden-brown. The time to avoid, if planning strenuous walking, is high summer. The temperature is too high for any kind of exertion, and it is easy to succumb to sunburn, dehydration and sunstroke if you fail to exercise due care.

Spring is an especially colourful time to explore the Maltese islands

Even in the winter be prepared to cover up, use sunscreen and drink plenty of water, but in high summer it is essential to take every precaution against the sun. As always in strong sun and high temperatures, it is best to rest in the shade at intervals and remember to drink plenty of water. Malta's national soft drink is *Kinnie*, based on bitter oranges and aromatic herbs. The national alcoholic drink is *Ċisk* lager, but all types of familiar products are on sale around the islands.

After the searing heat of summer, the cooler days of autumn slowly appear. Walking can be pleasant as autumn gives way to winter, but the landscape may look exhausted as all the crops have been harvested and everywhere seems barren. Still, the islands will be quiet and some splendid days can be spent exploring. Bear in mind that once the winter rains appear, the ground, and especially the slopes of Blue Clay, can get very sticky, causing heavy clods of earth to stick to footwear. Be careful while exploring valley routes and riverbeds if there is a risk of flooding during heavy rain.

Wind direction has an influence on Maltese weather. The *tramuntana* from the north brings cool weather, while the *xlokk* brings uncomfortably hot and humid weather from the south-east. The *grigal* from the north-east and *majjistral* from the north-west can send waves crashing into the cliff coasts, so care is needed when walking close to the sea and bathing may be inadvisable.

LANGUAGE

First, be assured that almost everyone you meet on the Maltese islands speaks English. Furthermore, practically all signs and notices are in English and are often displayed in other languages too. Malta was under British rule from 1800 to 1964 and so English became a natural second language, and it remains very much in use around the islands. However, Maltese is the true language of the islands – part of the Semitic group of languages that includes Arabic and Hebrew. It is the only language within that group to be written in a Latin script, although there are four letters that have distinct

Maltese forms. These letters are used in place-names throughout this book, and affect the pronunciation of words as follows:

- *Ċ* or *ċ* is pronounced as the 'ch' in 'check', so *Ċenċ* = 'Chench'
- *Ġ* or *ġ* is pronounced as both 'g's' in 'George', so *Ġorġ* = 'George'
- *Ħ* or *ħ* is pronounced as the 'h' in 'hello', so *Ħamrun* = 'Hamrun'
- *Ż* or *ż* is pronounced as in 'fuzz', so *Żabbar* = 'Zzabbar'
- *Għ* or *għ* is silent, but lengthens the next vowel, so *Għar* = 'aar'.

Standard letters are pronounced mostly as in English, except:

- *H* or *h* is silent
- *J* or *j* is pronounced as 'y' as in 'yes', so *Bajjada* = 'Bayyada'
- *Q* or *q* is simply a glottal stop (although a 'k' sound might be acceptable)
- *X* or *x* is pronounced 'sh', so *Xlendi* = 'Shlendi'
- *Z* or *z* is pronounced 'ts' as in 'sits', so *Balzan* = 'Baltsan'.

Some words beginning with *M* followed by a consonant are pronounced as though they have a letter 'i' at the beginning, so *Mdina* and *Mtarfa* are pronounced as 'Imdina' and 'Imtarfa'.

When all the pronunciation rules have been mastered, place-names such as *Baħar iċ-Ċagħaq* or *Mġarr* should present no problem, but never be afraid to check any pronunciation with a Maltese person. They will usually be delighted to offer assistance and will welcome your interest in their language and your efforts to pronounce it.

Listening to Maltese people speaking is quite an education even if you don't understand the language. At times their speech sounds as if it has an Arabic or Italian tone, although when referring to numbers they will often use English. Listen carefully to hear them go to the market, or *suq* (Arabic), and say 'thank you' for a service rendered and *ciao* (Italian) when they depart!

See Appendix D for a topographical glossary which you may find helpful for interpreting maps and signs as you explore the islands.

RELIGION

The Maltese islands are overwhelmingly Roman Catholic, and so is almost every ecclesiastical structure. That is not to say that they all belong to the Roman Catholic church, however, since many small country chapels, while undoubtedly 'Catholic', are privately owned, as the old estates were obliged to build private chapels for the use of their workers and employ a priest to minister to them. Many of these chapels bear a marble plaque inscribed *'non gode l'immunita ecclesias'*, meaning that outlaws couldn't claim immunity by sheltering inside them. In the towns and villages, people take great pride in their churches, and some of the more outstanding structures were financed and built

Ta' Pinu Church near Għarb is a major pilgrimage centre on Gozo (Walk 32)

entirely through local donations. The Church authorities used to own large areas of land in Malta, but much of that land was handed over to the state after independence. It is interesting to note that 'God' is referred to as *Alla* in Maltese, and 'Lord' is *Sultan*.

In most towns and villages, churches are open throughout the day. Visitors are expected to be quiet and respectful, and keep their arms and legs covered. Wearing shorts and T-shirts may result in being barred from admission. Photography may or may not be permitted – look out for notices or ask for advice. In some of the more popular churches or cathedrals, there may be an admission charge, but in any case it is good practice to leave a donation after a visit. Many Maltese churches are architectural treasure-houses, and the costs of upkeep and maintenance are enormous.

Churches and chapels may be festooned in coloured lights and decorations as each and every one of them celebrates its own special feast-day. These festivals, while rooted in religion, often have a carnival atmosphere, with food, drink, fireworks, bands, songs and long processions. Tourist information centres and the local press have lists of over a hundred festivals taking place around the Maltese islands, and even if you have no wish to take part, you will be very aware of any that are taking place!

MALTESE WILDLIFE

The Maltese islands offer gorgeous displays of wild flowers each spring, and it is difficult to believe that there was once extensive tree cover across the islands. Birds can be spotted, but bear in mind that they are ruthlessly hunted on Malta and Gozo. Other animals may only rarely be observed. Walkers who have a particular interest in wildlife should obtain the encyclopædic *Wildlife of the Maltese Islands*, published by BirdLife Malta and Nature Trust Malta. The following brief notes offer only a bare outline of what might be seen while walking around the islands.

The distribution of wildlife depends, of course, on the habitats that are available. As the islands are very built up, some habitats are under great pressure. Perhaps the most prolific habitat is the surrounding sea, although that specialised environment is not covered in the notes below. Rocky shores and sand dunes are extreme habitats, where the species count may be low, but specialised. Marsh lagoons are scarce, but are extremely important sites. Watercourses rarely run throughout the year, and rainwater pools are even more precarious. The main habitats are the rocky cliffs, clay slopes and steppes, rocky steppes, *garigue* (patchy rock and shrubs), *maquis* (thick thorny scrub) and woodland.

Maltese trees and flowers

It is thought that when human settlers first arrived on Malta, the islands were covered largely in holm oak. Woodlands were quickly cleared for hut construction, fuel and to make

Maltese Everlasting grows only round the cliffs of Dwejra Bay on Gozo (Walk 27)

space for agriculture. While this may have had a devastating effect on the forest, leading to soil erosion and the creation of large areas of bare rock, it also opened up areas for colonisation by other species. Flowers and thorny scrub were quick to gain a root-hold in even the most precarious situations. With increased agriculture, and waves of new settlers, came the introduction of new plant species, both intentional and unintentional, so that gradually a particular Maltese 'assemblage' of plants evolved.

Woodlands are of limited extent, and most of the larger ones are forest schemes, such as on the Bajda Ridge. Aleppo pines were introduced to the islands and offer year-round shade in arid places. Acacia is another introduced species that spreads rapidly and can be a nuisance. Fig trees, and more especially carob trees, have been planted for their enduring food value through the centuries. Malta's national tree is the rare *sandarac* (*Tetraclinis articulata*). Another uncommon tree is the 'chaste tree', whose leaves were once eaten by monks to control their sexual urges! Bushy tamarisks of African and European types exist, as well as varieties of palm trees.

Flowers are a bewildering study as there are so many species, including some that are endemic to the islands. Malta's national flower is the cliff-hugging Maltese Rock Centaury, a primitive species classified as *Palaeocyanus crassifolius*. Dwejra Bay, on the island of Gozo, is the only place in the world where you can find the Maltese Everlasting, or *Helichrysum melitense*, but at least it grows abundantly there. However, even common species such as the Crown Daisy are to be admired, and can turn even a heap of builder's rubble into a mass of golden bloom each spring! Crumbling landslip slopes of Blue Clay are often bound together by esparto grass and covered in masses of *sulla*, which forms crimson carpets of flowers in spring.

The garigue and maquis areas show how well a variety of plants have been able to adapt to the harsh, dry areas of limestone pavement around the islands. Some species have succulent leaves, such as the Golden Samphire, which enable it to store precious fluid and thrive where everything else has given up. Shrubby tree spurges protect themselves by having a poisonous latex sap. Other species rely on thorns, while wolfbane bushes sport a remarkable double-horned seed pod. Fragrant wild thyme used to be collected ruthlessly each winter as decoration for Christmas cribs, but it now enjoys protection and thrives in tiny hollows in the limestone.

The best way to become familiar with a good representative range of Maltese trees and flowers is to visit the Elysium nursery, run by the Gaia Foundation, at Golden Bay. Around 40 species are constantly being reared for eventual transplantation into the wild. The aim is to re-establish a specific range of Maltese flora in areas where ground cover has been damaged or destroyed. Initial areas where such work has taken place include Golden Bay and Għajn Tuffieħa Bay on Malta, as well as around Ramla Bay on Gozo.

Agriculture is still an important activity in Malta, although most foodstuffs are now imported. It can be quite entertaining to scan the terraces and tiny fields to see what fruit and vegetables are currently being raised. Oranges grow well in the floors of old quarries. Providing a steady drip-feed of water can be maintained, all kinds of things can be grown, and a lot of produce is sold from roadside stalls.

Maltese birds

Birds are often a sore point of discussion around the Maltese islands. There is a strong shooting lobby of some 17,000 licensed hunters, plus a number who hunt illegally, even if that means shooting at protected species on nature reserves! Shooting huts, hides and traps are dotted all over the islands, and some of them have been erected illegally on public land. A referendum to restrict hunting was held early in 2015 and was defeated by the narrowest of margins. The most popular game birds are turtle doves and quails, which are far less common than they used to be. There are few resident species of birds around the islands, which are mainly visited by birds migrating between Africa and Europe. Around 370 species have been recorded, but some are rare one-off visitors.

The Maltese islands were once famous for falcons, and two Maltese falcons formed the traditional annual 'rent' paid by the Knights of St John to the King of Spain and the Viceroy of Sicily. Small kestrels or hobbies might be seen, or more rarely a peregrine. Buzzards and marsh harriers can be spotted, while kites or ospreys are rare vistors. The chances of seeing owls are slim. Malta's national bird is the blue rock thrush, or *merill* in Maltese.

The sea around the islands is home to shearwaters and cormorants, while some species of herons and waders will occupy the seashore for a short time while on migration. There are plenty of gulls around the shores and occasional flocks of ducks. The lack of freshwater habitats inland, in the form of rivers and ponds, limits the appeal of the islands to many species. However, the development of bird reserves around lagoons at Għadira and Is-Simar has been an outstanding success. Little bitterns have managed to breed successfully at Is-Simar. Visit the bird reserves at weekends on Walks 9, 10, 11, 13, 14 or 15 for up-to-the-minute information about visiting species as and when they are spotted. The whole island of Comino, visited on Walk 33, is a major reserve where shooting and trapping is completely banned.

Woodland areas are of limited extent, and while they are favoured by turtle doves, they are also targeted by hunters. Open country, such as the wild and rocky steppes, garigue and maquis, are home to finches, warblers, flycatchers, sparrows, wagtails, thrushes, pipits, buntings and larks. Many of these fly low and are well camouflaged, feeding off seeds and insects. Some of them nest in rocky holes or thorny scrub, where they are safe from predators.

Maltese animals

There are few animals to be seen around the Maltese islands. Even farm stock is rather sparse. On sunny days, lizards of various hues can be seen basking, then promptly scuttling for cover. Wart-covered wall geckoes do pretty much the same thing. Skinks are curious creatures that look like fat lizards, if you see their tiny legs, or stubby snakes if you don't see their legs. There are a few snakes, which are all basically harmless, and the most commonly observed are the fast-moving whipsnakes.

Almost all the reptiles feed on insects, and the full tally of insect species has yet to be fully recorded. Most insect species are barely noticed, but butterflies are abundant while there are flowers to provide nectar. Beekeeping has a long history on the islands, and wasps can be seen building paper nests on buildings, walls or cliffs. The Maltese freshwater crab and painted frog are rarely seen, being restricted to small and rapidly dwindling habitats.

Wild mammals are few and seldom seen. Bats, rats, mice and shrews keep a low profile. Hedgehogs do not hibernate in such a warm climate, but remain active. Rabbits are bred in captivity to appear later on Maltese menus, but they are also seen in the wild. Weasels are most elusive and

A knobbly-skinned wall gecko basks in the sun and catches insects

are seen only on Malta, being absent from Gozo and Comino. The only other wild mammals likely to be seen are occasional common or bottle-nosed dolphins, and the chances of seeing these are greatly improved by taking one of the many extended cruises around the islands.

PROTECTED AREAS

Malta is so densely populated that there are few open areas that the state can control and protect adequately. There is a 'National Park' at Ta' Qali in the middle of Malta, but on closer inspection it turns out to be a large public park and sports stadium. However, in recent years efforts have been made to protect certain areas of land. Two bird reserves were established, which is quite an achievement when one of the national sports involves shooting birds. Shooting has been banned in other areas, notably the island of Comino and many coastal cliffs around the islands.

There are four 'schedules' governing the protection of limited areas of landscape. Schedule 1 is the highest level of protection, covering areas such as Il-Karraba at Għajn Tuffieħa and the adjacent Il-Majjistral Nature and History Park; Schedule 2 offers lesser protection; and Schedules 3 and 4 may be little more than buffer zones. The amazing landforms around Dwejra on Gozo have been proposed for World Heritage Site status. Ancient monuments are in theory protected, although this does not always keep some of the less well-known sites free of damage or destruction either by developers, landowners or wanton

Fungus Rock at Dwejra Bay on Gozo (Walk 27)

vandalism. Malta does have a problem with litter, rubbish dumping, dereliction and squalor in places, but many Maltese people are becoming more and more anxious to deal with these problems.

Conservation bodies such as the Gaia Foundation, BirdLife Malta and Nature Trust Malta (see Appendix B) are gradually raising the awareness of Maltese people and visiting tourists of the fragile and priceless nature of the islands. These organisations visit schools in an effort to reach young people, and would welcome the support of visiting tourists, so that ultimately the state might be persuaded to take more action. Most Maltese governments operate with slender majorities and are loath to tackle some issues for fear of losing a percentage of the votes.

GETTING TO THE MALTESE ISLANDS

Flights

Air Malta is the national airline of Malta (tel 2166 2211, www.airmalta.com), operating services to and from the island from Europe and North Africa. The national airlines of other countries operate flights throughout the year to Malta. There are plenty of charter flights available, as well as budget airlines, as this is a popular destination. Simply pick a flight at a time and price that you're happy with, but be prepared for a bewildering choice! All flights to and from the islands operate from Malta International Airport. To visit Gozo or Comino, onward arrangements have to be made.

Gozo Channel Line ferries run early until late, linking Malta and Gozo

Ferries

The only year-round ferry service to and from Malta is operated by Virtu Ferries (www.virtuferries.com) between Valletta in Malta and Pozzalo in Sicily, although it's unlikely that many people would travel overland through Italy and then catch a ferry to Malta. More often, people use the ferry to make day-trips between Malta and Sicily. The 'standard tour' involves an early morning high-speed ferry from Malta to Pozzalo, followed by a coach tour to Mount Etna and the bustling historic town of Taormina, with a return to Malta on a late-night ferry. Most tour operators on Malta can sell this tour, or a simple ferry ticket could be bought if you wish to do your own thing.

GETTING AROUND THE MALTESE ISLANDS

Ferries

Gozo Channel Line runs fast, frequent and cheap ferries between Ċirkewwa at the northern end of Malta and Mġarr at the southern end of Gozo. Queues can be long, but there's a quick turnaround and it isn't necessary to book in advance. Buses and taxis meet virtually every ferry, so there are seldom any significant delays. There are also one or two sailings per day from Sa Maison (handy for Valletta and Sliema) to Mġarr on Gozo. It's a good idea to check the times of these sailings and perhaps also to book in advance: tel 2210 9000, www.gozochannel.com.

A cruise trip around the islands is a fine way to explore the cliff coast

Several small ferries operate from the northern end of Malta or from Mġarr on Gozo to the little island of Comino. These are quite numerous in the summer, but many cease running in the winter months. The Marsamxetto Ferry simply runs back and forth between Sliema and Valletta, usually every hour, offering a different perspective than you would see on a bus journey through the urban sprawl.

Cruises

A variety of cruises enable visitors to view the cliff coasts of Malta and Gozo, but check details carefully with cruise operators. Some cruises simply head out to sea for a quick spin and promptly return, or simply tour the Grand or Marsamxett Harbours. Others make a circuit all the way around the coast of Malta, or Gozo, or both. Some cruises involve a little time onshore, perhaps at a popular location such as the Blue Lagoon on Comino. Cruise details can be checked at Sliema on Malta, at Mġarr on Gozo, or at tourist information centres, where a variety of cruise leaflets may be available.

Car hire

Hiring a car on Malta is not advisable, although there are plenty of vehicles available and hiring can be arranged either at the airport or through a hotel. Visiting motorists tend to find the road systems confusing, the volume of traffic stressful, and the likelihood of having an accident dramatically increased. Car parks may be crowded to capacity at times, and signs threatening to have illegally parked cars towed away are fastened to almost every lamp-post in the urban areas.

From a practical point of view, bearing in mind that most of the walks in this book are linear, a car is more of a liability than a convenience – and the walks are designed to tie in with the frequent bus services. Learn to use and trust the buses and your enjoyment of the islands will be greatly increased!

On the island of Gozo, bus services are rather patchy in some places, and a car might be a little more useful. Cars cannot be taken to the little island of Comino, which is one of the reasons why that place is so refreshing – especially after experiencing the traffic conditions elsewhere!

Bus services

Malta and Gozo used to be served by ancient, brightly coloured, owner-operated, ex-British public transport buses. These were withdrawn from public service to comply with EU directives, although a few were spared to provide 'vintage bus' tours. A fleet of air-conditioned 'King Long' buses was imported from China, including 'bendy buses' on some routes, all operated by the big transport company Arriva. The entire fleet, plus a few more buses, is now operated by Malta Public Transport (tel 2122 2000, www.publictransport.com.mt). To distinguish public transport buses

Malta Public Transport operate the islands' buses

from tour buses and private buses, their number plates include the word 'BUS'.

Bus transport is remarkably cheap, with routes visiting most parts of Malta and Gozo, often operating at intervals ranging from 10 minutes to one hour. This means that buses are generally available when you want them. There are variations between summer and winter, with more routes available in summer. Using buses ensures that there is no problem enjoying an alcoholic drink (but not too much!), and anyone feeling tired after a long walk in the hot sun can let the driver take them home in coolness and comfort.

The first thing to do before using the buses is to get hold of current timetables. A selection of these can be obtained at the City Gate bus terminus at Valletta, as well as from bus stations and tourist information centres. It's unlikely that all the timetables you want will be available in print, but they are all available online. There are different ticket types, which is difficult to grasp for a first-time visitor, but feel free to ask for advice at bus stations. The most basic ticket is for a single journey lasting up to two hours. Huge discounts are available by purchasing 'Tallinja Cards', and in 2015 unlimited bus transport for a whole month around Malta and Gozo cost only €26.

The bus route numbering system and spaghetti-like route maps take time to understand, and in many instances several buses run along the same roads, despite displaying different numbers and destinations. To make best use of the bus network, find accommodation close to the bus terminus in Valletta on Malta, or the bus station in Victoria/Rabat on Gozo. The bulk of tourist accommodation on Malta is located in Buġibba and Sliema, and those places also have good bus services, although it may be necessary to change buses to reach some destinations. Buses prefixed with an 'X' serve the airport, while buses prefixed with an 'N' run through the night. The night buses aren't listed in this guidebook, but any walkers planning to stay out very late may need to use those services.

If in doubt about how the buses operate, just ask any employee, or ask any local person in the bus queue for assistance. Always keep hold of your bus ticket, as there's a fine of €50 if you can't produce a ticket. To get on a bus, give a clear hand signal from a bus stop or bus shelter. To stop a bus, press a button, but watch for the 'stop' light to show or for a bell or tone to sound so that you know it worked. Watch how local people do things and take your cue from them!

There are no buses on the little island of Comino, where everything is done on foot.

Taxis

Taxis are usually white and are available at stands in most of the cities and towns around Malta and Gozo. Their number plates include the word 'TAXI'. While most drivers operate using a meter or a set scale of charges, others may prove open to negotiation. It is always a good idea to check the likely fare before getting into the car, as a few drivers are unscrupulous and give the rest a bad name. If a taxi is needed at an unsociable hour, for something like an early morning airport run, it is usually best to let your hotel make the booking, as they will invariably deal with someone of proven reliability. However, it's best to double-check that a booking has actually been made.

Karrozzin

Lovely horse-drawn carriages, or *karrozzin*, are often found in the more popular cities and towns around the Maltese islands. For a hefty fee, these take visitors on leisurely trots around the streets, passing popular sights. (The shiny marks left on the roads by the wheels will give an indication of the available routes.) Karrozzin were once the only real public transport option around the islands, and they were quite often prepared to take visitors on full-day journeys. From time to time in the countryside, milestones are noticed, marked with the distance from Valletta. The British planted these so that anyone using the karrozzin would know the distance and wouldn't be overcharged on a long journey. The milestones were deliberately defaced so as not to give potential invaders any kind of advantage during the Second World War.

Triq ir-Repubblika – the main shopping street through Valletta (Walk 1)

MONEY

The Euro has been the currency of Malta since the beginning of 2008, replacing the Maltese Lira and its enormous 'pound' coins. Large denomination Euro notes are difficult to use for small purchases, so avoid the €500 and €200 notes altogether, and avoid the €100 notes if at all possible. The rest – €50, €20, €10 and €5 – are fine. Coins come in €2 and €1, bearing striking Maltese Cross designs. Small denomination coins come in values of 50c, 20c, 10c, 5c, 2c and 1c. Banks and ATMs are available on Malta and Gozo. Many hotels accept major credit and debit cards, as will large supermarkets and shops, but small bars, shops and cafés deal only in cash.

ACCOMMODATION

Many people who travel to Malta do so as part of a package deal. If booking a package, take particular note of where the accommodation is located. The Maltese islands may be small, but some places are a long walk from a good bus route. Places such as Paċeville and St Julian's are very popular with young people, so anyone wanting a good night's sleep should avoid apartments or hotels sandwiched between noisy, late-night-early-morning discos! Buġibba and Mellieħa Bay are popular budget package destinations on Malta; while on Gozo, Marsalforn is the main resort. The standard of accommodation is gradually moving up-market, with prices increasing accordingly.

Hotels and guesthouses

Avoiding package deals is easy, as there are plenty of hotels and apartments around the Maltese islands that can be booked online. There are a handful of hotels and guesthouses in Valletta, as well as several apartments, which are all handy for the bus station. Many visitors believe that the quiet culture of the city is far superior to the rowdy resorts. Tourist information centres offer up-to-date lists of hotels, guesthouses and apartments on Malta and Gozo. On Gozo, farmhouse apartments, often housed in traditional stone buildings, are a growing business, especially in the north-west of Gozo, and some of them are most luxurious.

Tourist information offices

The main contact point for information about the Maltese islands is Visit Malta, www.visitmalta.com. While touring the islands, a freephone number is available: tel 8007 2230. Tourist information offices are listed below.

Malta International Airport, Arrivals, tel 2369 6073
229 Merchants Street, Valletta, tel 2291 5440
Pinto Wharf, Valletta Waterfront, tel 2122 0633
Inquisitor's Palace, Birgu, tel 2180 0145
Torre Dello Standardo, Mdina, tel 2145 4480
Misrah Iż-Żjara tal-Papa Gwanni Pawlu II, Mellieħa, tel 2152 4666

An old windmill above Qala, on Gozo, has been incorporated into a hotel

Local Council Sub Office, St Paul's Bay, tel 2141 9176
17 Independence Square, Victoria, Gozo, tel 2291 5452

MAPS OF THE MALTESE ISLANDS

The most detailed maps of the Maltese islands are published by the Malta Environment and Planning Authority (MEPA). One large map covers Malta and a smaller map covers Gozo, both at a scale of 1:25,000 with contours at 10m (33ft) intervals. These are similar in style and content to a previous imperial edition used for the map extracts throughout this guidebook, with route overlays. To obtain the maps it is best to go in person, Monday to Friday (except holidays), to Mapping Shop, Malta Environment and Planning Authority (MEPA), St Francis Ravelin, Floriana (tel 2290 1007, www.mepa.org.mt). This is only a short walk from the City Gate bus terminus at Valletta.

Maps of Malta can be ordered in advance from specialist suppliers such as Stanfords, 12–14 Long Acre, London WC2E 9BR, tel 0207 836 1321, www.stanfords.co.uk; The Map Shop, 15 High Street, Upton-upon-Severn WR8 0HJ, tel 01684 593146, www.themapshop.co.uk; or Cordee, 3a De Montford Street, Leicester LE1 7HD, tel 0116 254 3579, www.cordee.co.uk. Free street plans for most of the interesting towns on the islands can be obtained from tourist information centres. Anyone wishing to have comprehensive street plans for the whole of the Maltese islands should obtain a copy of *The mAZe Street Atlas*. GPS-compatible digital maps are available online, and can be used on mobile devices.

COUNTRYSIDE ACCESS

There are many paths and tracks that are regarded as rights of way around the Maltese islands, but these are seldom waymarked, nor is information about rights of way shown on maps or easily obtainable from government offices. There are many paths and tracks where responsible walkers are tolerated, but which are actually private. Landowners often go out of their way to indicate private property by various signs and marks. Signs reading 'Private', 'No Entry', 'Privat', 'Tidħolx' and 'RTO' all essentially mean the same thing – 'Private Property, Keep Out!' The words 'Post Privat' might be used to indicate a building to which there is no access.

Another method used to denote private property involves marking rubble walls with blobs of white paint at intervals. The idea is that you should not pass anything marked in this way, although walking alongside is usually fine. There have been problems where people have marked areas as private when in fact they are owned by the state, where there might be no objection to people crossing the land. It can happen that while a

Enjoying the view from roadside cliffs on the way towards Dingli (Walk 6)

Maltese 'trespasser' might get a good telling off, a visiting tourist might be allowed free passage, or vice-versa! In some cases, those much-maligned bird hunters will point out one or two good routes for visitors. It is not unknown for visitors to be allowed to use a private track or path after a polite request, although some landowners get a bit jaded with long processions of walking groups.

There should be no access problems with the routes in this guidebook, but tempers sometimes get frayed when walkers meet hunters shooting birds. Hunting may be legal or illegal, depending on who's doing it, when they're doing it, where they're doing it, and what they're shooting. Hunting in Malta is now in theory subject to EU legislation, but there is still a lot of passionate debate. A referendum aimed at restricting hunting was narrowly defeated early in 2015. If there seems to be a lot of shooting taking place in a particular area, it may be best to choose another walk. If you object strongly to hunting, consider supporting BirdLife Malta (see Appendix B) rather than engaging in unproductive face-to-face arguments with hunters.

The Ramblers' Association of Malta

The Ramblers' Association of Malta (www.ramblersmalta.org) was founded in 2005 to address access issues. The organisation promotes walking as a healthy lifestyle, as well as a means of enjoying the countryside and its cultural heritage. Members aim to safeguard and maintain publicly available paths, despite the lack of rights of way legislation.

The scenery around the cliff coast of the Maltese islands is dramatic (Walk 27)

They lobby the government on issues of access and conservation, and challenge inappropriate developments in the countryside. They also campaign against illegal hunting and support a range of environmental organisations. Members organise programmes of walks, which are open to visiting walkers.

Great Walks in Malta and Gozo
Jonathan Henwood, a Maltese environmental scientist, regularly leads walks around the Maltese islands. Walks on Saturdays are generally open to anyone, but it's also possible to book specific tours on request. For full details see greatwalksmalta.com.

USING THIS GUIDE

The walking routes in this guidebook start with a short heritage trail around the city of Valletta (Walk 1). This could be completed in a morning or afternoon, or it could take all day. Next, a series of walks are arranged roughly clockwise around the coastline of Malta (Walks 2–17), moving inland to explore some of the ridges and valleys later (Walks 18–23). The walks on Malta conclude with a heritage trail around Mdina and Rabat (Walk 24).

Walk routes on the island of Gozo start with a heritage trail around Victoria (Walk 25). This is followed by a clockwise exploration of spectacular coastal walking that allows a complete circuit of the island (Walks 26–31). The final walk on Gozo wanders over a series of little hills further inland (Walk 32). The last walk in the book (Walk 33) might be regarded by some as the best of all – a circuit around the lovely little island of Comino.

Looking towards Miġnuna Point from St Thomas Bay (Walk 3)

The information boxes at the start of each walk contain at-a-glance details of the distance covered, the start and finish points, the relevant map, the nature of the terrain, transport options, and the likely availability of food and drink along the way. The grid references for the start and finish points are not absolutely essential, but if you use the 1:25,000 maps you can pinpoint them exactly.

GPX tracks for all the routes are also available free on the Cicerone website at: www.cicerone.co.uk/822/GPX.

Up-to-date bus timetables are needed, and it's wise to check in advance the opening times of any visitor facilities along the way, if wishing to incorporate them in your explorations. Tourist information offices have lists of all the major attractions along with their current opening times. In the route descriptions, place-names that appear on the maps are indicated in **bold**.

A table summarising all the routes described in this book is included as Appendix A, to help you choose.

Terrain

Bear in mind that nearly all walking surfaces in Malta are hard underfoot. Roads, concrete or gravel tracks, limestone and hard-baked earth form the bulk of walking surfaces. Ensure that footwear is both comfortable and capable of taking a pounding. Stout shoes may be better than boots, although with care even training shoes and sandals might be used, but only if you've walked confidently in them before.

The exception to these hard surfaces is the crumbling Blue Clay, which is notoriously sticky when wet and forms huge, heavy clods on all types of footwear.

Għajn Tuffieħa Tower and the Ras il-Waħx headland beyond Golden Bay (Walk 8)

WALK 1

Valletta Heritage Trail

Start/Finish	City Gate, Valletta (557 727)
Distance	5km (3 miles), plus an optional 4km (2½-mile) extension
Time	(walking time) 2hr
Terrain	City streets, steps and garden paths, with some exposed rock ledges on the optional extension
Maps	1:25,000 Malta sheet. Town maps available from tourist information offices.
Refreshments	Abundant shops, bars and restaurants of all types are found at frequent intervals around Valletta.
Transport	Most Malta Bus services operate from outside the City Gate at Valletta. Bus 133 makes a circuit inside the city. Taxis and horse-drawn *karrozzin* are also available. The Marsamxetto Ferry serves Valletta from Sliema.

A whole week could be spent quartering Valletta and it wouldn't be sufficient to penetrate every nook and cranny. This route offers a very basic tour of the city, at first via the top of the stout defensive walls, and then wandering along some of the more interesting streets before exploring outside the walls. A free detailed map of the city can be obtained from the tourist information office, or a copy of *The mAZe Street Atlas* can be used for greater detail. A selection of interesting structures and visitor attractions are pointed out, but 10 times more features can be found with careful exploration.

THE DEVELOPMENT OF VALLETTA

The important thing to remember is Valletta's relatively short history. It was founded on the Sceberras headland in March 1566 by Grand Master Jean de la Vallette, of the Knights of St John, only months after the devastating Turkish attack and siege of the island in 1565. The initial plan was to level the hilly headland and to use the stone gleaned from it to construct most of the buildings. However, the construction was rushed and many of the hills remain, so that some of the streets are not actually roads, but flights of steps! The grid-plan of the streets shows that this was a carefully planned settlement. Innovative methods brought in water and dealt with sewage, while niches on street corners once held blazing torches as an early form of street lighting.

The Knights of St John (see Appendix C for more information) could rely on vast amounts of money from their estates around Europe, and it's plain that no expense was spared. The complexities of the defensive walls are all the more remarkable considering that they were raised in only three years. In fact, by 1571 the Knights of St John had moved in solemn procession to take possession of the new city, which by 1600 was filled with an assortment of splendidly ornate buildings.

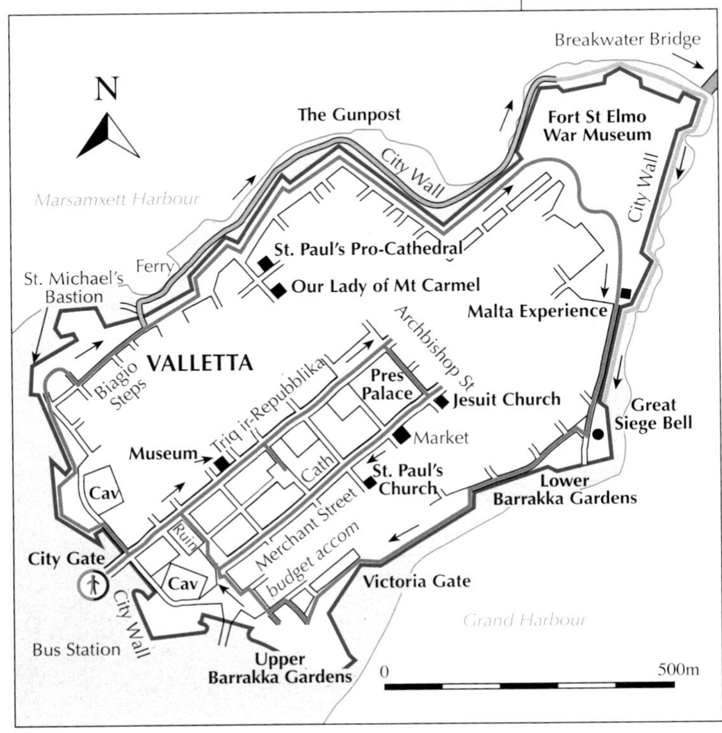

Start at the **City Gate** just outside Valletta, where most of Malta's bus services turn around the Triton Fountain, and taxis and horse-drawn karrozzin are available for hire. While entering the City Gate, note the deep rock ditches on either side, where stone was cut and hoisted to build the defensive walls above. Also note how the walls are shaped so that the gate could be overlooked and defended from all angles. Walk into the city and immediately turn left up a long and broad flight of 66 steps.

The cavalier once housed soldiers whose main function was to defend the City Gate.

Walk through gardens on top of the defensive wall and pass close to **St John's Cavalier**. ◂ More garden paths lead to **St Michael's Bastion**, where the complexity of the walls can be studied and fine views are available across Marsamxett Harbour. Beyond the fortified Manoel Island, sprawling resort developments can be seen. If the wall is followed onwards, buildings push you slightly into the city, so walk down Triq Sant Andreja, Triq San Bjaġju and the **Biagio Steps**. A total of 108 steps drop to a road linking with the **Marsamxetto Ferry**, so if arriving by ferry pick up the route here, inside the city wall.

Stay on top of the city wall and follow Triq Marsamxett in the direction of a tall spire. Steps on the right lead up to this spire, which is **St Paul's Pro-Cathedral** of the Anglican Diocese of Gibraltar in Europe. Further uphill

The city wall rises from a rock ledge, with a view of the Breakwater Bridge

is the dome of the Roman Catholic Sanctuary Basilica of **Our Lady of Mount Carmel**. If these places are visited, walk back down the steps to continue along the top of the city wall afterwards.

The road leads to a corner at **The Gunpost**, where there is a view across the little bay of Il-Fossa to a fort at the end of the headland. Pass the Auberge de Baviere to reach **Fort St Elmo**. ▸ Follow the road gently uphill and downhill alongside the fort to reach **The Malta Experience**. Here, an audio-visual show offers a basic grounding in the turbulent history of Malta, and opposite is the site of the Chapel of Bones. Continue walking along the top of the city wall, looking back to see the stout breakwater that shelters the **Grand Harbour**, to reach the Second World War siege memorial.

The original fort on this point pre-dates the construction of Valletta. It contains the War Museum, but other parts of the site cannot be visited.

The memorial contains the **Great Siege Bell**, erected in 1992. The bell rings every day at noon, and you're warned not to stand beneath it! The monument commemorates the award of the George Cross to Malta, honouring over 7000 service personnel and civilians who were killed during the Siege of Malta between 1940 and 1943.

Enjoy views across the Grand Harbour to the fortified headlands of the Three Cities, each one of which could warrant careful study. Closer to hand, the Maltese ball game of *boċċi* might be taking place on a small pitch.

Walk up Triq il-Mediterran, passing the ornate **Lower Barrakka Gardens** on top of St Christopher Bastion. Stay close to the city wall by walking along Triq Santa Barbara. This leads to a complex intersection of roads and steps, spanned by bridges, above the **Victoria Gate**. ▸ Climb up Triq Sant' Antnin, where a series of small signs point towards the Lascarris War Rooms, and a short detour reveals the Second World War operations rooms where the first invasion of Axis-controlled Europe was planned.

A number of budget accommodation options in Valletta are located around here, including the British Hotel, Grand Harbour Hotel and Asti Guesthouse.

If not visiting the War Rooms, continue up steps and keep climbing until it's possible to turn left into the **Upper Barrakka Gardens**. The gardens are surrounded by arches

The former Auberge de Castille serves as the office of the Prime Minister

and memorials, with superb views across the Grand Harbour to the Three Cities, as well as into the dockyards and neighbouring Floriana. Walk out of the gardens to pass the Castille Wine Vaults and Auberge de Castille, also noting the church of Our Lady of the Victories. Pass a ruin where the stumps of stone columns remain, entering a busy square close to the **City Gate**.

For the second part of the tour, walk straight into Valletta along the busy Triq ir-Repubblika. There are plenty of shops, bars and restaurants along its length, as well as souvenir shops and an assortment of attractions. The National Museum of Archaeology is on the left, housed in the former Auberge de Provence. Enter it to see some of Malta's most ancient treasures and stonework.

Further along the busy street, a right turn up Triq San Ġwann leads to **St John's Co-Cathedral**, which incorporates a fine museum. On the left of Triq ir-Repubblika, meanwhile, are the Courts of Justice. At Queen Victoria Square, the old Bibliotheca faces the former Treasury of the Order of St John. Palace Square is dominated on the right by the **Presidential Palace**, originally used by the Grand Masters of the Order of St John. Also take note of the ornate front of the Hostel de Verdelin.

Turn right alongside the Presidential Palace, along **Archbishop Street**. The **Jesuit Church** is on the left at the end, but turn right instead along Merchant Street. On the left is the **Market**, or Is-Suq tal-Belt. Lots of little signs urge you to go down to the left to see **St Paul's Shipwreck Church**, rightly described as a gem of Maltese architecture. ◂

The exterior is so plain you could walk straight past it, but the interior is richly decorated.

Keep walking along Merchant Street to find the Palazzo Parisio, where Napoleon stayed for one week from 12 to 18 June 1798, when Malta capitulated to his forces. The building faces the former Auberge d'Italie, which is now the Ministry of Tourism. At the end of the street, turn right and left, passing the modern parliament building before returning to the **City Gate**.

Extension to Fort St Elmo and Breakwater Bridge

An extension to the route could be made by retracing steps along the first part of the tour, going back down the Biagio Steps. This time, walk down the road as if intending to catch the **Marsamxetto Ferry**, but stay on the road as it runs along the foot of the massive city walls. The road leads all the way to **Fort St Elmo**, by which time visitors will appreciate just how formidable the defences really are. In stormy or windy conditions, it might be inadvisable to continue further, as the route runs across bare, uneven rock that is occasionally washed by waves.

A feature of interest is the **Breakwater Bridge**, which can normally be crossed, although sometimes it is locked in the interest of safety. The breakwater allows fine harbour views but leads nowhere, so it's necessary to keep following the rugged, rocky platform beneath the wall. Eventually, all manner of tiny buildings are passed, squashed into the space between the wall and the sea. At this point, climb back to the top of the walls and continue as before from the **Great Siege Bell**.

After leaving Valletta, **urban explorations** could continue into the neighbouring fortified city of Floriana, or to the defensive Cottonera Lines across the Grand Harbour, and even into the fortified Three Cities. There's no shortage of Maltese history and heritage hidden in the urban sprawl – including the mysterious ancient underground Hypogeum and the Tarxien Temples.

WALK 2

Rinella to Marsaskala

Start	Fort Rinella (578 725)
Finish	Marsaskala (605 690)
Distance	7km (4½ miles)
Time	2hr
Terrain	Easy walking along roads and tracks on a low, rocky coast
Maps	1:25,000 Malta sheet
Refreshments	Bars at Smart City and Xgħajra. Plenty of shops, bars and restaurants at Marsaskala.
Transport	Bus 3 serves Fort Rinella and Smart City. Buses 94 and 120 serve Xgħajra. Buses 91, 92, 93, 124, 135, 204 and X5 serve Marsaskala.

Walkers who wish to trek all the way around the coastline of Malta would have to endure a long and intricate walk through the built-up areas surrounding the Grand Harbour. There are interesting features at the start of this walk, such as Fort Rinella and the world's biggest cannon, and the Mediterranean Film Studios and their enormous water tanks. Unfortunately, the rocky coastline is inaccessible at Rinella and currently has to be gained at Smart City. An easy coastal track links Xgħajra and Marsaskala, but the scenery is occasionally blighted. Walkers looking for a more scenic coastal walk might skip this stretch and start their explorations with Walk 3 from Marsaskala to Birżebbuġa.

Check whether a path on the left has been re-opened, and if so, follow it down to the coast and turn right to reach Smart City.

Start from the late 19th-century **Fort Rinella** (www.fortrinella.com), where a remarkable 100-ton Armstrong gun, reckoned to be the biggest cannon in the world, can be studied. Follow the road past a junction overlooking the Mediterranean Film Studios, where it's possible to glimpse the huge water tanks where watery movies such as *James Bond* and *Titanic* were filmed.

A crossroads is reached where access to the coast has been temporarily closed. ◂ Walk straight ahead into

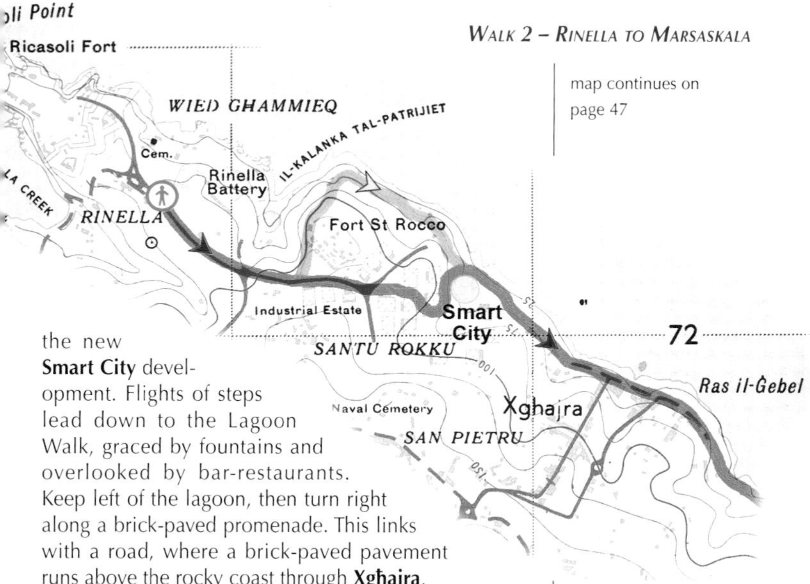

map continues on page 47

oli Point
Ricasoli Fort
WIED GHAMMIEQ
IL-KALANKA TAL-PATRIJIET
Cem.
Rinella Battery
LA CREEK
RINELLA
Fort St Rocco
Industrial Estate
Smart City
SANTU ROKKU
72
Ras il-Ġebel
Naval Cemetery
Xgħajra
SAN PIETRU

the new **Smart City** development. Flights of steps lead down to the Lagoon Walk, graced by fountains and overlooked by bar-restaurants. Keep left of the lagoon, then turn right along a brick-paved promenade. This links with a road, where a brick-paved pavement runs above the rocky coast through **Xgħajra**.

A dirt road leaves the village, blighted by fly tipping, but it's possible to pick a way along the low, rocky shore for better scenery, linking broad rocky ledges and short stretches of path. Every so often small rocky coves, such

Waves beat against the rocky coast at Xgħajra

An old film prop at the Mediterranean Film Studios

as **Ġorf l-Abjad**, bite into the cliffs. ▶ The dirt road leads to the Dive Med centre on **Zonqor Point**, where a snack bar and toilets are located and an intricate series of salt pans has been cut into the rock.

There are a number of lookouts along the way, ranging from a 16th-century stone tower to concrete Second World War structures, as well as shooters' huts.

Follow the paved promenade path beside the road running alongside **Marsaskala Bay**. This leads to the centre of **Marsaskala** at the head of the bay, where food and drink are readily available. Little fishing boats, or *luzzu*, painted in traditional colours, bob on the water. Head straight inland from the head of the bay to find the little bus station, or continue around the bay as described in Walk 3.

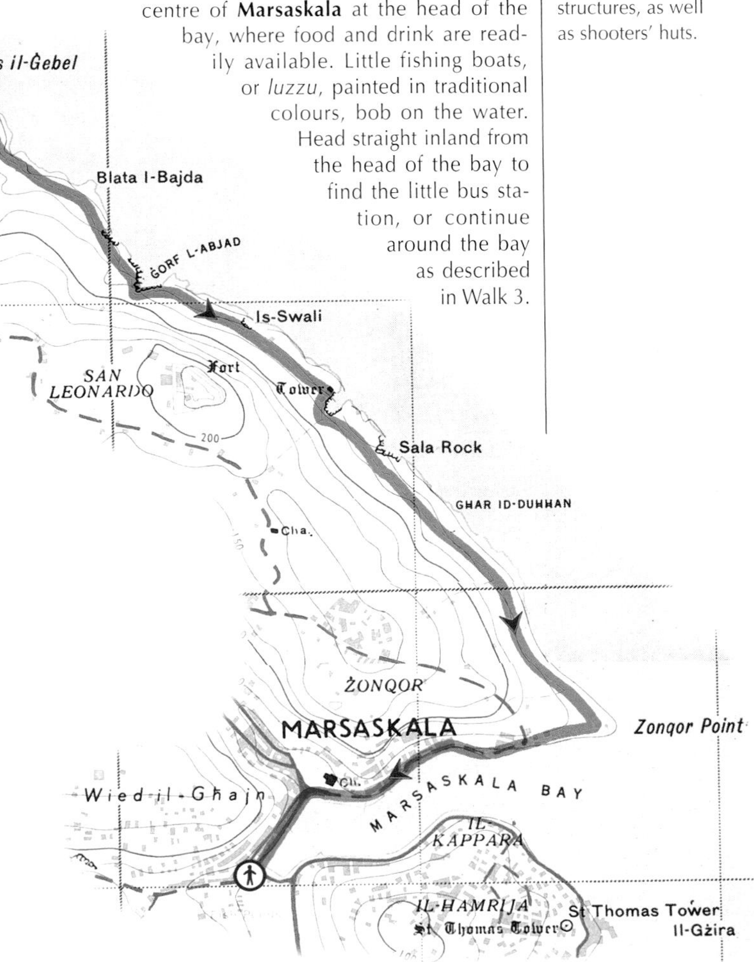

WALK 3

Marsaskala to Birżebbuġa

Start	Marsaskala (605 690)
Finish	Pretty Bay, Birżebbuġa (574 649)
Distance	18.5km (11½ miles)
Time	5hr 30min
Terrain	A mixture of coastal roads and tracks, with narrow cliff paths and some detours inland
Maps	1:25,000 Malta sheet
Refreshments	Plenty of shops, bars and restaurants around Marsaskala. A couple of bars and restaurants around St Thomas Bay. Shops, bars and restaurants at Marsaxlokk and Birżebbuġa.
Transport	Buses 91, 92, 93, 124, 135, 204 and X5 serve Marsaskala. Buses 81, 85 and 206 serve Marsaxlokk. Bus 119 links Marsaskala, Marsaxlokk and Birżebbuġa. Buses 82, 210 and X4 serve Birżebbuġa.

The eastern coastline of Malta is a succession of headlands and bays. Some of these can be walked around, while others have to be omitted, but the scenery changes constantly as the walk progresses. The towering chimney of the Enemalta power station is often in view, and towards the end of the walk the scenery becomes very industrial around Marsaxlokk Bay. Some walkers will be happy to finish at Marsaxlokk, which is an attractive little town. Others might like to continue around another headland to reach Birżebbuġa. The scenery deteriorates towards the end, but there are points of interest.

Start in the centre of **Marsaskala** and walk along the southern shore of **Marsaskala Bay**, admiring the colourful traditional fishing boats (luzzu) while following a paved promenade walkway. This often overlooks intricate salt pans carved in rock, and leads past apartments. Take a look at the fort of **St Thomas Tower** near a derelict hotel. ◄

The fort, surrounded by a deep ditch, was built after a Turkish raid in 1614, when the inland town of Żejtun was attacked.

Drop down onto the rocky shore beyond the derelict hotel and walk past more salt pans. Step up to a blockhouse and continue up along a crumbling cliff path on **Miġnuna Point** towards a road. Either follow the road, or take care following the crumbling cliff edge, and walk down to a car park on a low point.

A promenade path leads past gardens, toilets, a snack cabin and the San Tomaso Bar Restaurant. Continue along a battered dirt road, passing scruffy holiday homes that are squashed close together at the head of **St Thomas Bay**. The dirt road ends at a barrier gate where a narrow track climbs inland, offering a short-cut.

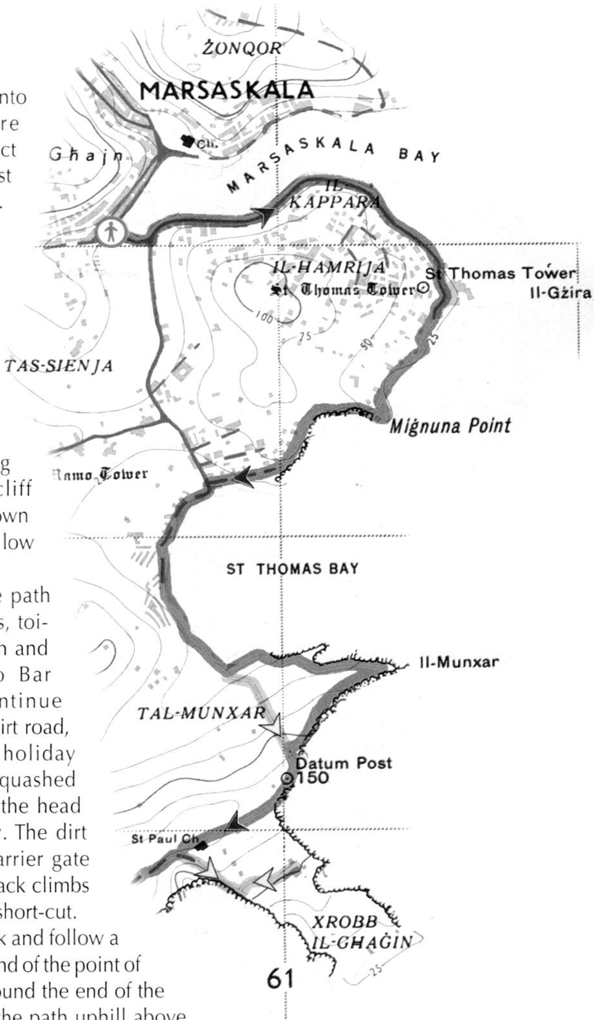

Leave the track and follow a path towards the end of the point of **Il-Munxar**. Turn round the end of the point and follow the path uphill above sheer white cliffs, re-joining the track. Turn left to follow the track along the crumbling cliff edge, which is flanked by a line of aloes. The track omits the rugged headland of **Xrobb il-Għaġin** and

map continues on page 50

map continues on page 53

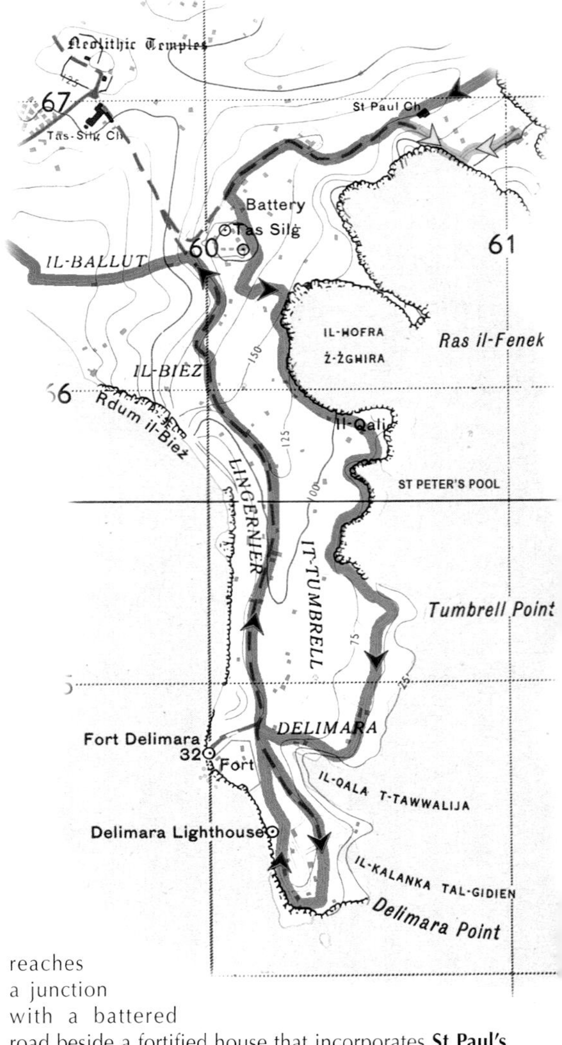

A left turn can be made down the road, turning left again into the Xrobb il-Għaġin Nature Park. Short nature trails are available, but steps have to be retraced afterwards.

reaches a junction with a battered road beside a fortified house that incorporates **St Paul's Chapel**. ◂

Turn right to follow the battered road away from St Paul's Chapel. The road swings right and left, passing junctions with tracks. Pass a big house tucked away behind gates, then turn left along a track. It's worth passing this junction briefly, just to see the entrance to the **Battery Tas Silġ**, which now operates as an animal sanctuary. ▸

Passing the fort altogether by road short-cuts the entire Delimara peninsula from the route.

Follow the track until it joins a concrete road, then turn left along another track, which runs down to a junction with a path. Follow the path, but bear in mind that it runs close to a cliff edge that's undercut in places, passing high above the bay of **Il-Ħofra iż-Żgħira**. It's quite likely that one day this path will collapse, in which case it would have to be closed, and walkers would have to detour inland by road to continue.

Continue along the cliffs by following a concrete road, turning right beyond **Il-Qali**, through a gate and along a path. The path quickly reaches a rocky inlet. Turn round the head of the inlet, then go down steps for a closer look at a remarkable rocky cove. ▸ Continue along the top of the cliffs, linking with a track set back from the edge. Turn left at a junction and walk round the other side of a cove, almost reaching a turning space at the end of the track.

This is St Peter's Pool, but rather confusingly, maps mark the next cove as 'Peter's Pool'.

Just before the turning space, turn left along a lesser track on **Tumbrell Point**. This leads to a dwelling set above salt pans, where several chained dogs will start barking. Leave the track and keep well to the right of the dwelling to pass it, continuing along another track set back from the coast. Aim to pass between a couple of cabins that are seen ahead, then follow a dirt road to a ruin and a turning space on a tarmac road. Enjoy views around the inlet of **Il-Qala t-Tawwalija** and walk up to a road junction.

Turn left and walk gently down a track. At the last minute, don't walk to a huddle of buildings, but branch to the right, turning round the end of **Delimara Point**, overlooking salt pans. Pass the weather-beaten **Delimara Lighthouse** and follow a battered road back to the road junction reached earlier.

Traditional fishing boats, or luzzu, *moored at Marsaxlokk Harbour*

It's worth considering a left turn here to reach the entrance of the 19th-century **Fort Delimara** and for a view around **Marsaxlokk Bay**. The Enemalta power station and the enormous Freeport are blots on the landscape – a decision was made in the past to concentrate most of Malta's industries in the south-east of the island.

Return to the road junction and turn left, following the road high above the power station. ◀ After passing the station there is later a narrow road down to the left and another road rising to the right, but avoid both of these roads and keep walking straight ahead, almost back to the **Battery Tas Silġ**. Turn left down a concrete road, which quickly becomes a rugged track leading down to a wide road. Turn right, then left for **Marsaxlokk**.

Views are dominated by the power station's towering chimney, which has been a recurrent feature throughout the day.

Pass the Hunter's Tower Restaurant and a harbour-side car park. There are toilets and plenty of places offering food and drink. A bus stop is located between the church and the harbour, while the harbour itself is full of gaily painted luzzu, attended by a dwindling number of fishermen. There are often market stalls alongside the harbour, selling all kinds of goods.

> **Marsaxlokk Bay** was too wide to be effectively defended in the past. The Turkish fleet under Dragut Reis dropped anchor here during the Great Siege of 1565, followed in 1798 by the French during the Napoleonic Wars. The Cold War was concluded by the American and Russian premières while they were aboard a warship anchored in the bay in 1989.

The walk can be ended at Marsaxlokk, but it's no hardship to continue onwards to Birżebbuġa. Simply keep close to the coast when leaving Marsaxlokk to follow a good track around **Qratjen Point** and a cliff path around

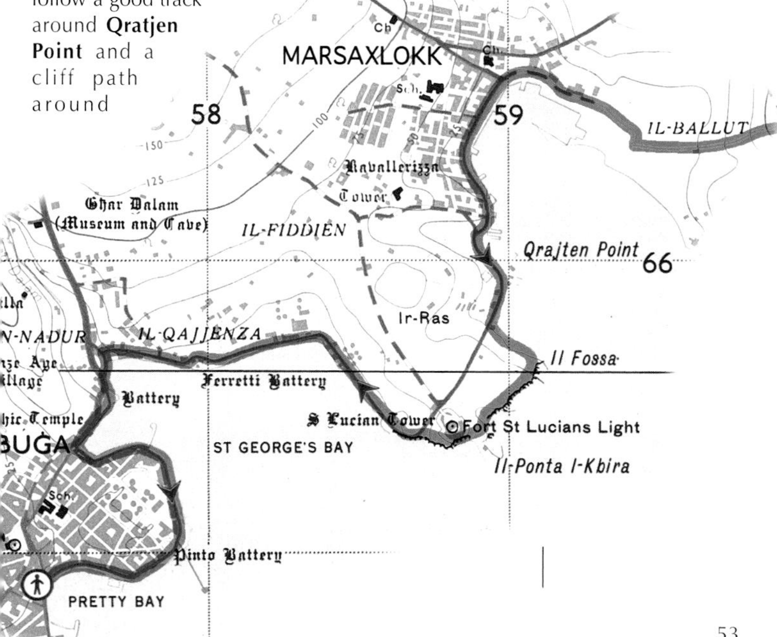

Pretty Bay and its white sand beach faces the enormous Freeport

The 'Bronze Age Village' marked on maps is a remarkable feature, surrounded by a formidable walled enclosure, but is unfortunately closed to visitors. To arrange a visit, tel 2295 4307.

Il-Fossa. The old **Fort St Lucian** is now used as a fisheries station. Follow the road down past the St Lucian Oil Company and continue past the derelict **Ferretti Battery** to approach Birżebbuġa, where there are bar-restaurants along the road, as well as buses. ◄

To finish the walk, either catch a bus near a roundabout at the head of the bay, or walk straight into the centre of town to find a bus stop near the parish church. It's possible to follow the coastal road a little further, round to **Pretty Bay**. Unfortunately, there is nothing pretty further ahead, where huge container ships are unloaded at the Freeport.

WALK 4

Birżebbuġa to Gudja

Start	Birżebbuġa (575 654)
Finish	Gudja (551 675)
Distance	5km (3 miles)
Time	1hr 30min
Terrain	Easy tracks, paths and roads, generally heading uphill
Maps	1:25,000 Malta sheet
Refreshments	Several shops, bars and restaurants at Birżebbuġa. A few little bars around Gudja.
Transport	Buses 82, 210 and X4 serve Birżebbuġa. Buses 135, X5 and X7 serve Gudja, and more buses serve the nearby airport.

Anyone trying to walk around the south-eastern coast of Malta beyond Birżebbuġa will find all sorts of obstacles stacked up against them. The area is very shabby and run-down and is essentially an extensive industrial area. The only decent walk in this part of the island heads inland. A fine, short valley-walk leads to the confluence of the Wied il-Qoton and Wied Ħas-Sabtan, from where quiet country roads lead up to the little village of Gudja. The village sits alongside Malta International Airport, so expect low-flying aircraft throughout this short walk. Walkers who want to get the most out of a visit to Malta could save this short walk for their final day, and extend it to finish at the airport!

Start at a roundabout at the head of a bay, where the bus runs into the heart of **Birżebbuġa** along Triq Birżebbuġa. Follow this street, then turn right up Triq Id-dar ta' Pultu. This quickly becomes a track, leaving the little town and continuing through fields. The surface gives way to bare rock as the track runs along a broad terrace of Lower Coralline Limestone. There's barely a crack or fissure in the rock, which is remarkably smooth. The terrace curves gently to the left to form a natural amphitheatre overlooking a verdant valley. A narrower path continues along a higher, narrower terrace. ▶

Note how the limestone has been hammered into little ribs to provide a non-slip walking surface.

The track dwindles to a walled path. Another track is joined and a left leads towards a substantial ruined house called **Casa Ippolita**. Just before reaching it, turn left down another track to reach a hut deep in the valley, where thickets of cane grow. Walk uphill and turn right along a concrete track to cross both the **Wied il-Qoton** and **Wied Ħas-Sabtan** valleys. The latter valley is crossed using a small bridge, then a concrete road leads uphill, neatly sliced deep into the limestone bedrock. The road rises past the Giebja Borehole and levels out at a converted Second World War pillbox called **Ta' Kusinu**. The scene is of fields and farmland all around.

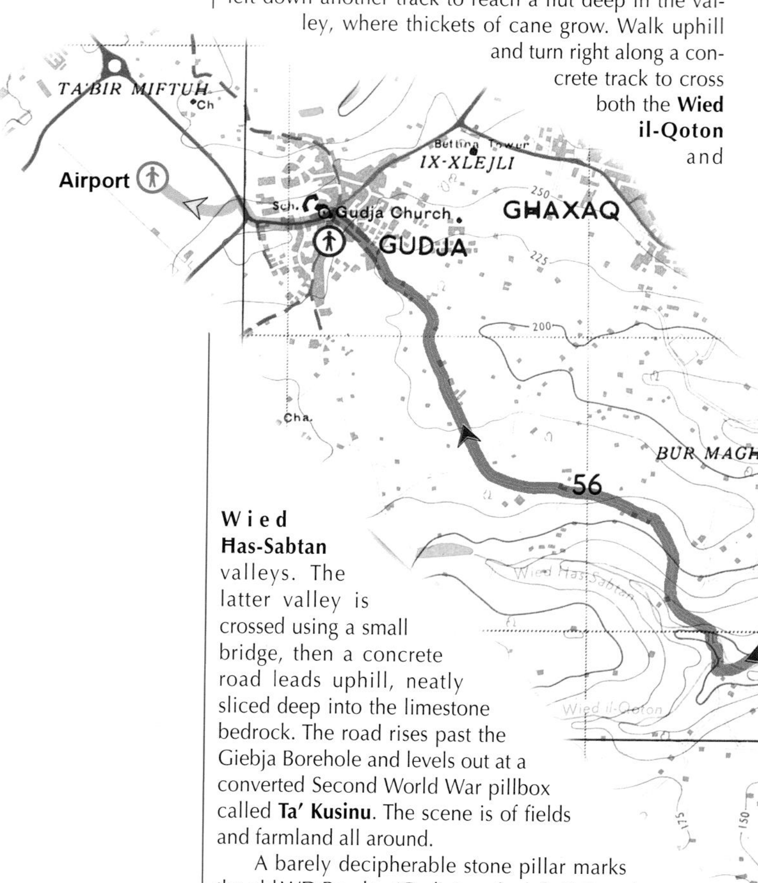

A barely decipherable stone pillar marks the old WD Road to 'Gudia' on the left. Follow the road until a point is reached where tracks cross each other. Walk straight ahead down a narrow road, looking

Walkers follow a concrete road in the Wied Ħas-Sabtan valley

far ahead to spot the church in the village of Gudja. The road winds and wriggles, then reaches a crossroads on the outskirts of **Gudja**. Walk straight ahead along Triq San Ġorġ and Triq San Ċiru, heading directly to the church in the middle of the village. Refreshments are immediately available, and if a quiet, shady spot is required while waiting for a bus, there's a sizeable garden tucked away behind the church, where toilets and a refreshment kiosk are located.

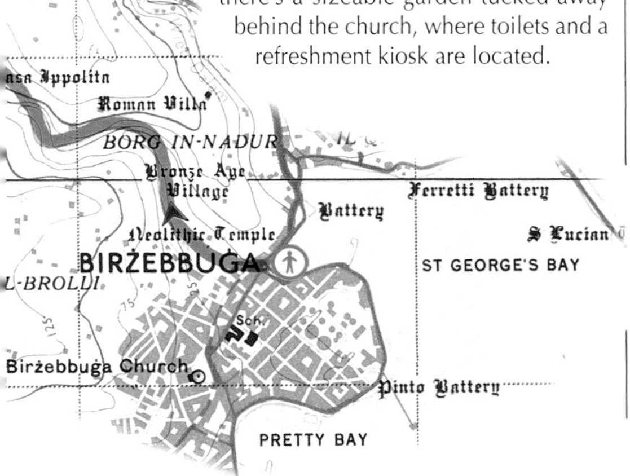

WALK 5

Żurrieq to Siġġiewi

Start	Żurrieq church (526 655)
Finish	Siġġiewi church (493 681)
Distance	14km (8¾ miles)
Time	(walking time) 4hr
Terrain	Roads, tracks and cliff paths. Some of the cliff paths are narrow and exposed, requiring care
Maps	1:25,000 Malta sheet
Refreshments	Shops, bars and restaurants in Żurrieq. Bars and restaurants at Wied iż-Żurrieq. Bar-restaurant at Ħaġar Qim. A couple of bar-restaurants at Għar Lapsi. A few shops, bars and restaurants at Siġġiewi.
Transport	Buses 71, 73, 117, 118 and 201 serve Żurrieq. Buses 71 and 109 serve Għar Lapsi in summer only. Buses 62, 109 and 209 serve Siġġiewi. Bus 201 links Żurrieq, Ħaġar Qim and Siġġiewi.

This is an action-packed day's walk – not particularly long, but with lots of interesting things to see along the way. If starting early, then an initial road-walk is necessary from Żurrieq. If starting later, then a bus can be used to reach Wied iż-Żurrieq, although there might be queues for the popular boat rides into the Blue Grotto. Next on the walk is the Ħaġar Qim/Mnajdra Archaeological Park, which takes time to explore properly. An exciting rocky coastal walk leads to Għar Lapsi, where summer bus services might allow an early finish; otherwise a long road-walk inland leads to buses in the town of Siġġiewi.

Start in the middle of **Żurrieq** and follow roads signposted for Wied iż-Żurrieq and the Blue Grotto. The roads in town are quite convoluted, but the main road away from town is more direct and has a pavement alongside for most of the way. Enjoy fine views along the cultivated valley of **Wied Babu** to a rocky ravine leading to the sea. A splendid viewpoint lies to the left, planted with aloes, allowing people to watch little boats nudging in and out of the awesome rock arch of the Blue Grotto. ▶ Buses stop at a nearby junction, but these don't operate early in the morning.

A sign at the viewpoint informs visitors of the likely sailing times, weather permitting, which can be checked in advance: tel 2164 0058 or 2164 9925.

Walk down the road towards Wied iż-Żurrieq, but watch for a short-cut down a walled track that cuts a big bend from the road. There's a large car park at **Wied iż-Żurrieq**, as well as bar-restaurants, a 17th-century stone tower, toilets and souvenirs.

Tickets for the **boat trips** are available from a kiosk on the way down to the water's edge. Queues can be very long once the tourist coaches roll in, so arrive as early as possible to avoid waiting. The boats visit five caves and pass through the towering arch of the Blue Grotto.

After the boat trip, there's no need to retrace steps up the road. Instead, pick a way around the cliff edge, starting from the boat landings and keeping just seawards of the stone tower. ▶ The **Blue Grotto** is directly underfoot at one point, but is not seen to good advantage. Look out for a few little steps that lead back to the road junction and bus stop passed earlier in the walk.

Bear in mind that the cliff edge is undercut as you climb higher and higher towards the road.

Turn left as signposted for Ħaġar Qim,

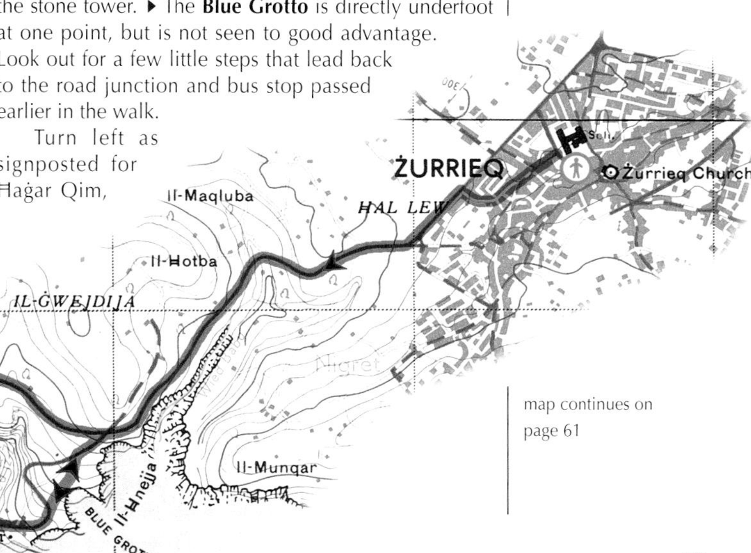

map continues on page 61

following the road gently uphill, while looking down a rocky ravine to Wied iż-Żurrieq. Continue up the road alongside **Wied Ħoxt** to reach a couple of bus stops and turn left along a road leading to a car park for the Archaeological Park. Decide whether to go into the visitor centre to buy a ticket for access to Ħaġar Qim and Mnajdra, or go to the Ħaġar Qim Bar Restaurant for food and drink.

Very little is known about the purpose of the complex stonework structure that is **Ħaġar Qim**, or of the lives of the people who constructed it over 5000 years ago, but it was undoubtedly a ritual site. Huge slabs of stone surround the roughly circular form, while inside, other slabs and walls define a handful of oval chambers. It's thought that a wooden roof once covered the whole structure. These days, it's covered by a huge tent-like structure to protect it from the weather.

Walk around the outside of the perimeter fence to find a straight paved path leading down to a similar site at **Mnajdra**. A ticket is required to enter the fenced compound, otherwise the site has to be studied from a distance. ◄

There are three interlocked structures, built over a period of 600 years. In essence they appear similar to Ħaġar Qim, but have particular orientations.

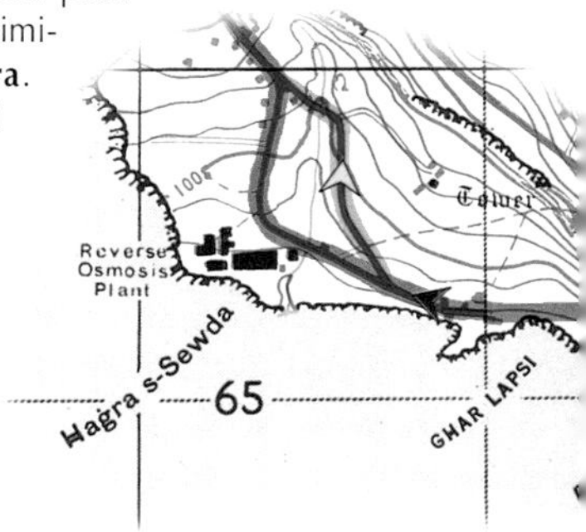

Leaving the fenced enclosure, walk back towards Ħaġar Qim, but turn right along a track and follow a path towards the 17th-century **Ħamrija Tower**. Retrace steps along the path and head for the prominent Congreve Memorial. An inscription reads: 'Sacred to the memory of His Excellency Sir Walter Norris Congreve, Governor of Malta, buried at sea on the 4th March 1927 between this spot and Filfla Island.' ▶

The little island of Filfla is protected as a nature reserve.

There's a way down the cliffs below the monument, but spend a few minutes looking carefully to spot it. To get down safely requires shoes that grip well on the rock; otherwise adopt 'Shufflebottom's Approach' and go down on your backside until safer ground is reached below. Swing right and keep well above the lower cliff line. There are faded painted arrows, but these occur infrequently, so keep an eye on the rather vague path along the cliff coast.

Aim for the little rocky inlet of **Il-Mitqub**, which has a white cobbled beach. The coastline is very complex, with little rocky points and coves, as well as occasional rock arches. ▶ A path continues across the rocky slope beyond, while a varied scrub includes wolfbane and tree spurges. After passing a couple of huge boulders, the path drops down closer to the sea.

Some broken rock bears drill marks and has tumbled from an old quarry higher up the cliffs.

Cross the mouth of a valley called **Wied Magħlaq** and look up through a ravine cut into the cliffs which is full of tree spurges. Painted arrows at the valley mouth urge walkers to keep left at a path junction, but whichever path is chosen, climb high above a cliff-bound cove at **Ras Ħanżir**. Pick a way across the steep and rocky slopes, which are not as bad as they look at first, but

map continues on page 62

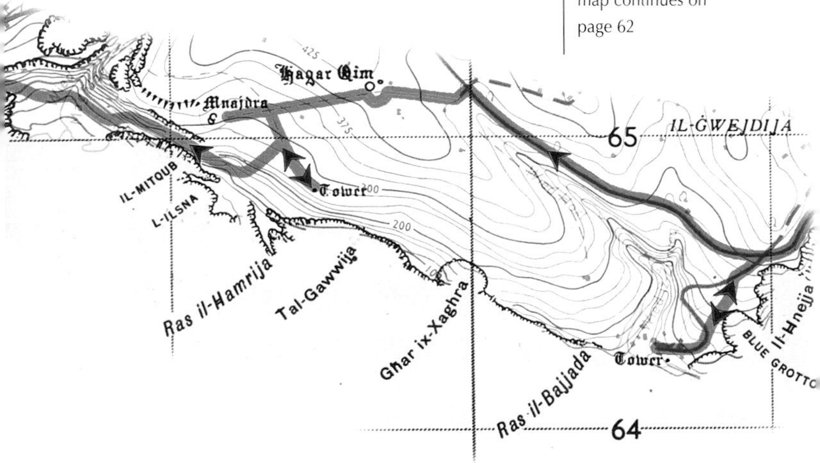

Għar Lapsi is a huddle of buildings above a small rocky cove

The Blue Creek and Lapsi View offer food and drink, and there are toilets, a car park, a play area and a summer-only bus service.

bear in mind that the sea cliffs are often undercut. Walk straight into **Għar Lapsi**. ◂

Follow the road uphill and inland, keeping either left to pass the **Reverse Osmosis Plant** or right to cut across a rugged slope where a castle-like building is a feature of interest. Both roads join at a higher level, then pass above a splendid rocky ravine at **Ix-Xaqqa**. The road bends right and climbs past the Caqnu Hardstone Quarry. Keep left at a roundabout, as signposted for Siġġiewi, and follow the road up past a big building at **Tal-**

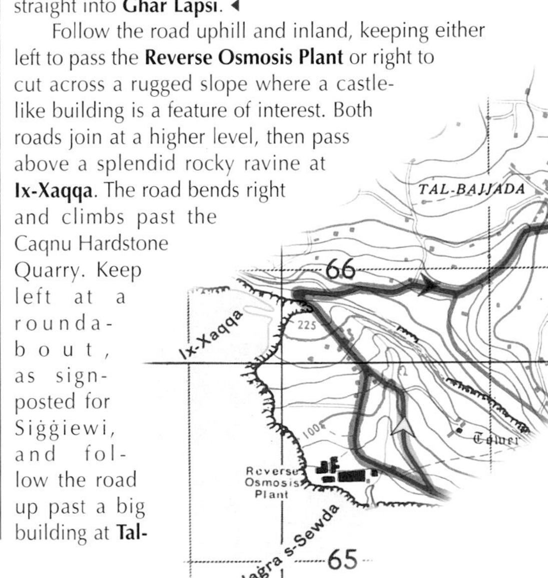

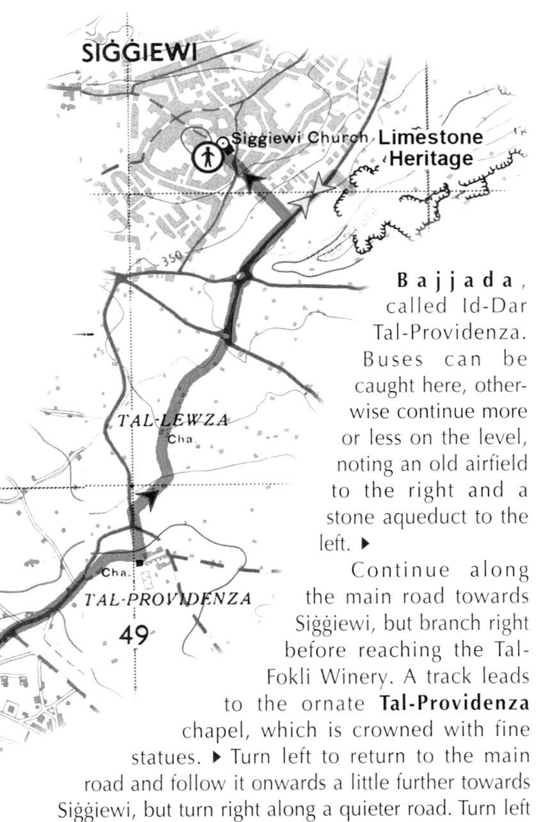

Bajjada, called Id-Dar Tal-Providenza. Buses can be caught here, otherwise continue more or less on the level, noting an old airfield to the right and a stone aqueduct to the left. ▸

A left turn along a road at this point continues the coastal theme as Walk 6 to Dingli.

Continue along the main road towards Siġġiewi, but branch right before reaching the Tal-Fokli Winery. A track leads to the ornate **Tal-Providenza** chapel, which is crowned with fine statues. ▸ Turn left to return to the main road and follow it onwards a little further towards Siġġiewi, but turn right along a quieter road. Turn left at the next junction to follow a very narrow road, which eventually reaches a roundabout on a busy road. Go straight across this, and another roundabout, to continue along the Siġġiewi bypass. A left turn up Triq Nikola Saura leads to the church in the middle of **Siġġiewi**, where a couple of shops and bars are set around a fine square. Buses run from this square to Valletta.

A little window allows a view of the rich artwork inside the chapel.

WALK 6

Siġġiewi to Dingli

Start	Siġġiewi church (493 681)
Finish	Dingli (443 689)
Distance	10km (6 miles)
Time	3hr
Terrain	Mostly roads and tracks, but towards the end the rugged cliff edges can be followed
Maps	1:25,000 Malta sheet
Refreshments	A few shops, bars and restaurants at Siġġiewi and Dingli. Possibly a snack van beside the Maddalena Chapel.
Transport	Buses 62, 109 and 209 serve Siġġiewi. Buses 52 and 202 serve Dingli. Bus 201 links Siġġiewi and Dingli.

This walk attempts to stay close to the coast, but is often set well back from the sea, and high above it. The route starts at Siġġiewi and follows roads, gradually moving closer and closer to the coast. There are interesting chapels along the way, and in due course there are splendid views of the cliffs. The highest parts of Malta, around 250m (820ft), are passed on this walk. The famous Dingli Cliffs are actually formed of two lines of cliffs; those closest to the sea are hardly seen on this walk, but then a rugged, cultivated slope leads up to a higher cliff line, which is followed quite closely at times.

If time can be spared turn left, then right, to reach the Limestone Heritage Park and Garden, which is located in a former softstone quarry and is well worth a visit. (See Walk 21).

Start at the church in **Siġġiewi** and walk down from a statue in the square to reach the Siġġiewi bypass. ◂ Turn right along the bypass to go straight past a roundabout. Go straight past another roundabout and continue along a narrow road that becomes even narrower. Turn right at a junction and walk to the main road. Turn left to walk up to the ornate **Tal-Providenza** chapel, which

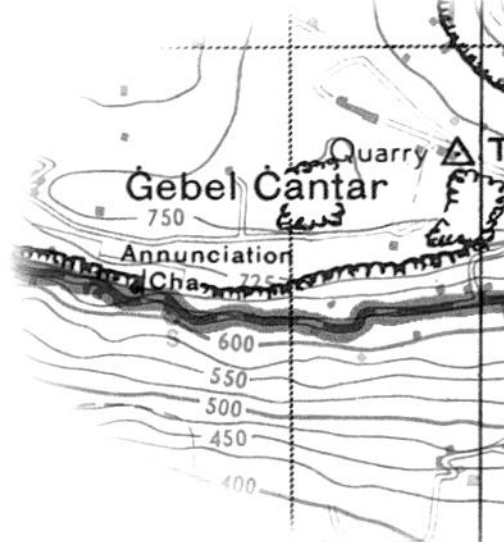

is crowned by fine statues. ▶ Turn right to pass the Tal-Fokli Winery and continue along the main road to reach a crossroads.

A little window allows a view of the rich artwork inside the chapel.

Turn right to follow a quiet country road, with fields to either side and a prominent aqueduct away to the left. Follow the road up to a large building called The Hermitage and turn left along a battered road. At a fork in the road, right leads up to a quarry at **Ġebel Cantar**, so keep left and begin to drop in stages from terrace to terrace as the road cuts across a cultivated slope. Cliffs rise above the cultivated terraces, and the old Kappella tal-Lunzjata, or **Annunciation Chapel**, is passed. Continue past occasional houses to reach the domed Underground Chapel at the end of the road, at **il-Fawwara**. ▶

A path beside the chapel leads down to the 'underground' part.

Follow a track onwards from the road-end, passing round a rocky natural amphitheatre, with an impressive overhanging cliff on the right and cultivated slopes behind a block

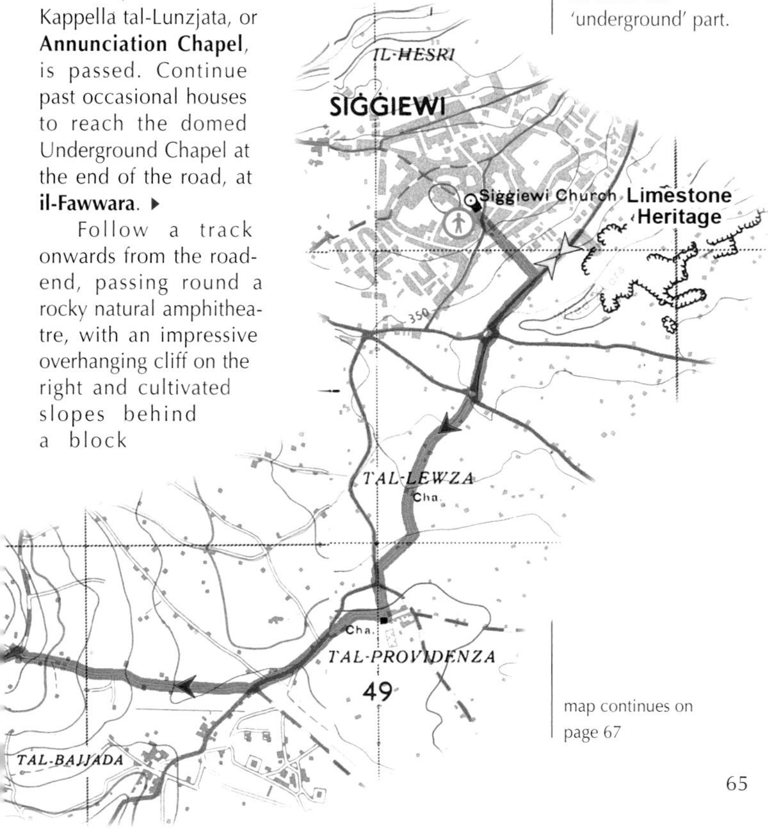

IL-HESRI
SIĠĠIEWI
Siggiewi Church
Limestone Heritage
350
TAL-LEWZA
Cha.
Cha.
TAL-PROVIDENZA
49
TAL-BAJJADA

map continues on page 67

wall on the left. The track zigzags up past attractive stumps of rock, with Maltese rock centaury, wolfbane, Mediterranean heath and all sorts of tangled scrub clinging to the rock-faces, and the views open up splendidly.

The track passes a wall, and if you stand back you can discern the letters 'NAZAC' built into the stonework. The track is very rugged and has been cut deep into the rock as it climbs up to a road at **Ta' Zuta**. Turn left to follow the road; a noisy hardstone quarry lies out of sight, cutting into one of Malta's high points, to the right of the road at 253m (830ft). When the road forks, keep left, then either follow the road or walk on the rough and rocky cliff edges of **Rdum Dikkiena** whenever possible. Looking ahead, the dumpy form of the Maddalena Chapel can be seen and a short, rugged climb leads towards it if the cliff edge is still being followed. ◂

An old lookout stands alongside, in danger of collapse, and there might be a snack van parked nearby.

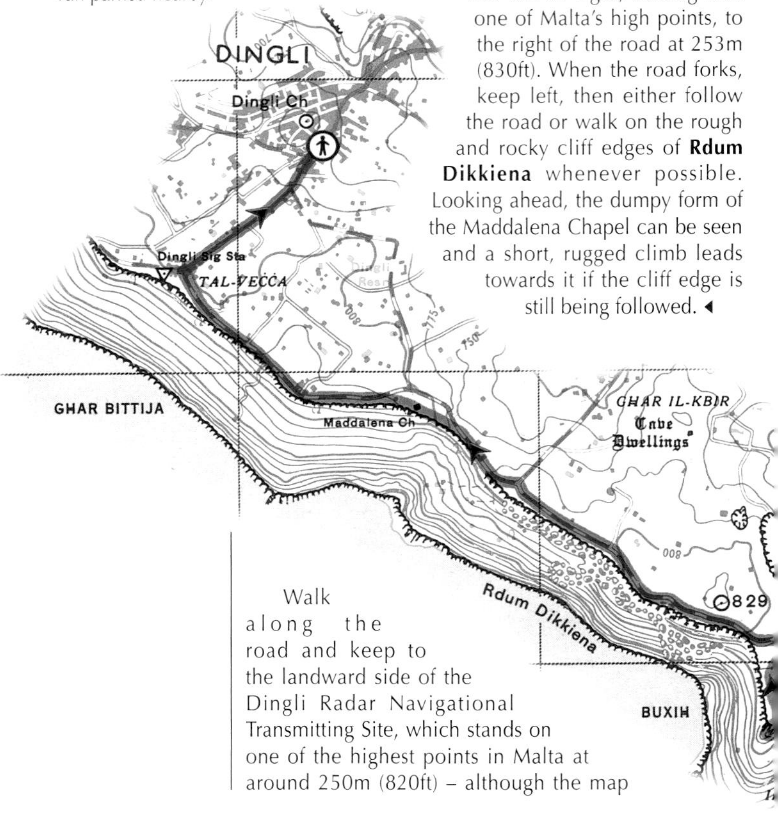

Walk along the road and keep to the landward side of the Dingli Radar Navigational Transmitting Site, which stands on one of the highest points in Malta at around 250m (820ft) – although the map

A view along the edge of the Dingli Cliffs before finishing at Dingli

gives no precise value for its height. Again, it's possible to walk along the edge of the Dingli Cliffs, but the road has a much easier pavement.

> **The Cliffs Interpretation Centre** (tel 2145 5470, www.thecliffs.com.mt) is worth a visit. It occupies a 1960s military site and contains information about wildlife. Its café offers an interesting menu flavoured with locally gathered produce. All kinds of plant communities are tucked into every hollow in the limestone pavement, and there are views down rugged, cultivated slopes.

When a military lookout is reached at **Tal-Veċċa**, leave the cliffs and turn right inland. The road is Triq it-Turretta, which leads to the Mater Dolorosa cemetery, where keeping straight ahead leads onto Triq il-Kbira. Walk straight into **Dingli** and either finish at the bus stop, shops and bars, or make a detour up to the imposing church before leaving.

WALK 7

Dingli to Mġarr

Start	Dingli (443 689)
Finish	Mġarr church (429 754)
Distance	19km (11¾ miles), with a 3.5km (2¼-mile) extension
Time	6hr–7hr
Terrain	Mostly roads and tracks, with some hill and cliff paths that require careful route-finding
Maps	1:25,000 Malta sheet
Refreshments	A few shops, bars and restaurants at Dingli and Baħrija. Snack cabins at Ġnejna Bay. A few shops, bars and restaurants at Mġarr.
Transport	Buses 52, 201 and 202 serve Dingli. Bus 109 serves Baħrija. Buses 101 and 102 link Ġnejna Bay with Mġarr in summer. Buses 38, 44 and 225 serve Mġarr.

There's plenty to see on this walk, but it's a long walk that can only be broken easily in the middle, at Baħrija. Leaving Dingli, a fine cliff-walk quickly gives way to a lengthy detour around the huge and well-cultivated Mtaħleb valley. Afterwards, there's an optional detour down a winding road to a rocky chasm at Miġra Ferħa. Bear in mind that the long climb back uphill in the heat of the day can be exhausting. Another short detour leads to a Bronze Age village on the way to Baħrija. A useful bus service at Baħrija allows a break of journey; otherwise another detour inland is followed by a traverse across the hill of Pellegrin. The coast is reached at Ġnejna Bay before a long road-walk inland to finish at Mġarr. The road has a bus service in the summer months.

The village of **Dingli** is huddled around a fine church on elevated ground. Start from the bus stop at a road junction below the church and follow signposts for the Dingli Cliffs. Leave the village along Triq il-Kbira and keep right of the Mater Dolorosa cemetery to follow Triq it-Turretta. The road leads to a junction at a military lookout; turn right as signposted for Is-Simblija and the Bobbyland Restaurant.

Enjoy brief views of the **Rdum Depiro** cliffs, pass the restaurant (noting its collection of antiques) and continue down the road. Keep straight ahead at a road junction to pass a stout cliff-top house called Ridum Depiro. Climb a little, then follow the road to a junction near a securely fenced explosive factory at **Il-Qaws**.

Turn sharp right at the junction, as if following the road straight back towards Dingli. Keep straight ahead at another road junction. ▸ Avoid tracks leading left and right to properties, then turn left when another road junction is reached and follow the road across a dip.

Turning left offers a scenic road-walk above the fertile Mtaħleb valley, but every track and path leading off it is private, and steps would have to be retraced from the end of the road.

map continues on page 71

Walk straight ahead at the next junction, turn left along a busier road at yet another junction at **Ta' Cassia**, then continue straight through a staggered crossroads. When a triangular road junction is reached, turn left along a quiet road. Reach a complex road junction at **Ta' Baldu**, turn right only a short way uphill, then immediately turn left towards a little house.

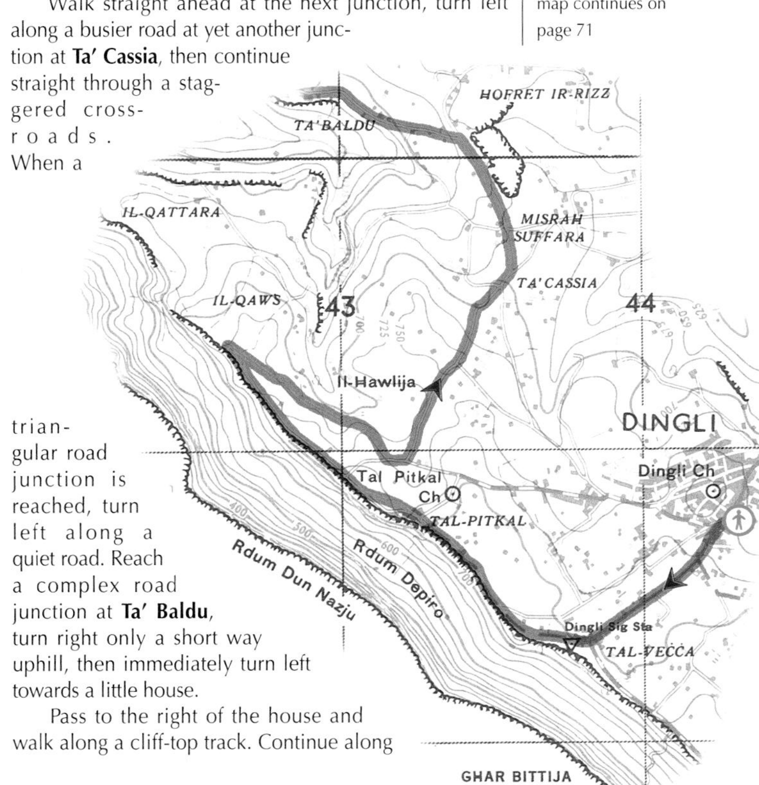

Pass to the right of the house and walk along a cliff-top track. Continue along a stoutly walled track that drifts away from the cliffs and runs through fields. ◂ The track leads out onto a road, which seems to end abruptly on a cliff edge. However, a huddle of buildings lies unseen below, built into the cliffs overlooking **Wied ir-Rum**.

This is a great place to spot wall geckos, as they have to run a long way to find gaps to hide in the wall.

Stay on the cliff top and follow a vague path across bare limestone, soon noting a series of 'cart ruts' cut deep into the rock. Some parts of the path are overgrown, but by staying close to the cliff edge a few buildings are reached on a road bend. Turn right to follow the road to a junction, then quickly turn left and left again to pass the Mtaħleb Unit, which houses young offenders. Follow the road to the cliff-edge **Mtaħleb Chapel**. ◂

This 17th-century structure sits on the site of two earlier chapels.

Walk back along the road from the chapel and turn left down some concrete steps to a lower road. Turn right and walk to a road junction just to the left of the Mtaħleb Unit. Turn left to continue along the road, turning left and right in quick succession at junctions with other roads. In effect, stay on the widest road as it winds through a dry and desolate area of stony steppes. Reach yet another road junction among acacia trees at **Tal-Merħla**. Here you have the option of a detour to the sea, so take account of your available time and energy.

Extension to Miġra Ferħa

The road down to the left leads to the remarkable chasm of Miġra Ferħa, at sea level. This out-and-back detour involves 180m (590ft) of descent and ascent, and an additional hour of walking. As the road winds downhill, cultivated slopes give way to tamarisk, aloes and bare rock by the time a couple of cliff-top car parks are reached. Note the deep, rocky cleft, which contains a narrow, stepped path leading all the way down to the sea at **Miġra Ferħa**. There are splendid views of the cliffs, but take care when big waves are beating against them. ▸

Roger the Norman is said to have invaded Malta at this point, ending the Arab rule of the island in 1091.

Eventually, turn round and climb all the way back up to **Tal-Merħla**. Just before reaching the junction among the acacia trees, it's possible to turn left along a quieter road running parallel to the main road, and both roads soon join.

Continue along the road, roughly parallel to the cliffs of **Rdum tal-Vigarju**, with views inland to the huddled village of

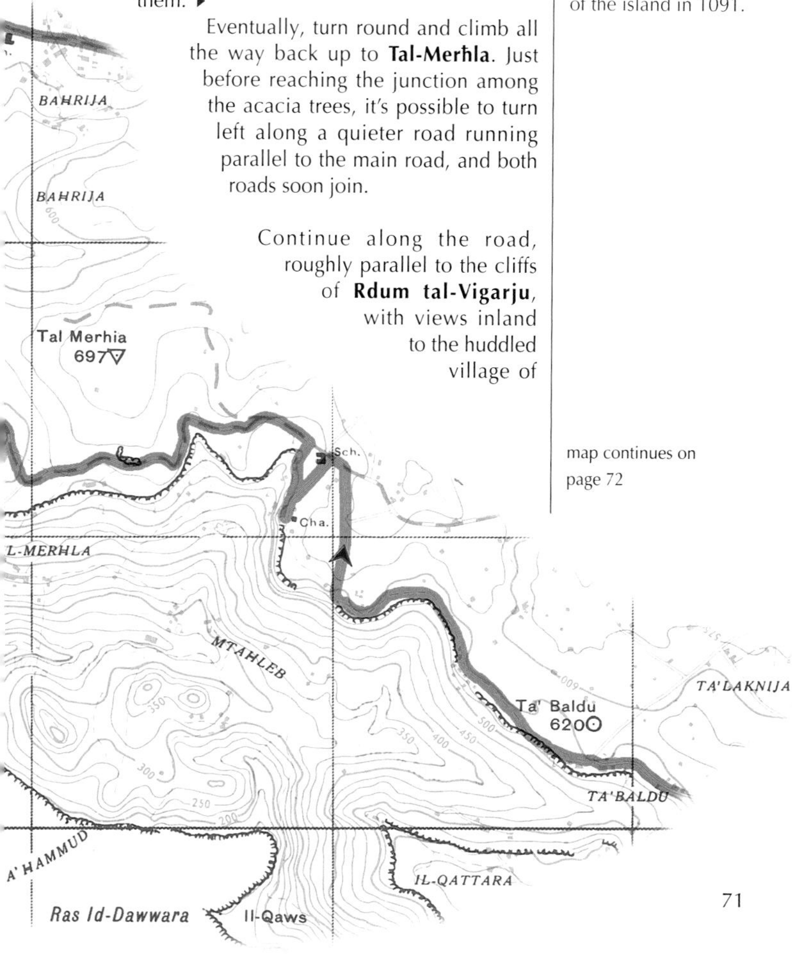

map continues on page 72

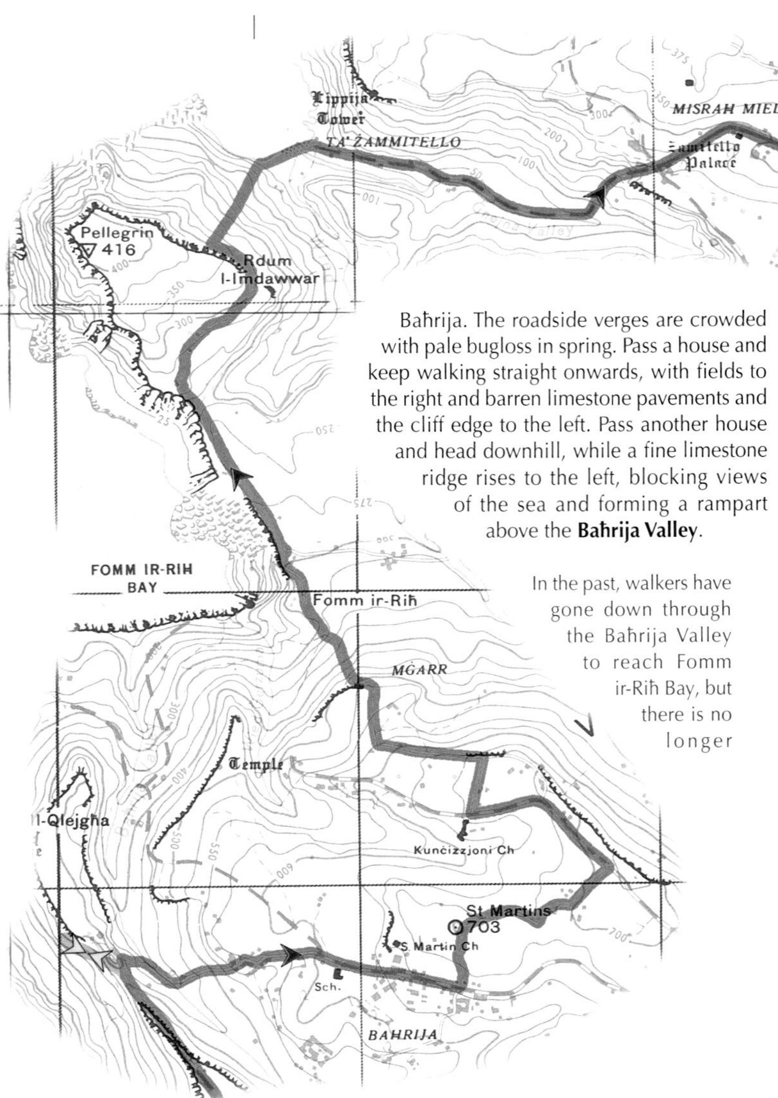

Baħrija. The roadside verges are crowded with pale bugloss in spring. Pass a house and keep walking straight onwards, with fields to the right and barren limestone pavements and the cliff edge to the left. Pass another house and head downhill, while a fine limestone ridge rises to the left, blocking views of the sea and forming a rampart above the **Baħrija Valley**.

In the past, walkers have gone down through the Baħrija Valley to reach Fomm ir-Riħ Bay, but there is no longer access between the bay and the slopes of Pellegrin beyond.

When the sea is revealed again, in a view from a gap, it's worth making a short detour left along a track to see the cave dwellings of a Bronze Age village. Steps have to be retraced afterwards. When walking down into the Baħrija Valley, keep turning right down a concrete track and follow a little watercourse upstream. Cross the stream in a thicket of cane, where there are also a couple of stout prickly pears. The track becomes a road as it climbs to some houses. Keep straight on along the road to reach the village of **Baħrija**.

Baħrija is clustered around a central garden and play park, offering refreshement at a handful of bar-restaurants. The 16th-century St Martin's chapel is a point of interest, contrasting markedly with the modern St Martin's church. Bus 109 offers the only exit from the middle of this long day's walk, leading to Rabat and other bus services.

To continue walking, follow the road through the village, turning left up Triq Dun Saverin (FX) Bianco. Pass to the right of St Martin's church to follow a stony track. Keep right at a junction, heading downhill and bending right, then turn left through a gap in a wall to pass a huddle of farm buildings. Follow an access road to a road junction and turn left. The road soon bends left and reaches the **Kunċizzjoni Chapel**, which stands next to a stone gateway inscribed 'Fondazione Paola 1731'.

Turn right and follow the road to a memorial and a fine viewpoint on the Victoria Lines. ▶ Turn left to follow the road parallel to the wall, overlooking distant Mġarr. The road becomes a track, serving a derelict searchlight battery, so turn left along another track before reaching it. The 'No Trespassing' notice at this point is a mystery

See Walk 18 for a long day's walk along this impressive defensive wall.

A boat moored at Ġnejna Bay before the walk heads inland to Mġarr

to local people! Walk down the track to reach the stout stonework of the Victoria Lines again, and turn left to follow the wall downhill.

The path beside the wall is quite rugged and passes a blockhouse. The wall itself crumbles away further downhill. Pick a way down the steep and stony path to join a concrete track. Turn right, then almost immediately left at a track junction. Walk straight through an intersection of tracks and later reach a road high above **Fomm ir-Riħ Bay**. Enjoy views around the bay. If time is pressing, turn right to short-cut by road to Mġarr, otherwise turn left to follow the road and complete the full walk, later passing a cliff-top villa.

The road passes a couple of small houses and becomes a track. Fork right at a junction and cross the lower slopes of a hill called **Pellegrin**, keeping to the clearest path. The path rises gently, then it suddenly gives way to a concrete path on the right, which drops below a cliff line. ▸ Follow the path as it rises a little past vines and fruit trees, then it suddenly drops downhill. The path is steep and grassy, but worn to crumbling earth on slopes of Blue Clay, which can be messy when wet. At the bottom turn right to reach the beach at **Ġnejna Bay**, then head for the car park and toilets. There might also be snack vans available.

There are fine views over Ġnejna Bay, Għajn Tuffieħa and other headlands beyond, with the island of Gozo in the distance.

Follow the road inland from the beach, rising through the **Ġnejna Valley**, climbing steeply to reach a crossroads. Go straight through and follow the tree-shaded road past the **Żamitello Castello** restaurant to reach the little town of **Mġarr**.

The domed church in **Mġarr** was built in 1912, financed from the sale of eggs, and is known locally as the Egg Church. Food and drink are readily available, and there are bus stops on a nearby corner.

WALK 8

Għajn Tuffieħa circuit

Start/Finish	Golden Bay (411 770)
Distance	4km (2½ miles)
Time	1hr 30min
Terrain	Mostly along easy coastal and cliff paths, but also through a jumbled area of huge boulders that needs care
Maps	1:25,000 Malta sheet
Refreshments	Bar-restaurants at Golden Bay. Possible ice-cream van at Għajn Tuffieħa.
Transport	Buses 44, 101, 102, 223 and 225 serve Golden Bay/ Għajn Tuffieħa.

Golden Bay is a very popular destination dominated by a huge Radisson hotel. There are well-trodden paths around the bays, headlands and cliffs. Those who wish to find out more about the plants and wildlife of the Maltese islands – especially on a first visit to Malta – should visit the Gaia Foundation nursery at 'Elysium'. The Gaia Foundation operates an Integrated Coastal Project Management scheme along the coast and cliffs covered in this walk, actively re-establishing plants in the area and finding ways of coping with increasing numbers of visitors.

Start at the bus terminus at **Golden Bay**, which is beside the Apple's Eye Restaurant. A road runs down to a popular sandy beach, but stay inland and follow the road past the Apple's Eye. A fenced enclosure on the right is home to 'Elysium' – a nursery propagating Maltese flowers, shrubs and trees.

A site visit offers an excellent grounding in **Maltese flora**. Some 10,000 endemic plants grow on this site, which was formerly a sewage treatment plant for a British army barracks. The Gaia Foundation was instrumental in obtaining special protection in 1996 for the nearby cliffs, including the highest possible protection for the nearby headland of Il-Karraba.

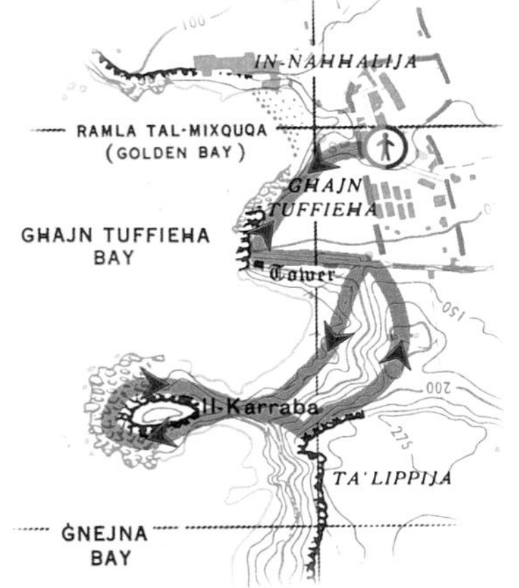

Leaving Elysium, follow a track alongside the perimeter fence, admiring the dense flowery scrub that has been re-established on the once-denuded headland. Also admire the 17th-century **Għajn Tuffieħa Tower**, which is sometimes open to visitors in the evenings. It overlooks both Golden Bay and Għajn Tuffieħa Bay, but beware of the cliff edge, where rocks are splitting apart.

Follow a clear track towards a derelict building that was once a hotel, reaching a car park beside it. ▸ Turn right at the exit from the car park and follow a path down a slope of Blue Clay. Avoid paths leading all the way down to the beach at **Għajn Tuffieħa Bay** and instead cut across the clay slopes covered in tamarisk, grass and fiery red carpets of sulla in the spring.

The intriguing Gaia Peace Grove lies beside the track and is threaded by a network of paths.

Għajn Tuffieħa Bay with the headland of Il-Karraba rising beyond

The headland of Il-Karraba is slowly crumbling away

With geology as unstable as this, take care if walking all the way around the headland. If it looks too dangerous, omit the headland!

Aim for a bare clay gap between the headland of **Il-Karraba** and the higher cliffs, from which there is a view across the gap of **Ġnejna Bay** and the headland of Pellegrin. Walk towards Il-Karraba, noting how its cap of Upper Coralline Limestone overhangs on almost all sides. It's supported by a thin, crumbling layer of Greensand, which is in turn supported by the crumbling Blue Clay. ◂

Keep to the left-hand side for an easy start, but beware of the dangers of rock-falls and landslips. Traverse the steep and crumbling slopes to reach massive jumbled boulders at the end of the headland. Watch out for red paint blobs, which indicate a path that wriggles between – or even underneath – the boulders, and admire the bushy tree spurges, fig trees, golden samphire and all kinds of flowery plants that have found a niche in this chaotic terrain. The path leads all the way around the headland and returns to the crumbling clay gap.

Climb straight uphill towards the higher cliffs, but watch for a path heading off to the left before the final rock-face. The path traverses a scrubby slope and passes acacia, tamarisk and pine trees before reaching a gap. Climb straight up a bare little hill, whose Blue Clay slopes are crowned with crumbling Greensand. An old reservoir structure stands nearby, and a clear path runs straight down to the car park beside the derelict hotel.

A road can be followed straight back to Elysium and **Golden Bay**, otherwise steps can be retraced along the path to the stone tower to return around the headland.

WALK 9

Mġarr to Għadira

Start	Mġarr church (429 754)
Finish	Għadira Nature Reserve (414 812)
Distance	16km (10 miles)
Time	5hr
Terrain	Mostly cliff paths, with a few linking roads and tracks
Maps	1:25,000 Malta sheet
Refreshments	A few shops, bars and restaurants at Mġarr. Bar-restaurants at Golden Bay. Bar-restaurant at the 'Popeye Village'. Beach bars near the Għadira Nature Reserve at Mellieħa Bay.
Transport	Buses 44 and 225 serve Mġarr, while 101 and 102 link Mġarr and Golden Bay/Għajn Tuffieħa. Bus 237 serves the 'Popeye Village' in summer. Buses 41, 42, 101, 102, 221, 222 and X1 serve Għadira.

This walk takes in some of the most scenic and dramatic cliffs on Malta. It includes a visit to Il-Majjistral Nature and History Park, which is Malta's closest equivalent to a national park. The cliff tops are mostly Upper Coralline Limestone, which lies on a crumbling layer of Greensand that is barely supported by even more crumbling Blue Clay beneath. As a result, the cliff edges are often fractured and huge detached boulders form a wild and jumbled 'undercliff' where few walkers venture. Among the boulders are sheltered sun-traps that have been pressed into use for cultivation.

The walk can be shortened by starting at Golden Bay, or finished early by catching a bus from the remarkable 'Popeye Village'. Strong walkers could continue to Ċirkewwa for a bus, but most would be happy to cut across the island to catch a bus at Għadira.

Before leaving Mġarr, it's worth visiting the Ta' Ħaġrat Temples, signposted off Triq Fisher. An interesting wartime shelter can be visited on Triq il-Kbira.

To start the walk, face Mġarr church, keep to the right, and follow Triq il-Kbira out of the little town. The road passes the **Żamitello Castello** restaurant and reaches a crossroads. Turn right up a battered road, passing the Villa Copperstone. As the road levels out, turn left along a track, passing a little house to reach the 17th-century **Lippija Tower**, perched on a cliff of Upper Coralline Limestone overlooking Ġnejna Bay.

map continues on page 82

Turn right to follow the cliff edge gently downhill. Keep an eye open for a path that cuts below the cliff edge, and continue across a steep slope of Blue Clay until a crumbling ridge is reached, stretching down to the rugged little headland of **Il-Karraba**. (A path around the headland is described in Walk 8.)

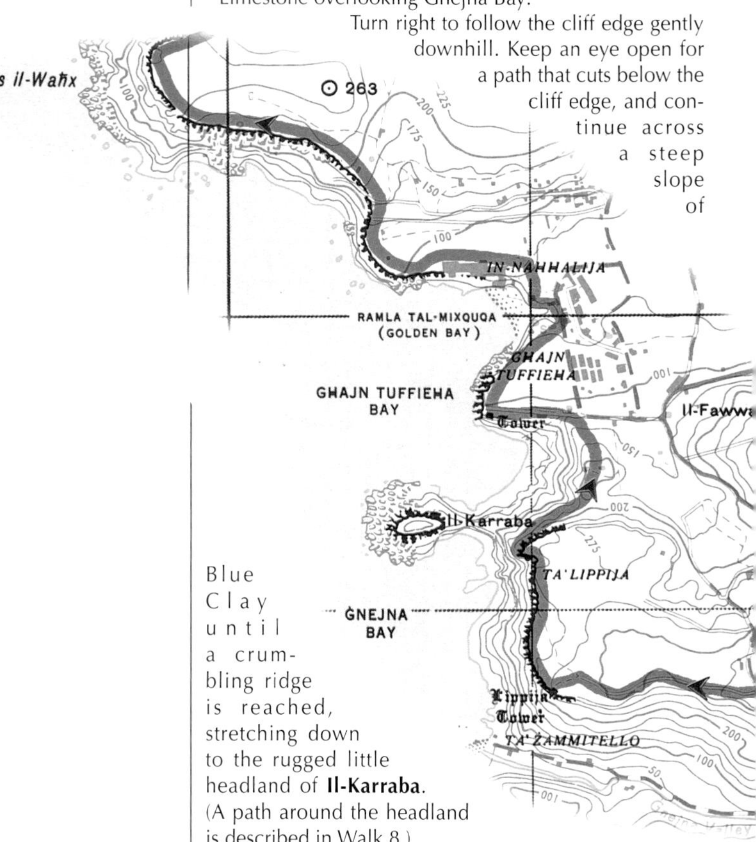

The 17th-century Lippija Tower sits on a cliff above Ġnejna Bay

Cross the ridge and follow a path that traverses a scrubby slope below the cliffs, passing acacia, tamarisk and pine trees before reaching a gap. Climb straight up a bare little hill, whose Blue Clay slopes are crowned with crumbling Greensand. An old reservoir structure stands nearby, and a clear path runs straight down to a car park beside a derelict hotel at **Għajn Tuffieħa**.

Follow a track from the derelict hotel to the 17th-century **Għajn Tuffieħa Tower**. ▶ This commands fine views over Għajn Tuffieħa Bay and Golden Bay, and a clear track leads onwards round the headland, running alongside the perimeter fence of 'Elysium' – a nursery propagating Maltese flowers, shrubs and trees (see beginning of Walk 8).

The intriguing Gaia Peace Grove lies beside the track and is threaded by a network of paths.

Turn left along the road to reach the Apple's Eye Restaurant, a large car park and bus stop. A road runs down to a popular sandy beach at **Golden Bay**, if a detour is required, otherwise stay on the higher road and follow it inland round a corner. Almost immediately, turn left as if going to the large Radisson hotel. However, turn right when a notice is seen about Il-Majjistral Nature and History Park. ◂

There's a visitor centre, but it lies off-route beyond a scout camp (tel 2152 1291, mt.majjistral.org).

A path runs between the hotel boundary wall and a fence surrounding a scout camp. It then turns left, still running between the wall and the fence, then later crosses open ground towards a cliff edge. Turn right to follow the cliff edge, but bear in mind that it's often undercut. A stony track passes a few stone buildings as it climbs up a slope, but avoid another track running down through a cutting onto the 'undercliff'.

Keep climbing, and a good stony path runs round the headland, with views of lush, cultivated areas down on the chaotic bouldery slopes. ◂ At the top of the headland, overlooking **Ras il-Waħx**, a concrete lookout is embedded in the ground. Steps lead down into it, revealing herringbone bedding in the

The headland is like a rock garden in spring, with wolfbane growing in conspicuous clumps.

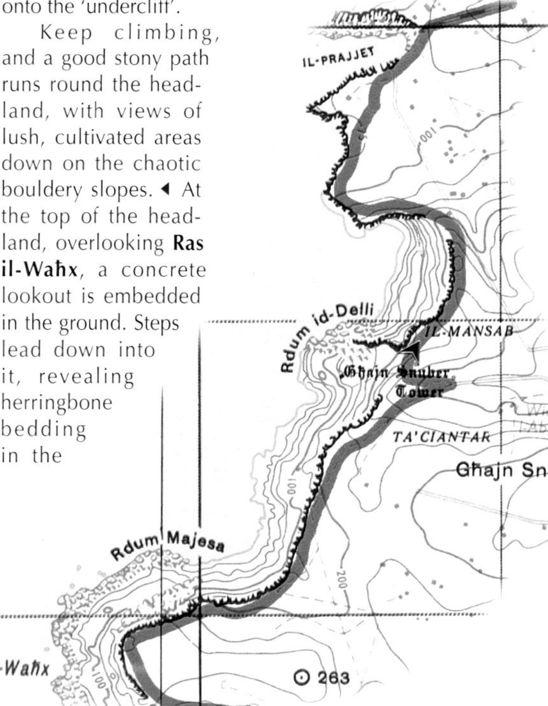

map continues on page 83

limestone. Old terracing can be seen on the bouldery slopes of **Rdum Majesa**.

Views stretch along the coast of Malta to the southern cliffs of Gozo. Keep following the cliff edge, but if the rugged terrain underfoot becomes too difficult, a handy track can be used a bit further inland. (Views from the edge, however, are excellent and should be enjoyed even if it means slow progress.) Rock steps lead down to cultivated patches among the boulders, although these are marked as private. A track leads gently uphill, drifting away from the cliffs, with rubble walls alongside as it climbs to the restored 17th-century **Ghajn Żnuber Tower**.

Take care with route-finding when leaving the tower. The best thing is to double back sharp left from the tower, then keep right along a track. Watch out for a series of narrow paths descending to a couple of huts beside a line of prickly pears. Turn right and cross a rocky fissure choked with boulders and fig trees. Scramble up and walk along the cliff edge, heading gradually uphill, overlooking the bouldery slopes of **Rdum id-Delli**.

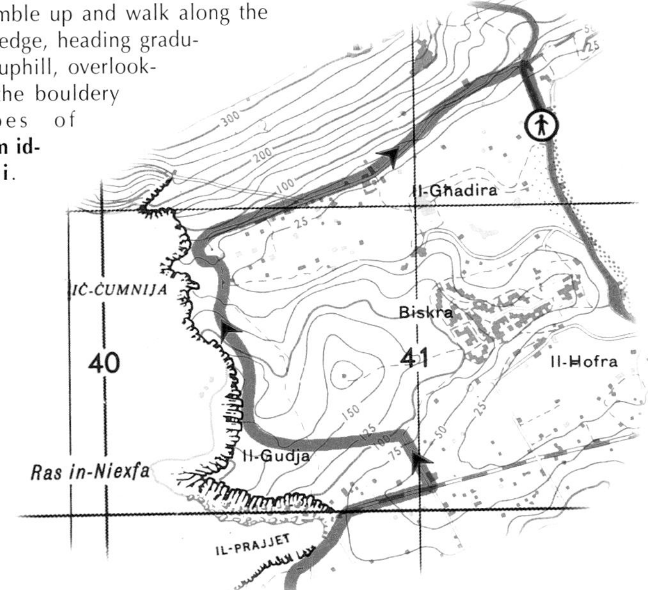

The whimsical 'Sweethaven' where Popeye was filmed in 1980

Beware of cracks and fissures and keep back from the edge, which is often undercut.

Descend along the cliff edge overlooking a rocky bay and walk out onto a barren headland. Turn round the headland and continue downhill, bearing in mind that the cliffs overhang dramatically. ◂ Look out for caves cut into the base of the cliffs, and reach a track close to a sewage outfall. It's best to follow the track inland to a road, then continue round the inlet of **Il-Prajjet**. There are views of the 'Popeye Village' and walkers can decide whether to make a visit.

The rocky slopes support only golden samphire and sparta grass, but often it's only the samphire that survives.

Sweethaven, or the **'Popeye Village'**, was built purely as a film set in 1980. The film starred Robin Williams with bulging biceps as Popeye, and Shelley Duvall in a most unflattering dress as Olive Oyl. The film was a flop, but the village has endured!

Nineteen wooden buildings were constructed at drunken angles, with much of the wood being imported from Canada. The set has been retained an attraction (tel 2152 4782, **www.popeyemalta.com**) and there's an entrance fee. There's a bar-restaurant on site, as well as toilets and a chance to see the *Popeye* film and documentaries. A rather incongruous addition to Sweethaven is an animated Christmas wonderland!

Follow the road inland until a point is reached where there are vehicle tracks heading right and left. ▶ Turn left and follow the track until it climbs, then turn left through a gap in a wall. A vague path runs across a rugged slope towards a fenced cliff edge. Turn right to climb steadily. The ground is rough and rocky at first, but becomes easier at the top of **Il-Gudja**. Walk along the cliff-top then head down towards a bay. There's a fine semi-circular cove at **Iċ-Ċumnija**, spoiled by being too close to a sewage works and dumped rubbish. Follow a road uphill from the works and turn right.

The road offers an obvious short-cut straight to Mellieħa.

The road runs coast-to-coast across a narrow neck of cultivated land. ▶ Reach a busy main road above **Mellieħa Bay** and turn right down it. Either head for a bus stop, toilets and beach bar, or include a visit to the **Għadira Nature Reserve**.

To continue to Cirkewwa, as described in Walk 10, turn sharply left uphill at a junction.

GĦADIRA NATURE RESERVE

The reserve is open at weekends from November to May and can get very crowded. A visitor centre is full of information boards, overlooking a lagoon surrounded by trees and bushes. Bird hides are available and BirdLife Malta (www.birdlifemalta.org) keeps a record of all visiting species.

Sixteenth-century maps showed this area as a salt pan, but it fell into disuse when the Knights of St John developed salt pans at Salina. Għadira silted up, but contained water in winter, which attracted ducks, then it dried out in the summer. It was eventually used as a summer car park.

In 1978 Għadira was declared a bird sanctuary and by 1980 it had become Malta's first nature reserve. The area was enlarged and deepened and is now permanently flooded. Islands were created, then trees and shrubs were planted. The area was fenced and the visitor centre and hides were built. The Għadira Nature Reserve was officially opened in 1988.

WALK 10

Marfa Ridge circuit

Start/Finish	Mellieħa Bay (414 814)
Distance	16km (10 miles)
Time	5hr
Terrain	Roads, tracks and rugged cliff paths
Maps	1:25,000 Malta sheet
Refreshments	Beach bars at Mellieħa Bay. Bar-restaurant at Paradise Bay. Bar-restaurants at Ramla Bay and Armier Bay.
Transport	Buses 41, 42, 101, 102, 221, 222 and X1 serve Mellieħa Bay and Ċirkewwa. Bus 37 serves Għadira and Armier Bay. Gozo Channel Line ferries link with Mġarr Harbour on Gozo.

The northern part of Malta is essentially a broad limestone ridge, steeply sloping on its southern side and gently sloping on its northern side, with dramatic cliffs to the west and east. The Marfa Ridge is almost a separate island, tethered to the rest of Malta by a narrow neck of land at Għadira. A complete circuit is possible, or bus services can be used to cover the route over two separate trips.

A busy main road crosses the Marfa Ridge, carrying traffic to and from the Gozo Channel ferries at Ċirkewwa. Views from the ridge are excellent in places, stretching back through Malta and across to the neighbouring islands of Comino and Gozo. The conspicuous Red Tower was built on the Marfa Ridge in the 17th century as a signal tower.

Start on the main road at **Mellieħa Bay**, at the bus stops nearest to the access road for the Mellieħa Bay Hotel. Instead of turning towards the hotel, leave the main road opposite the turning, where a notice beside a gate explains about the Foresta 2000 reserve and the paths that allow the forested slopes to be explored.

Walk up a stretch of the old main road, where vegetation now creeps across the tarmac. Fork left at a junction and a flight of 70 log steps climbs a steep slope. Turn

The Red Tower is worth a detour for extensive views over the Marfa Ridge

left along a road, quickly reaching a road junction. The route turns left downhill, but it's well worth continuing straight ahead first to visit the **Red Tower**.

> The **Red Tower** is also known as St Agatha's Tower and it dates from 1649, built on the orders of the Grand Master Lascaris. The National Trust for Malta (dinlarthelwa.org) restored it, and it opened to the public in 2001. An impressive flight of 33 stone steps climbs to its entrance, while a further 41 spiral wooden steps climb to the gun platform on the roof. A splendid panorama takes in most of this walk, as well as overlooking the lagoon and islands of the Għadira Nature Reserve.

Back at the road junction, walk down past a large, derelict stone building to reach a small car park. Pass a gate and follow an easy path across old cultivation terraces, now planted with trees but with plenty of gaps for views. ▶ Walk past a gate at the end of the terrace path and go down to a concrete road. Turn right and pass between two concrete huts, enjoying splendid cliff

When a stand of eucalyptus trees is reached, it's possible to turn sharp right, then left, to climb to a road high on the Marfa ridge.

views from the road. When a junction is reached, climb a steep concrete track and continue straight up a flight of 62 overgrown concrete steps. Reach a road and turn left along the **Marfa Ridge**.

The road runs towards a small huddle of buildings at a radar station at **Ras il-Qammieħ**. This is the highest part of the ridge, at 129m (424ft). However, before reaching the buildings turn left at a black marker post, following a vague path to pick a way around the

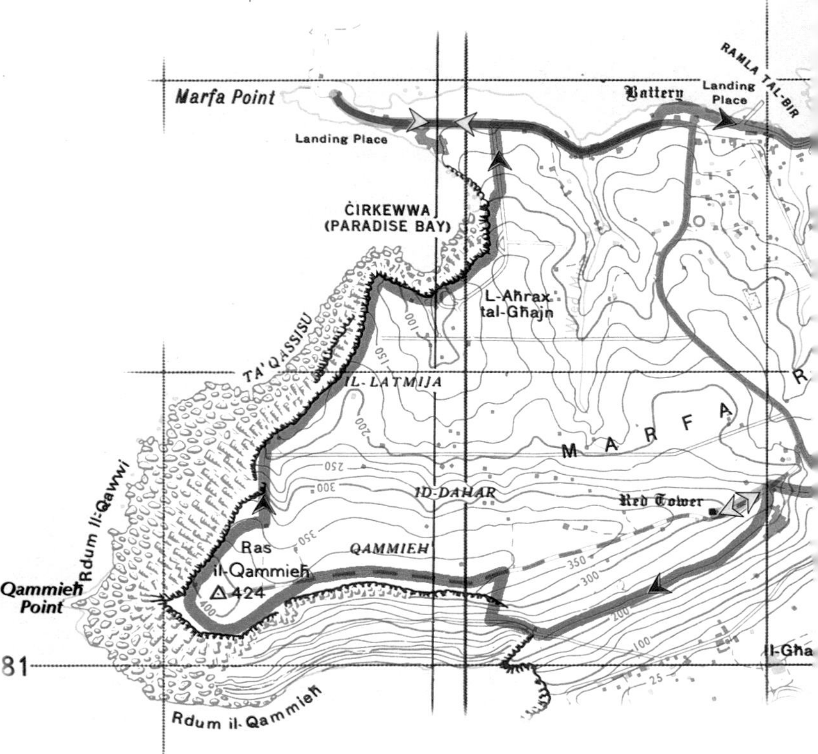

cliffs. Keep an eye on the ground to avoid deep fissures, and look over the cliff edge to see a well-tended farmstead near the jumbled boulders of **Rdum il-Qammieħ**. Keep to the cliff edge, still

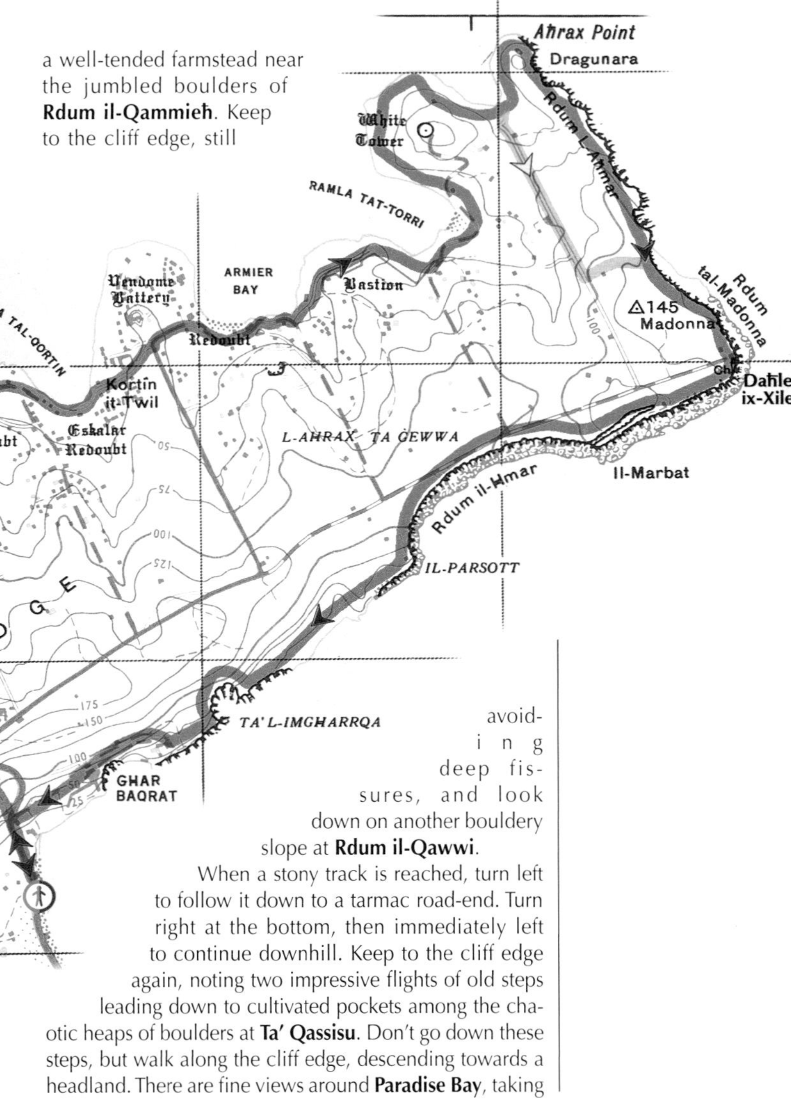

avoiding deep fissures, and look down on another bouldery slope at **Rdum il-Qawwi**.

When a stony track is reached, turn left to follow it down to a tarmac road-end. Turn right at the bottom, then immediately left to continue downhill. Keep to the cliff edge again, noting two impressive flights of old steps leading down to cultivated pockets among the chaotic heaps of boulders at **Ta' Qassisu**. Don't go down these steps, but walk along the cliff edge, descending towards a headland. There are fine views around **Paradise Bay**, taking

Go down a flight of steps on the left if a break is required at the Paradise Bay Bar Restaurant, where there are toilets and a small sandy beach.

There are a couple of bus stops along the way, as well as the Malta/Gozo pipeline, which shares water between the islands.

in a hotel on the far side, as well as the Gozo Channel Line ferries and the islands of Comino and Gozo.

Turn right to reach the head of the bay. ◂ The cliffs beyond are brightly coloured and overhanging. Walk up 44 steps to a reach a turning area and a car park. A road runs over a rise, then heads down towards a junction with a busy main road, but there's a good cliff path that could be used part of the way, joining the road later.

A left turn at the road junction leads off-route to **Ċirkewwa**, the Paradise Bay Hotel, the Gozo Channel Line ferries, Comino ferries and bus services, if any of these are required. If not, then turn right along the busy road and walk from the Reverse Osmosis (desalination) plant on the corner, noting how water pipelines run parallel to the road. ◂ Turn left as signposted for **Ramla Bay**. Alternatively, there's a path along the coast, passing seawards of a battery. A ferry serves the island of Comino from opposite the Riviera Resort and Spa. (See Walk 33 for a route around Comino.)

Follow a gravel path round Ramla Bay and pass inland of the Ramla Bay Resort. Use the resort access road to leave, but quickly switch to an uneven concrete road beside the sea, then walk along a stretch of beach at **Ramla tal-Qortin**. Walk straight up a concrete road past several dull holiday homes, then branch left just after a small statue of the Virgin. Follow Triq ir-Ramla Ta' Kejli and go through a crossroads. Later, pass between the Victoria Bar Restaurant and Mambo Restaurant at **Armier Bay**. Turn right along the beach in front of the Mambo Restaurant, then follow a road to reach Ray's Lido.

Walk up a road and turn left along a dirt road before reaching a statue of Sant' Anna. Pick a way around a low point on bare limestone, noting a stout bastion wall, then pass more cramped holiday huts. The Liberty Kiosk take-away cabin is at the head of **Ramla tat-Torri**, where you continue along a road. Either follow the road inland, keeping right of the **White Tower**, or follow a vague vehicle track round a low point, always keeping left of the White Tower. Either way, continue along a rough track towards **Aħrax Point**. When the rocky ground dips, look

A small rock arch might be noticed near the point at Il-Parsott

There's hardly any vegetation on this, the most northerly point on Malta, but there are fine views across to Comino.

If this sounds too difficult, stay on the road, follow it uphill and later turn left along a track to reach the cliff path.

out for a huge hole that suddenly opens up, full of water, connected to the sea through a rock arch. ◂

An extremely rugged cliff-walk leads along the cliffs of **Rdum l-Aħmar**, but taken slowly and steadily there's no real problem. Don't try and go too fast, as this risks wrenching an ankle, as the rock is very uneven underfoot. Along the way, pass a small memorial and climb steadily uphill, peeping over the edge from time to time to see splendid scenery and a rock arch. ◂

The higher parts of the cliffs, around **Rdum tal-Madonna**, are much easier underfoot, and an area planted with aloes gives way to a wooded crest. The trees are predominantly acacia but include a few Aleppo pines, while the very last tree sitting on the edge of the cliff is a fig. A tamarisk grove has also been planted. Walk towards a small road-end chapel and a diminutive statue of the Madonna gazing out to sea.

There's no need to follow the road away from the chapel. Stay near the cliff edge, and a path can be followed either along the cliffs or just inside woodland. There's a stretch of cliff alongside the road at **Rdum il-Ħmar** that's badly fissured and is bound to collapse onto the bouldery slopes below one day.

The path swings downhill from the road later, with a fine view around a bay, then it turns around a point at **Il-Parsott**. Walk past a red-and-white navigation beacon and notice a stout stone wall just inland, while a small rock arch juts out into the sea. Walk along a coastal track and pass another length of defensive wall. A small cove is reached at **Ta' l-Imgħarrqa**, where it's necessary to climb uphill and downhill to get round to the far side.

Walk across a wooded slope that leads into the grounds of the Mellieħa Bay Hotel complex. Keep inland of the hotel to follow the access road away from it, then head straight for the busy main road where the circuit started earlier in the day. Turn left downhill to find toilets, beach bars and bus stops. The **Għadira Nature Reserve**, which is run by BirdLife Malta, is open at weekends, from November to May, and is well worth a visit (see end of Walk 9).

WALK 11

Mellieħa Bay to Xemxija

Start	Mellieħa Bay (418 805)
Finish	Porto del Sol, Xemxija (444 785)
Distance	8km (5 miles)
Time	2hr 30min
Terrain	Roads give way to rugged coastal paths and tracks, with roads again at the end
Maps	1:25,000 Malta sheet
Refreshments	Beach bars around Mellieħa Bay. A restaurant at Mistra Bay is open only in the evenings. Bars and restaurants at Xemxija.
Transport	Buses 37, 41, 42, 101, 102, 221, 222 and X1 serve Mellieħa Bay. Buses 37, 41, 42, 221, 222 and X1 serve Xemxija.

Few who travel along the main road between Mellieħa and Xemxija realise that there's a splendidly rugged coastline between both places. A succession of headlands lies between Mellieħa Bay and St Paul's Bay, and there are good coastal paths and tracks to facilitate explorations. Close-up views of St Paul's Islands are available, where St Paul was shipwrecked in AD60 on his way to stand trial in Rome. St Paul's time on Malta is recorded in the Acts of the Apostles, chapter 28, verses 1–10, and an important festival commemorating the event takes place each year throughout the Maltese islands on 10 February.

Start at a roundabout on the busy main road at the southern end of **Mellieħa Bay**. (The bus stop is known as 'Skrajda'.) Follow the coast as closely as possible, away from the main road, passing a boatyard beside the Westreme Battery, built in 1716. ▶ Keep to the seaward side of the building, then pass in front of rows of holiday homes, walking on concrete forecourts or tarmac roads. Keep looking ahead to judge the best way past the holiday homes, passing a small inlet at **Għajn Żejtuna**. The

This houses the Tunnara Museum, which deals with the former occupation of tuna fishing.

The Tunnara Museum is passed at the start of the walk on Mellieħa Bay

access road to the end of the rows of holiday homes is called ix-Xatt ta' Santa Marija; the last row is labelled as 'Section A' and there's a concrete forecourt in front of it.

Leave the forecourt at the far corner, where a narrow path traverses a rocky slope above the sea. Walk on bare rock for a while, taking care crossing a slimy patch where mint grows and there's a cane thicket uphill. Climb a little to join a higher path and aim for a crumbling lookout on the point of **Ras il-Griebeġ**. Swing right just before this point, or use a much rougher path around it instead.

Cross a crumbling landslip slope of Blue Clay, studded with boulders of limestone from the cliffs above. There's plenty of flowery scrub, as well as a clump of palm trees. Follow the path until a small car park and wartime lookout is reached in a cane-choked valley.

Walk down past a pill box, and a zig-zag path leads to a little beach at **Mġiebaħ**, or Imġiebaħ. Follow an undulating coastal path, climbing steeply before dropping down towards the next bay. ▸ The shattered cliffs of **Għajn Ħadid** were crowned with a 17th-century tower, but only the base remains, out of sight.

Yellow clover and fiery red carpets of sulla decorate the clay slopes in spring.

Pass some tamarisk bushes and cross a valley by switching to the highest path in view ahead. This cuts round the upper end of a watercourse choked with thickets of cane.

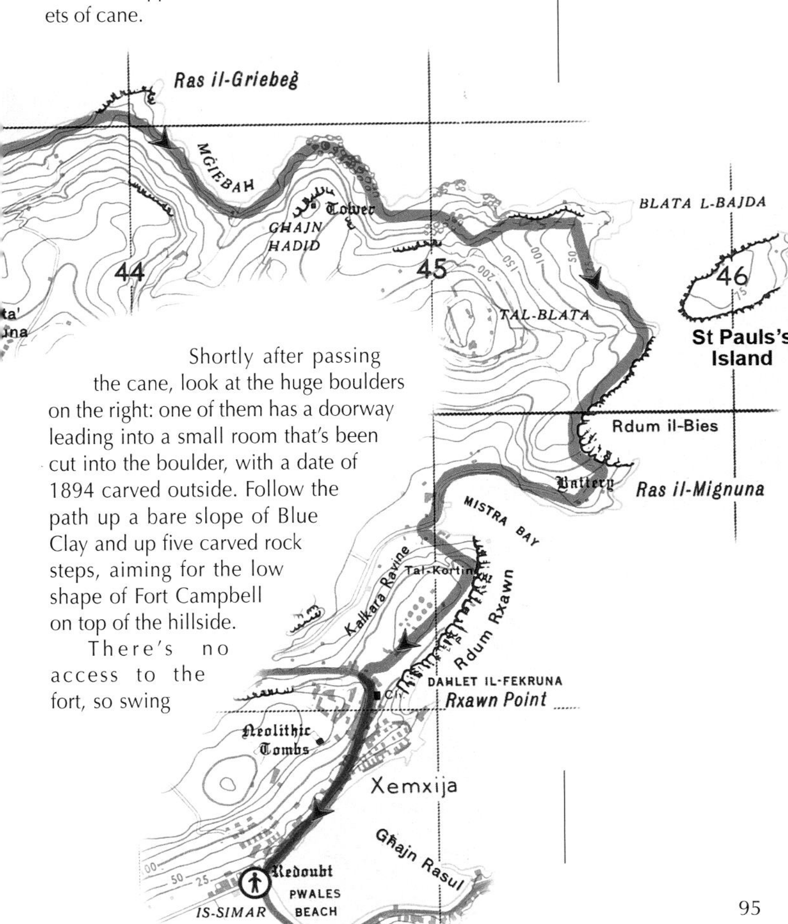

Shortly after passing the cane, look at the huge boulders on the right: one of them has a doorway leading into a small room that's been cut into the boulder, with a date of 1894 carved outside. Follow the path up a bare slope of Blue Clay and up five carved rock steps, aiming for the low shape of Fort Campbell on top of the hillside.

There's no access to the fort, so swing

St Paul's Island is passed on the way to Mistra Bay

sharply left back downhill, following a track on the ribbed, bare slope of clay. Old salt pans can be seen carved into the Globigerina Limestone along the coast, and the bare rock is blinding white in the full sun. A series of little lookouts and pillboxes are clustered around the point at **Blata l-Bajda**. Follow a path around the bay to reach the next low headland, which is as close as it's possible to get to **St Paul's Islands**. ◂

A statue of St Paul can be seen on the larger of the two islands, as well as a cross and the base of a 17th-century lookout tower.

Follow a path gradually uphill, taking occasional peeks over the cliffs of **Rdum il-Bies**. The higher parts of the path are broad and have been chiselled from the rock. Descend alongside the fissured cliff edge towards a small lookout on a low, rocky point at **Ras il-Miġnuna**. Enjoy views back towards St Paul's Islands, then walk to the old **Mistra Battery**.

Follow a road around **Mistra Bay**, looking into the shallow water to see meadows of sea grass. After passing Margo's pizzeria, the road suddenly turns right inland through the **Kalkara Ravine**. Leave the road and cross a beach beside a couple of buildings, then follow a path uphill. A flight of stone steps with holm oak alongside leads up to a crest covered in acacia trees.

Swing right from the crest, then left to walk alongside a stout stone wall. A fire station is passed and a busy road is joined at a roundabout at the top end of **Xemxija**, where a left turn leads to bus stops. Food and drink is available, with more options further down the road near **Pwales Beach**.

Just inland from the beach is the **Is-Simar Nature Reserve**, managed by BirdLife Malta (www.birdlifemalta.org), where shallow pools and bird hides are screened behind tamarisk bushes. It's generally open at weekends from September to May, and is worth visiting.

WALK 12

Selmun circuit

Start	Roundabout south of Mellieħa (434 792)
Finish	Road junction in the Mistra Valley (443 791)
Distance	5km (3 miles)
Time	1hr 30min
Terrain	Roads, tracks and a couple of short paths
Maps	1:25,000 Malta sheet
Refreshments	Bar-restaurant at Selmun and Selmun Palace. Other nearby refreshments are off-route at Mellieħa and Xemxija.
Transport	Buses 37, 41, 42, 101, 102, 221, 222 and X1 serve Mellieħa. Buses 37, 41, 42, 221, 222 and X1 cross the Mistra Valley. Bus 102 occasionally serves Selmun Palace.

Selmun Palace sits on the plateau-like Mellieħa Ridge, and most travellers on the road from Xemxija to Mellieħa will notice it. The palace was built in the 18th century for the Knights of St John, and was loosely modelled on the Verdala Palace in the hills near Dingli. Selmun Palace was planned as a summer residence, but was actually used as a hunting lodge, and is now part of a hotel complex. A selection of quiet roads, tracks and paths in the area leads walkers in a circuit that reveals a few little features of interest and a delightful hidden valley.

Start at a busy roundabout high on the Mellieħa Ridge on the southern outskirts of **Mellieħa**. ▶ Follow a paved path through the park to a drinks machine, then continue gently down the broad and quiet road of Triq Selmun, in the direction of Selmun Palace. A sign on the left announces three Punic tombs at Qabar, which are located a short distance from the road, tucked into a rocky cutting below a rubble wall.

This is a fine viewpoint, located at 107m (350ft), with a beehive-shaped storage hut, or girna, being a feature of interest in the Family Park off the main road.

Follow a track parallel to Triq Selmun, passing a row of houses, then a very short path rejoins the road. Turn left and follow the road past the Selmun Bar Restaurant. A small church to the right is dedicated to Our Lady of Ransom, while **Selmun Palace** lies straight ahead uphill. ◀ An interesting restored farmhouse complex can be studied nearby.

The palace was built in 1607 as a coastal lookout and hunting lodge. It was recently incorporated into a hotel complex, which closed in 2011.

Admire the fine stonework of the palace, then turn left along an access road to reach a small house. A path to the left side of the house drops down a slope, often worn to bedrock, landing on a quiet road. Turn right down the narrow road, which is initially flanked by holm oak, carob and a few pines. There are cultivated terraces and fig trees further down the Mġiebaħ valley, which is a delightful place.

The road swings suddenly to the right at the Tal-Mellieħa farmhouse, deep in the valley. At the next junction, walk straight ahead along a walled, grassy track, avoiding a left turn down to a beach at **Mġiebaħ**. Reach a small farm building and turn right to pass behind it. Follow a narrow path uphill, through a stone gateway. At the top, go through a gap in a stand of prickly pears to reach a road beside farmhouses.

Turn left along the road, passing tiny fields. When the road turns left, turn right instead and follow a walled track. Turn right again along a road that leads back towards **Selmun Palace**. Just before reaching it, however, turn left from a bend in the road and follow a concrete road downhill, which is steep

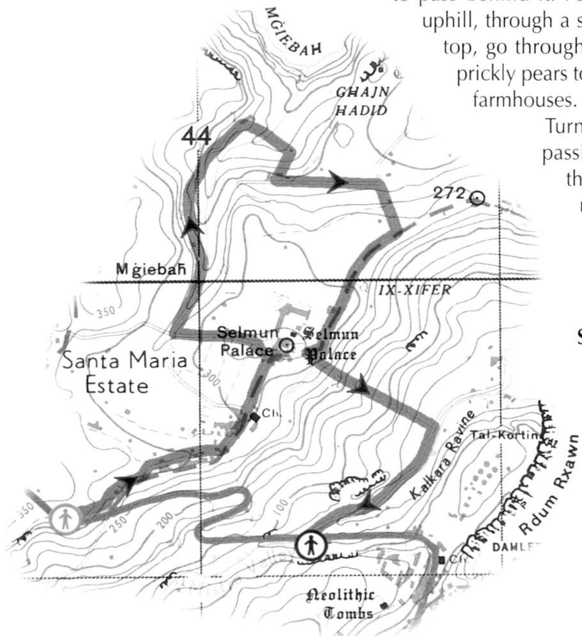

The 18th-century Selmun Palace was recently part of a hotel

and can be hard on the knees. There are fine views over Mistra Bay, then the middle part of the descent is stony and rather overgrown. Another stretch of concrete finally leads to a road at the bottom of the slope.

Turn right to follow the road up through the **Kalkara Ravine** to reach a busy main road on the outskirts of **Xemxija**. It's best to go beneath the road, through a tunnel, then use the nearest bus stops beside the main road. One bus stop stands opposite an imposing restored gateway to an estate that no longer exists. Following the busy road is not really recommended, but if that option is chosen, it's easier to walk down to Xemxija than up to Mellieħa.

Inter-connected Punic tombs cut into the limestone near Xemxija

WALK 13

Xemxija Heritage Trail

Start/Finish	Porto del Sol, Xemxija (444 785)
Distance	2.5km (1½ miles)
Time	1hr 30min
Terrain	A good track gives way to vague paths, finishing on roads. Although the route is never far from Xemxija, it needs to be followed carefully.
Maps	1:25,000 Malta sheet
Refreshments	A few bars and restaurants at Xemxija.
Transport	Buses 37, 41, 42, 221, 222 and X1 serve Xemxija.

The Xemxija Heritage Trail was created by a couple of local enthusiasts, with help from schoolchildren, backed by the local council. Over the years they identified numerous ancient sites, cleared back the undergrowth and partially rebuilt some of the ancient structures. Cairns were erected, bearing ceramic plaques showing the way from one site to another, taking in a wealth of features including a Roman road and Roman baths, fine stone apiaries, house sites and caves, burial sites and 'cart ruts'. While you can make your way from one site to another, it would be easy to miss some of them. If you have a chance to be taken on a guided walk around the trail it can be appreciated all the more.

Start at the head of St Paul's Bay at **Xemxija**, where there are bus stops at the Porto del Sol bar-restaurant and guest-house. Walk uphill around the back of the building, along Triq ir-Ridott, which is signposted for 'The Roman Road'. Follow the road up to the Porto Azzurro Hotel. Turn right uphill, then turn left off a bend, where a cairn marks a track as the Heritage Trail. The track is also known as Triq

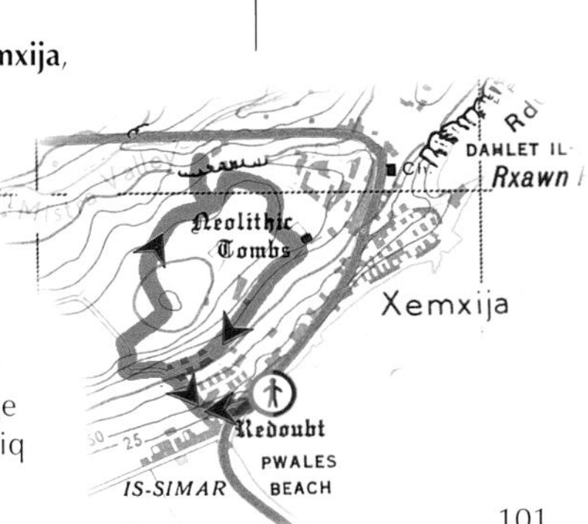

Inside a restored apiary that was once used as a burial chamber

Look out for ceramic plaques that mark specific sites, such as a menhir on the right and Għar ix-Xini (the 'Cave of the Galley'), which was once used as a dwelling.

Rumana (the 'Roman Road') and Triq il-Pellegrini (the 'Pilgrim's Way'). ◄

The track turns a bend and there's access on the right to Imġiebaħ – a Punico-Roman structure over 2000 years old. This is one of four stone-built apiaries in the area; it was almost completely intact when excavated and was re-roofed in an old style. Across the track is a 1000-year-old carob tree, Lill-ħarruba Xwejha. Tucked away behind it are two more apiaries and a cave with a barred entrance.

The apiaries were used as **burial sites** in late Roman times, over a thousand years ago.Most of the caves in the area have seen multiple uses, as burial sites, habitations, apiaries or agricultural storage.

Alongside the track is the more obvious Għar il-Midena – an ancient burial cave that may originally have had a smaller entrance, with stances and niches for oil lamps.

Follow the track through a rock cutting and note the rock wall on the left, which has a number of simple crosses etched into the surface, cut by pilgrims on their way to Mellieħa. ▶ There are fine views of St Paul's Bay and the Is-Simar Nature Reserve. On the highest part of the track, it's possible to divert left into a forest, where a path leads to an ancient temple site.

Sailors who survived storms or pirate raids were in the habit of making pilgrimages to Mellieħa to give thanks for safe deliverance.

Turn right off the highest part of the track, walking from a cairn to a gap between boulders in a rubble wall, which may be part of a deserted fortified village site. Walk through the gap, then look to the left to see a hole in the ground, which is a Punic tomb. Walk to a low stone building – a restored farmer's hovel called Gorboġ il-Bidwi – where there's an enclosure for animals and a nearby cave that was once used for burials, then later for habitation. ▶

Look carefully on top of the cave to spot a channel carved in the rock that would have carried running water into the cave.

Walk over the roof of the cave, heading for the top end of Xemxija. Look out for a hole called Fossa tal-Qamħ, which may have been used as a grain store before being converted into a well. Continue walking towards Xemxija, but drift slightly left towards a huddle of cairns. Look out for six deep holes, two of which are connected. These are more fine examples of Punic tombs.

Walk to a nearby road, Triq il-Preistorja, and turn left. Walk off the end of the road to a track, then turn right. A Second World War pillbox overlooks the valley; it was built to look like a rustic farm building, but later examples were made of concrete and painted to look deceptively like cottages.

Walk down steps below the pillbox to find the site of a Roman bath and a 16th-century façade above it. ▶ Looking downhill, there's a well-preserved old farmhouse beside a busy road, as well as an ornate stone gateway, which is best seen from the road rather than from above. Walk back up the steps and cross the track to find a set of excavated 'cart ruts' deeply cut into the limestone.

A cave cut into the rock used to be a burial site and later became a dwelling, which was inhabited within living memory. All sorts of curious features can be seen inside.

A clear set of 'cart ruts' excavated by Frank Scerri above Xemxija

Follow a road away from the cart ruts, turning right round the end of a building block, then walking uphill a short way on Triq Katerina Vitale. Turn right again onto Triq Piscopo Macedonia, then left down Triq il-Fuħħar. Turn right at the bottom to follow Triq Raddet ir-Roti, which eventually bends left, where the earlier steps of the day lead back down to the main road in **Xemxija**. The nearby **Is-Simar** Nature Reserve is managed by BirdLife Malta (www.birdlifemalta.org) and is generally open at weekends from September to May.

WALK 14

Bajda Ridge circuit

Start/Finish	Porto del Sol, Xemxija (444 785)
Distance	10km (6¼ miles)
Time	3hr
Terrain	Clear tracks and quiet country roads
Maps	1:25,000 Malta sheet
Refreshments	A few bars and restaurants at Xemxija.
Transport	Buses 37, 41, 42, 221, 222 and X1 serve Xemxija. Buses 101 and 102 follow a road near Għajn Żnuber.

The Bajda Ridge stretches coast-to-coast from Xemxija to the cliffs of Rdum Majesa. The broad crest runs roughly east to west and is flanked to the north and south by steep slopes. The middle part of the crest was planted with trees in an effort to re-establish some kind of forest cover in Malta; Aleppo pines, acacia and cypress are the three main species. The Bajda Ridge is sparsely populated and very dry at its western end, but there are a number of fine tracks and quiet roads that allow easy exploration. This walk starts in Xemxija, runs from coast to coast to the Għajn Żnuber Tower, then returns by a different route through the Mistra Valley.

Start at the head of St Paul's Bay at **Xemxija**, where there are bus stops at the Porto del Sol bar-restaurant and guesthouse. Walk uphill around the back of the building, along Triq ir-Ridott, which is signposted for 'The Roman Road'. Follow the road up to the Porto Azzurro Hotel. Turn right uphill, then turn left off a bend, where a cairn marks a track as the Heritage Trail. ▶

There are interesting features along this track, including a menhir, ancient caves used as burial sites, apiaries, dwellings and a thousand-year-old carob tree. For more details refer to Walk 13.

The track climbs and turns right round a bend. Continue through a rock cutting and climb to the highest part of the track. The Heritage Trail turns right at a cairn, but this walk runs straight ahead, over the crest of the **Bajda Ridge** and downhill a little.

Turn left at a track junction. There are pines and acacias up to the left and a cultivated valley down to the

A track leaves Xemxija, passing forested slopes above enclosed fields

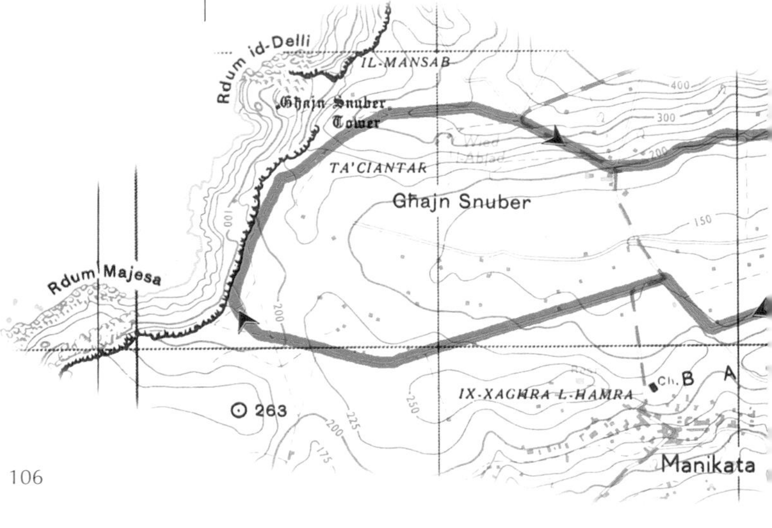

right. Follow the clear and obvious track gently downhill, then uphill, then down again to reach a road bend at **Miżieb**. Walk straight along and down the road, then continue straight along a dirt road. This stretch is cultivated, and there are a number of carob trees alongside, as well as the farm of Id dar il-Bajda.

After crossing a rocky crest the dirt road descends and rises gently. There are pines and cypresses to the left and cultivated slopes to the right. The road is concrete as it rises again, and for a short while it's wooded on both sides. When it finally leaves the woods, the dirt road swings right and heads down to a quiet country road, which carries bus services.

Turn left along the road, go over a slight crest and continue straight along another clear and obvious dirt road. This runs into Il-Majjistral Nature and History Park, crossing barren countryside and passing a handful of tiny farms. ▶ The track eventually splits in all directions, but follow any line that heads towards the lowest part of a cliff line seen ahead. Aim for a skeletal 'hut', which is no more than a concrete slab supported by four pillars.

This is the closest equivalent to a national park in Malta (**mt.majjistral.org**).

Enjoy views out to sea and along the north-western cliffs of Malta, with a glimpse of part of Gozo in the distance. Note the bouldery slopes of **Rdum Majesa** below the cliff, but don't be tempted down a path onto them. Instead, turn right and follow a track gently uphill.

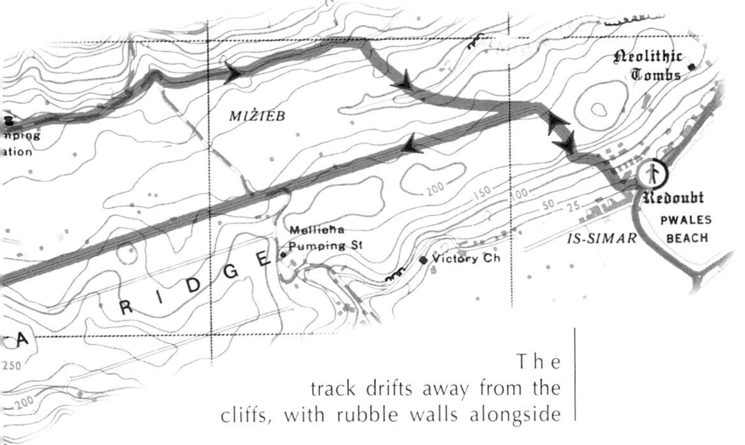

The track drifts away from the cliffs, with rubble walls alongside

A skeletal 'hut' on a cliff edge overlooking Rdum Majesa

as it climbs to the 17th-century **Għajn Żnuber Tower**. Technically, you are now standing on the Mellieħa Ridge, rather than the Bajda Ridge. Continue along the track, rising gently to reach a road bend at 100m (330ft), where bus services pass.

Turn right and walk steeply down the road towards a broad and cultivated valley, which is spanned by a splendid stone aqueduct. As soon as a huddle of buildings is reached, turn left along a track, then fork right. Follow the track onwards, with barren slopes and old terraces rising to the left and cultivated fields full of all kinds of crops to the right. Pass the **Miżieb Pumping Station** and continue along a road. When a road junction is reached, swing round to the right, then exit left along a track at **Miżieb**.

Follow the track alongside the **Mistra Valley**, and it eventually rises and crosses a stone-slab bridge. Turn right down a concrete road and cross a riverbed at the bottom of the valley. Walk up a broad, rough and stony slope using a narrow path flanked by low rubble walls some distance to either side. At the top, join and follow a clear track that was used earlier in the day, following it back across the crest of the Bajda Ridge. Simply continue down the Heritage Trail and join the road leading back down into **Xemxija**.

WALK 15

The Wardija Ridge

Start	Porto del Sol, Xemxija (444 785)
Finish	Wied l-Arkata, near Burmarrad (473 759)
Distance	12.5km (7¾ miles)
Time	3hr 30min
Terrain	Mostly quiet country roads, but some tracks and short paths too
Maps	1:25,000 Malta sheet
Refreshments	A few bars and restaurants at Xemxija. Shop at Bidnija.
Transport	Buses 37, 41, 42, 221, 222 and X1 serve Xemxija. Bus 401 occasionally serves Wardija. Bus 35 serves Bidnija. Buses 31, 37, 41, 42 and X3 serve Wied l-Arkata.

The Wardija Ridge is broad and sprawling. Its slopes are often steeply defined on the northern side, stretching from St Paul's Bay to Għajn Tuffieħa. There are a few fine palaces dotted around the higher parts of the ridge, and some of these have their own private chapels attached. This walk wanders around the Wardija Ridge, seeking out the old palaces and chapels. There is no public access to the vast majority of these sites, which have to be viewed from nearby roads, although Castello Dei Baroni, the International Headquarters and Diplomatic Centre of the Sovereign Order of St John of Jerusalem, can be visited by prior arrangement.

Start at **Xemxija**, where there are bus stops at the Porto del Sol restaurant and guesthouse. Walk down to a road junction, turn right and head straight inland, following the quiet Triq il-Pwales alongside the perimeter fence of the bushy **Is-Simar** Nature Reserve. ▶ The road passes a sewage disposal point and turns right. Soon afterwards, turn left at a gateway with pillars marked as 'private'. Walk along the road anyway, then continue up a concrete road and along a grassy track to reach the **Victory Chapel**.

The reserve is managed by BirdLife Malta (**www.birdlifemalta.org**) and is generally open at weekends from September to May.

Walk further along the grassy track and pass through a cane thicket to reach a road. Turn left down the road and cross the cultivated **Pwales Valley** to reach a junction and a bus stop. The junction is actually a crossroads, but trees have been planted on the far side, so make a quick left and right turn to continue along another road: Triq Ġnien Borg.

map continues on page 112

Keep left up a road marked 'no entry', pass Casa Galea and take the second turning on the left. Continue uphill, enjoying views back towards Xemxija. Huge walls and a pair of stout stone pillars stand to the left of the road, while further uphill, further away to the left, is a red arch at the entrance to **Palazz San Martin**. Still further up the road, also on the

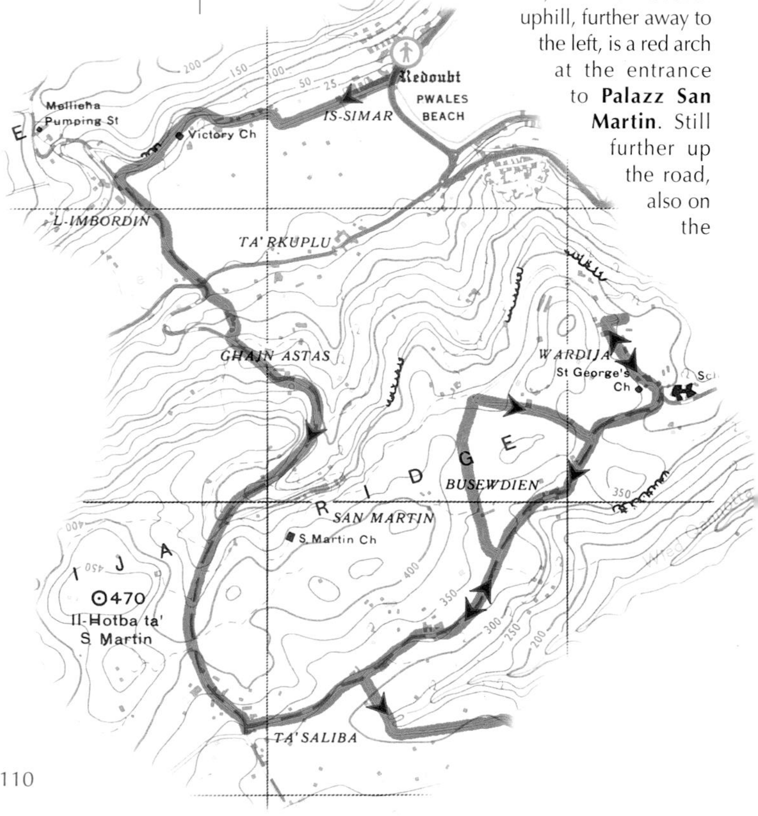

St Martin's Cave is passed by the road climbing above Palazz San Martin

left, is a shaded pine grove leading to St Martin's Cave, which contains a Lourdes grotto.

Keep walking up to the crest of the road, around 120m (400ft). ▶ Stay on the road and pass a stoutly enclosed housed called Il-Ħarruba. Also note several nearby redundant barrack buildings around **Ta' Saliba**. Turn left as signposted for Wardija, and follow the road past houses and farms, passing a small roadside shrine. Still further along the road, which is called Triq Busewdien, reach a triangular junction and turn left.

It used to be possible to follow a track towards a building incorporating St Martin's Chapel, but access is no longer permitted.

Follow the road until it turns left and is private, and instead continue straight ahead along a walled track which reaches a road bend where there's seating available. Continuing straight ahead leads to the **Wardija** Hilltop Village, so turn right instead to follow the road, called Triq il-Ballut, catching a glimpse of the Palazzo Busietta. When a road junction is reached, turn left and follow the road to another junction, then turn left again. Pass the Castello Dei Baroni, which is the International

Castello Dei Baroni is the international headquarters of the Order of Malta

Headquarters and Diplomatic Centre of the Sovereign Order of St John of Jerusalem.

Follow the road onwards, looking at fine properties to right and left, including **St George's Chapel**. When Castel Bertrand is reached, look straight ahead to catch a glimpse of Castello Tas-Sultan, but as this is private, turn right to have a look at the Palazzo Promontorio, which can be approached more closely. Afterwards, retrace steps along the road to Castello Dei Baroni and turn right.

Follow the road straight through **Busewdien**, all the way back to the small roadside shrine that was passed earlier. Walk past it again, then shortly afterwards, turn left down a concrete road. Follow the road across the head of the **Wied Qannotta** valley and turn left. There might be a huge muddy puddle to negotiate, then pass St Mary's Fireworks Factory and keep straight ahead as the track becomes gravel.

Pass round a clay pigeon range used by the Malta Shooting Federation and follow a road onwards, called Triq is-Sagra Familja. Turn left along a track and pass newly constructed walls and stabling. Turn right up a narrow road until Triq il-Bdiewa reaches a junction with Triq Tal-Milord in the little village of **Bidnija**. Turn left to pass between a fine little chapel and the Hilltop Self Service shop. Follow the road faithfully, passing Ras Riħana and avoiding a turning for 'The Funny Farm'.

The tarmac finally expires at a house called Ta' Catletti. Walk down a rugged track on the left, then keep right. (Keeping left reveals a vague field path leading to a concrete road running down to St Paul's Chapel and the village of Burmarrad.) A concrete track runs down through fields and runs close to **Santa Margerita Chapel** before landing on a busy main road at **Wied l-Arkata**. There are bus stops nearby and plenty of bus services on the road.

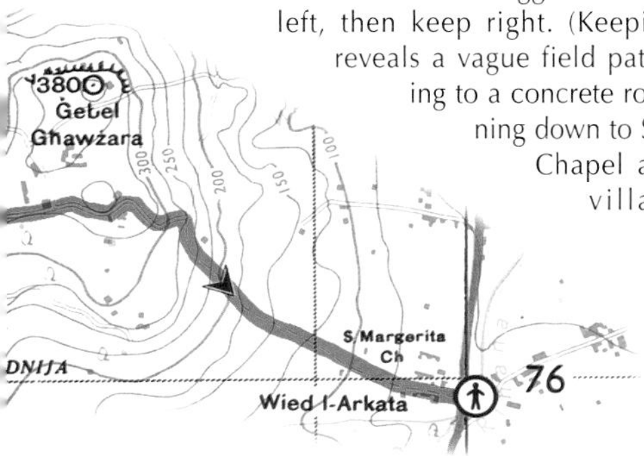

WALK 16

Falka Gap to Salina

Start	Falka Pumping Station (456 745)
Finish	Coastline Hotel, Salina (484 785)
Distance	11km (7 miles)
Time	3hr 15min
Terrain	Quiet country roads and clear tracks
Maps	1:25,000 Malta sheet
Refreshments	Shop at Bidnija. Bars and restaurants at Salina.
Transport	Buses 38, 44 and 225 serve Falka Gap. Bus 35 serves Bidnija. Buses 31, 37, 41, 42 and X3 serve Wied l-Arkata. Buses 12, 222 and X1 serve Salina.

This route meanders through quiet farming country, starting near the Falka Gap and crossing the broad head of the Għajn Riħana Valley. After climbing to the hilltop village of Bidnija, the route drops back into the Għajn Riħana Valley and follows a couple of riverbeds across a broad, level plain. A gentle, rolling upland route links narrow roads and tracks to head northwards to Għallis Tower, overlooking Għallis Point. A huge waste tip rose above the coast for some years, but is now in the process of being landscaped and planted with vegetation. A busy road leads quickly into Salina, where any spare time could be spent studying extensive salt pans.

Start north of the Falka Gap, where there are bus stops near the **Falka Pumping Station**, separated by a pedestrian crossing. A narrow road leaves the main road, passing a house called San Pawl. Follow the road ahead, then it later swings left down into a valley full of cultivated plots and small vineyards.

Cross a small streambed, follow a track across a rise, then cross a larger streambed in the **Għajn Riħana Valley** that might need to be forded after rain. Walk straight uphill along a road that passes other roads and tracks while gaining height, eventually reaching a broader road.

The little chapel at a road junction in the hilltop village of Bidnija

Turn left up to the village of **Bidnija**, which has a small chapel, Hilltop Self Service shop and a bus service.

Turn right along Triq tal-Milord and follow the road faithfully, passing Ras Riħana, but avoiding a turning for 'The Funny Farm'. The tarmac finally expires at a house called Ta' Catletti. Walk down a rugged track on the left, then keep right. (Keeping left reveals a vague field path leading to a concrete road running down to St Paul's Chapel and the village of Burmarrad.) A concrete track runs down through fields and runs close to **Santa Margerita Chapel** before landing on a busy main road at **Wied l-Arkata**. ◂

map continues on page 118

There are bus stops nearby and plenty of bus services on the road.

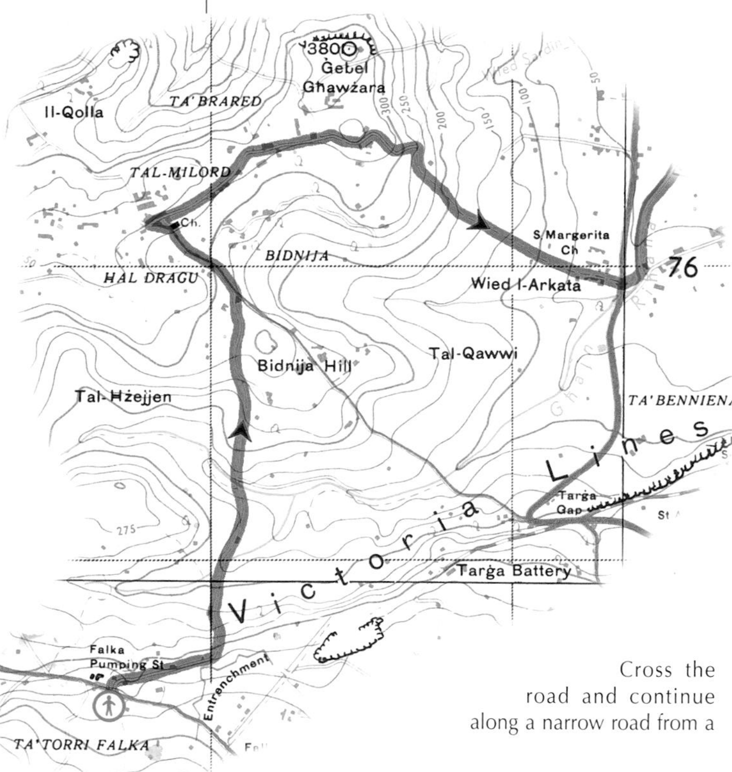

Cross the road and continue along a narrow road from a

A series of dams hold water in the valley beyond Wied l-Arkata

stand of shady pine trees. Cross a riverbed and turn left to walk downstream. The track passes water-spills where the river has been dammed to provide water for use in the adjacent fields. Eventually, turn right at a junction of tracks and head upstream alongside another riverbed in the **Wied il-Għasel**.

Watch out for a point where it's possible to cross the riverbed and use a track on the other side. Continue walking upstream, as if heading towards a noisy, dusty quarry eating into the cliffs. However, turn left along a dirt road, quickly followed by a tarmac road, to reach a busy main road at a sign for the Valle del Miele chicken processors, beside a few pines.

Cross the road and follow a narrow concrete track straight ahead and gently uphill, noting the weather-worn stone pillars bearing the letters 'PP', for 'private property'. The track later changes to a narrow road leading to a junction. Ġenna Żgħira lies to the left, but turn right to follow the road to a junction with a main road at **Il-Qadi**. Turn right again along the main road.

Turn left along a minor road called Triq it-Torri tal-Għallis, passing Neg Neg Farm, and keep following the road while avoiding all junctions to left and right. The road later becomes a track, and there are views across

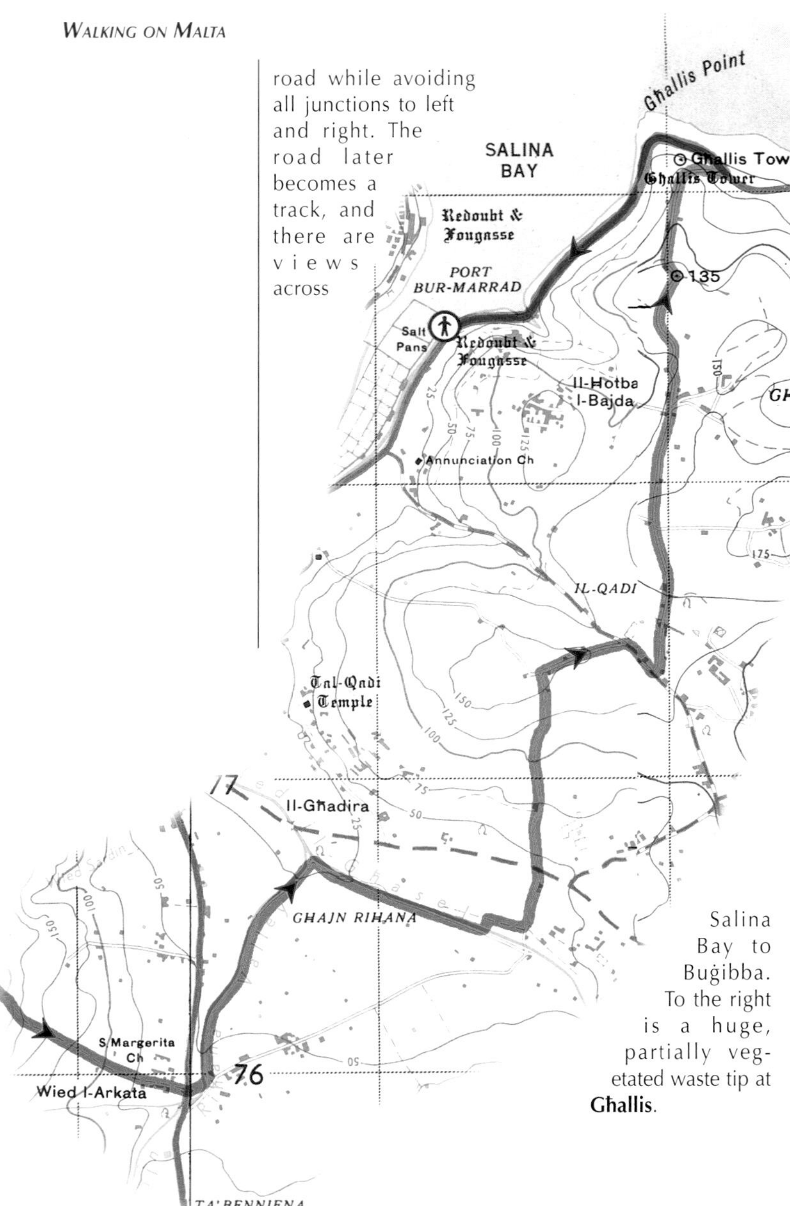

Salina Bay to Buġibba. To the right is a huge, partially vegetated waste tip at **Għallis**.

The 17th century Għallis Tower

The track wriggles along a crest that bears a sparse covering of trees. Turn left at a junction where there's a 'wall' of stone-filled barrels to reach the stout stone **Għallis Tower**, which was one of a series of lookouts erected in the 17th century and is now a National Trust for Malta property.

Walk down to the main coast road and cross to the other side. Turn left to follow the path alongside it, or pick a way along the shore. The road leads quickly round **Għallis Point** into **Salina Bay**. The little resort of **Salina** is soon reached, and there are bus stops in front of the Coastline Hotel.

The resort takes its name from the salinas, or **salt pans**, which fill the head of the bay. The salt pans were established by the Knights of St John, but fell idle in 1798, then were revived under British rule and continue to produce salt today. The Ximenes Redoubt stands beside the main road and has recently been restored.

WALK 17

Baħar iċ-Ċagħaq to St George's Bay

Start	Baħar iċ-Ċagħaq (509 775)
Finish	St George's Bay (540 760)
Distance	6.5km (4 miles)
Time	2hr
Terrain	Mostly tracks with some short paths and roads
Maps	1:25,000 Malta sheet
Refreshments	A couple of bars at Baħar iċ-Ċagħaq, and plenty of choice around St George's Bay.
Transport	Buses 12, 205, 222 and X1 serve Baħar iċ-Ċagħaq. Buses 13, 120 and 205 serve St George's Bay, with other services at the nearby Pembroke Park & Ride station.

The only stretch of coastal walking that anyone is likely to consider between St Paul's Bay and Valletta is the short distance from Qrejten Point, near Baħar iċ-Ċagħaq, to St George's on the edge of Malta's largest built-up area. This coastal walk is not particularly scenic and has been spoiled by military and holiday developments, but there are a couple of points of interest along the way, and anyone trying to complete a series of coastal walks around the islands might feel inclined to include this short walk. The middle part of the route features a reasonably good low cliff-walk.

Start at **Baħar iċ-Ċagħaq**, where an immediate decision needs to be made. Either set off in the direction of St George's Bay or head in the other direction to enjoy a short walk around Qretjen Point first. The latter course is recommended, but it involves walking beside a busy main road. Follow the road all the way past the point, then turn right and follow a track beside the inlet of **Qalet Marku**, where narrow ribs of bare limestone act as 'paths' up to the 17th-century **Qalet Marku Tower**.

Follow a track back towards the busy road and return to Baħar iċ-Ċagħaq, or walk along the rocky shore if sea conditions allow. ◄ Follow a quiet road further along the

A couple of snack bars, restaurants and toilets are available.

The 17th-century Qalet Marku Tower stands near Baħar iċ-Ċagħaq

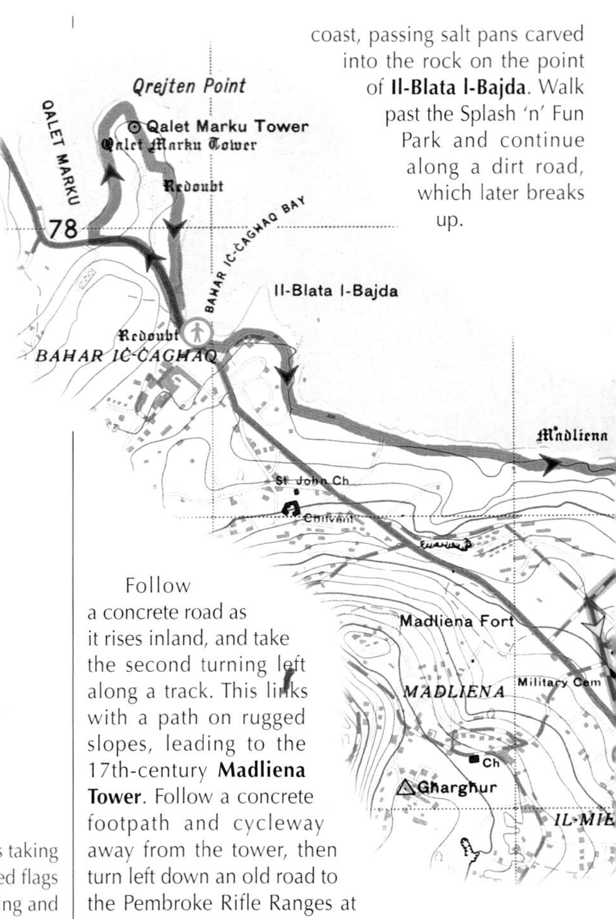

coast, passing salt pans carved into the rock on the point of **Il-Blata l-Bajda**. Walk past the Splash 'n' Fun Park and continue along a dirt road, which later breaks up.

Follow a concrete road as it rises inland, and take the second turning left along a track. This links with a path on rugged slopes, leading to the 17th-century **Madliena Tower**. Follow a concrete footpath and cycleway away from the tower, then turn left down an old road to the Pembroke Rifle Ranges at **Ras l-Irqieqa**. ◂

If firing is taking place, red flags will be flying and access will be forbidden. Instead, stay on the footpath and cycleway, and follow roads to the nearest bus stop.

Walk along clear tracks close to the coast. A series of pipes lead to a desalination plant outside the rifle range. Continue along another concrete footpath and cycleway. Pass between buildings and sports pitches, then climb a winding path through the attractive Pembroke Gardens, emerging close to the huge Radisson and Corinthia hotels.

There's a bus stop at the junction of Triq Manwel Buħaġiar and Triq Dun Luigi Rigord, allowing an early finish. Turn left downhill and head straight past a roundabout. Go through a staggered crossroads and drop steeply down a narrow road to reach the Villa Rosa on **St George's Bay**. Either walk round the head of the bay and wait for a bus or continue as far as you wish into the built-up Paċeville and St Julian's, where discos beat late into the night and early morning.

Much of Malta's holiday accommodation is based in this area, from budget options to the luxury end of the market. Urban promenades can be followed into the heart of Malta's largest conurbation, where more and more bus services become available.

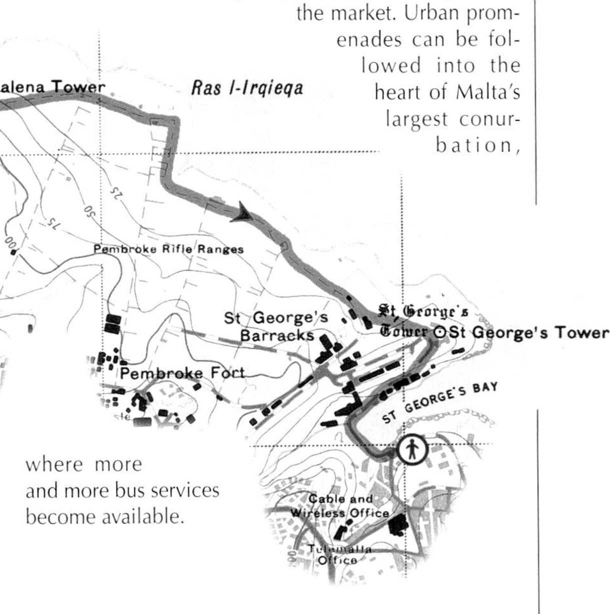

WALK 18

The Victoria Lines

Start	Mġarr church (429 754)
Finish	Baħar iċ-Ċagħaq (509 775)
Distance	22km (13¾ miles)
Time	8hr
Terrain	Remote uplands for the first half, giving way to more populated areas. Roads, tracks and paths are used, and some paths are steep and stony. It's not always possible to walk close to old fortifications.
Maps	1:25,000 Malta sheet
Refreshments	A few shops, bars and restaurants at Mġarr. Shops, bars and restaurants off-route at Mosta, Naxxar, Għargħur and Baħar iċ-Ċagħaq.
Transport	Buses 44 and 225 serve Mġarr. Bus 109 runs close to Binġemma Fort. Buses 38, 44 and 225 serve Falka Gap. Buses 31, 37, 41, 42, 225 and X3 serve Tarġa, near Mosta. Buses 35, 37 and 38 link Mosta and Naxxar. Buses 12, 205, 222 and X1 serve Baħar iċ-Ċagħaq.

China has its Great Wall. Britain has Hadrian's Wall. Malta has the Victoria Lines. The northern part of Malta was always vulnerable to invasion, and during times of strife it was often evacuated. A high ridge stretches from Fomm ir-Riħ to Madliena, running coast-to-coast across Malta. The British army strengthened this natural defence in the 1870s by building fortresses and walls, cutting deep ditches, and stationing soldiers and armaments at intervals along the ridge. These defences are known as the Victoria Lines and they stretch across the island – although the central parts, known as the Dwejra Lines, are the best preserved. The lines were abandoned in 1907 and largely left to crumble.

This is a long walk and there is no public transport to the start. Either arrange a lift to Fomm ir-Riħ or walk there from Mġarr. If the walk proves too long to cover in a day, it can be covered over two days by breaking at any of the bus routes along the way.

Start by facing Mġarr church and keep to the right, following Triq il-Kbira out of the little town. The road passes the **Żamitello Castello** restaurant and reaches a crossroads. Turn left and follow the road as it bends right around the head of the **Ġnejna Valley**. Pass a huddle of buildings at **L-Iskorvit**, then when the road bends left, watch for a track on the right. Follow this, and quickly turn left at a track junction, passing the head of a valley at **Il-Ħalqun**.

Always keep to the clearest track, eventually reaching a bend on a minor road. Turn left up this road, then turn right at a junction beside another huddle of buildings. Follow the road from **Ta' l-Abatija** until a bend is reached above the sea at **Fomm ir-Riħ Bay**. Turn left along a track, passing through an intersection of tracks, then turning right at another junction along a concrete track. Almost immediately, turn

map continues on page 126

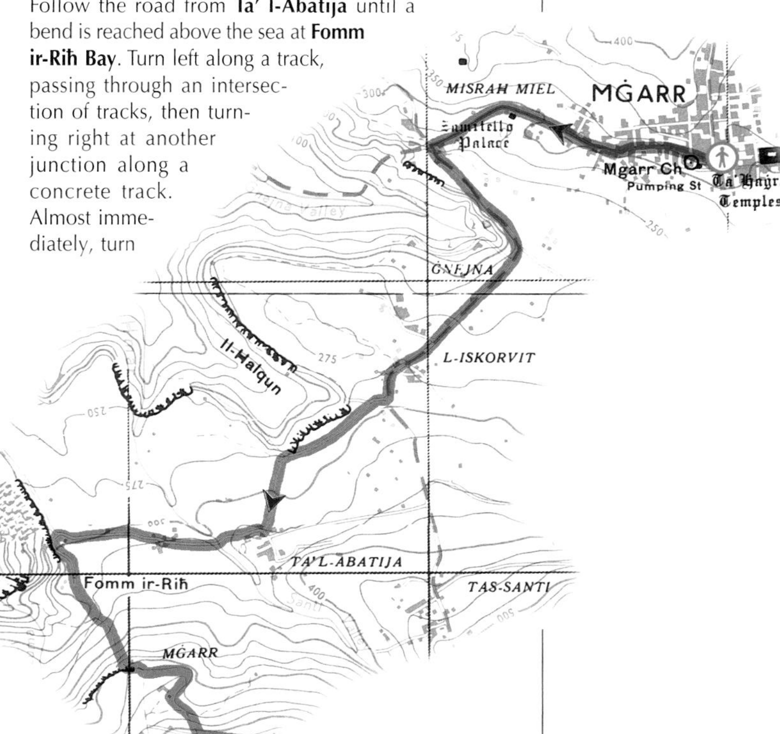

map continues on page 128

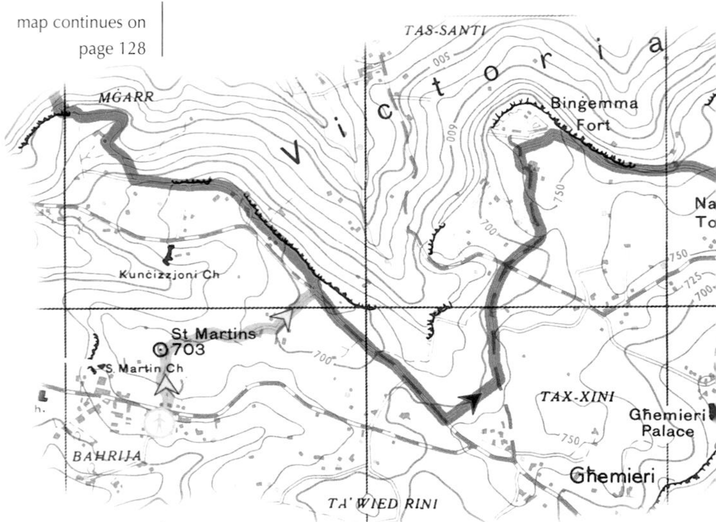

left up a path that soon begins to climb steep and rugged terrain. ◂

> Note the crumbling remains of a wall – the first stretch of the coast-to-coast Victoria Lines.

As height is gained, the wall becomes formidable and passes a blockhouse. Keep walking beside the wall, enjoying views back towards Mġarr and far beyond. The wall later swings right and quickly crumbles as it approaches a substantial derelict searchlight battery. Turn left to walk away from this site, which is rather awkward as the wall has been reduced to rubble and become overgrown. However, join a track and follow it for a few paces, then turn right up a path where over 50 stone steps climb to a road.

Turn left along the road, quickly reaching a corner where there's a memorial, and where a track leads straight ahead.Follow the track onwards, parallel to the wall, and later continue along a path, soon joining a road. ◂ Although the wall runs downhill parallel to the road, there's no access further along. Instead, turn right up the road and almost immediately left at a junction.

> For a shorter, gentler start to this day's walk, follow Walk 7 from Baħrija to this point. However, this omits part of the fortifications.

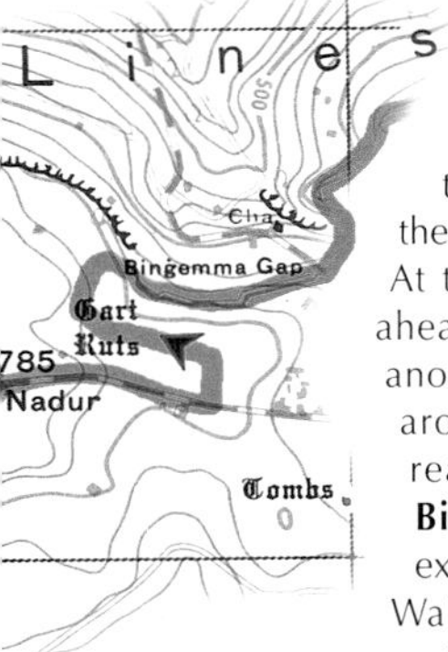

The road crosses a barren upland, then a clear track on the left quickly leads to another road. ▸ Turn left along the road and keep left at a junction. At the next junction, walk straight ahead uphill, and fork right at yet another junction. Turn left to pass around a house called Paradise, reaching a junction beside the **Binġemma Fort**, where a notice explains the Binġemma Countryside Walk.

Bus 109 runs along this road.

Keep right of the notice and fort, where the road quickly gives way to a track and cliff-edge path. Follow the path downhill and it's soon cut through bare limestone with the wall alongside. Pass occasional carob trees and eventually reach a concrete road and houses. Turn right up the road, reaching a junction around 240m (785ft), where the prominent 17th-century **Nadur Tower** stands to the right. ▸ Across the road lies a humble stone-built hut, or *girna*.

Extensive views take in Gozo beyond Golden Bay, Mellieħa, Buġibba, Għallis, the urban sprawl around Valletta, as well as Mtarfa, Mdina and Dingli.

Turn left at the junction and follow the road to a building called Dar il-Hena. Shortly afterwards, turn left past a barrier gate to follow a track. The ground alongside is rugged and covered in scrub, but watch carefully and pick a way downhill to join a splendid restored stretch of the old fortified wall. Turn right and follow it down to a road on the **Binġemma Gap**, where all kinds of explorations can be made.

The Kappella Binġemma lies only a short way down the road. ▸ There are also a few 'cart ruts' close to a sign for Mġarr. Looking down into the valley, notice how the cliffs are pockmarked with holes leading into ancient catacombs.

It is dedicated to the Madonna ta' l-Itria and was founded in 1680 by the nobleman Stanislaus Xara.

The Victoria Lines become the **Dwejra Lines** while crossing the gap. Rugged steps follow the wall down into a valley, then zigzag steps climb steeply up the other side, beside a cliff where a series of restored loopholes for armaments can be studied. A clear track leads

The Dwejra Lines fortified wall zig-zags across the Binġemma Gap

onwards, often with pines alongside; it's tempting to follow it because it's so easy, but in order to appreciate the scale and complexity of the fortifications, keep well to the left of the track and follow a narrow path beside a deep ditch cut into the limestone bedrock, passing a series of batteries.

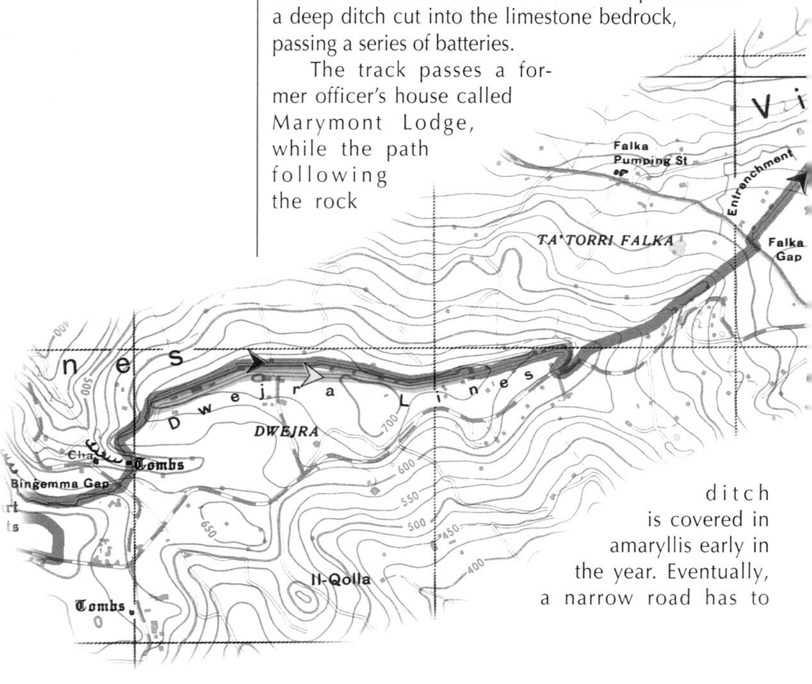

The track passes a former officer's house called Marymont Lodge, while the path following the rock ditch is covered in amaryllis early in the year. Eventually, a narrow road has to be followed and it passes a Boy Scouts' base. The road swings right and joins another road, then swings left before a dirt road runs left.

map continues on page 130

Turn right where boulders prevent vehicles from using a path, and follow the path downhill beside the wall until a track is reached below a farm. Dogs may bark furiously on top of the wall, but follow a narrow path along the base of the wall, later stepping up through a gap onto the higher side of the wall.

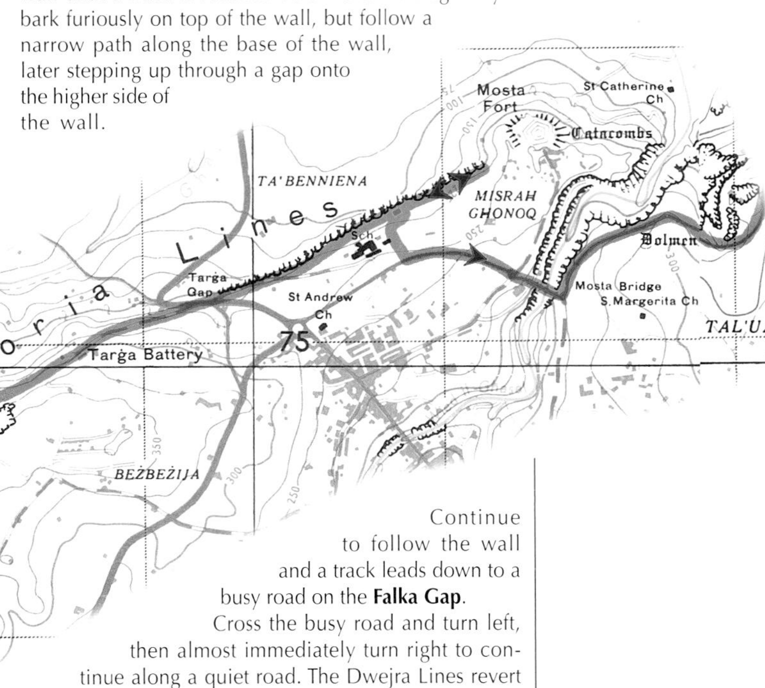

Continue to follow the wall and a track leads down to a busy road on the **Falka Gap**. Cross the busy road and turn left, then almost immediately turn right to continue along a quiet road. The Dwejra Lines revert to being called the **Victoria Lines** again, and the road passes alongside a deep quarry. Simply follow the potholed road gently downhill and admire stretches of the old wall alongside. Eventually, a junction is reached with a busy road on the **Tarġa Gap**, just outside **Mosta**. ▶

Plenty of buses pass here, where the route could be conveniently split over two days.

Just across the busy road is a quiet road signposted for the Ġnien l-Għarusa tal-Mosta public garden. Follow the road, then go down steps on the left to follow a splendid parapet walk along a spectacular stretch of the Victoria Lines, with cliffs down to the left and pine-shaded gardens rising to the right. When more steps are reached, there's an exit to the right, but it's worth continuing further along the parapet, passing a series of restored loopholes. However, in due course the way ahead is blocked by the security fence surrounding Mosta Fort, so double back and take the exit passed earlier.

The exit path links with a road beside the Art & Design Institute, reaching a busy road called Triq id-Difiża Ċivili. Turn left to follow this road, which has bus services, and pass a roundabout near **Mosta Fort**. ◄ Walk straight across a high-level bridge spanning the deep, cliff-bound valley of **Wied il-Għasel**, catching a fine view of the Mosta Dome rising above the town of Mosta.

The fort is used for storing munitions and explosives, as well as housing police dogs.

Turn left up another busy road, following a narrow path beside a line of pine trees to keep clear of the traffic. Peer into the deep valley to spot fragments of the Victoria Lines. However, as the road bends right, a deep hard-stone quarry has completely destroyed a whole section of the wall. Watch carefully alongside the road to spot a few short lengths of the wall that have survived near **Naxxar**. When a roundabout is reached at the **Naxxar Gap**, a couple of interesting V-shaped

map continues on page 132

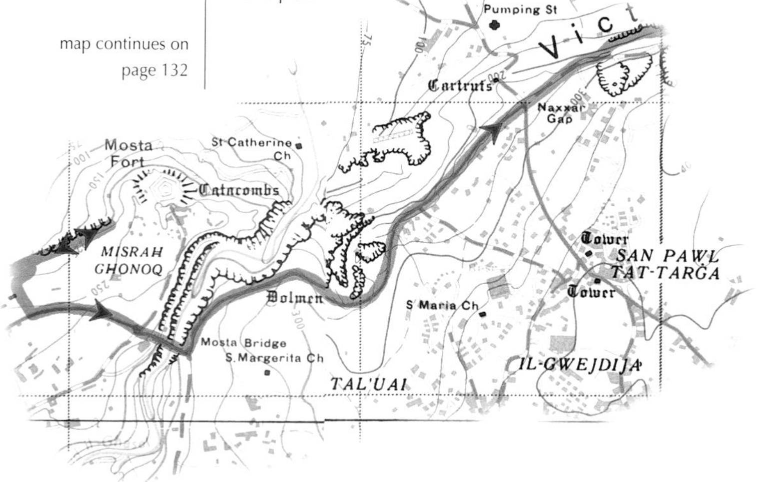

The Victoria Lines cross over the rugged valley of Wied il-Faħam

'redans' can be seen, where armaments were mounted to defend the road passing through the wall.

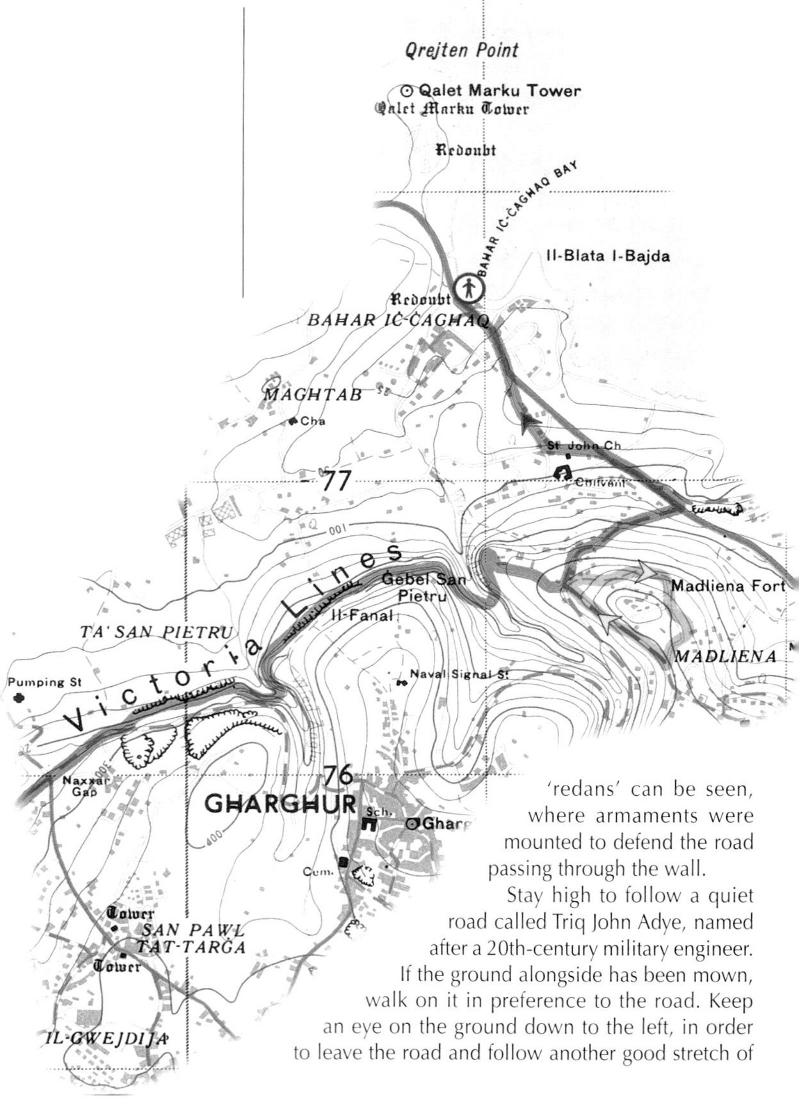

Stay high to follow a quiet road called Triq John Adye, named after a 20th-century military engineer. If the ground alongside has been mown, walk on it in preference to the road. Keep an eye on the ground down to the left, in order to leave the road and follow another good stretch of the old wall. There's a path alongside, but thorny scrub is encroaching on it.

The wall suddenly drops down a cliff face, with a long flight of almost 80 stone steps alongside. Cross the deep, rocky valley of **Wied Anġlu** and climb over 100 stone steps up the other side. There's a battery on top, now used as a picnic area, which once guarded a road leading into the valley.

Follow the wall onwards and upwards. ▶ Follow the road to another viewpoint, then leave it to follow a rugged path down beside another stretch of the wall. A steep and stony slope is followed by a flight of stone steps down into the steep-sided valley of **Wied il-Faħam**. More steps climb steeply, then a splendid rampart looks back across the valley. Stay close to the wall, squeezing past undergrowth to pass a few houses, reaching a cliff-top battery.

A viewpoint on top of a bunker at the 'Top of the World' enjoys fine views towards the sea and the village of Baħar iċ-Ċagħaq.

There's no onward access, so look for a small car park and pass between houses to follow an access road away from the wall. A crossroads is reached beside a wooded hilltop crowned by the **Madliena Fort**. (A forest path could be followed up towards the fort: by keeping right, the path encircles the old fort, which is occupied by radio communication dishes, then a road leads back down to the crossroads.)

To finish the walk, simply turn left and follow the road downhill. It passes through the last part of the Victoria Lines and drops to a busy main road. Turn left down the road to reach bus stops. By walking a little further along the road, the quiet Triq il-Wirt Naturali can be followed on the left, then a right turn at a chapel leads along Triq San Ġwann L-Evangelista. This leads back to the main road and more bus stops at **Baħar iċ-Ċagħaq**, where there are also bars and restaurants.

WALK 19

Fiddien to Mosta

Start	Fiddien Bridge (441 717)
Finish	Mosta Dome (483 743)
Distance	6.5km (4 miles)
Time	2hr
Terrain	Easy valley walking along quiet roads, tracks and paths. Parts can be wet and muddy after rain.
Maps	1:25,000 Malta sheet
Refreshments	Plenty of shops, bars and restaurants at Mosta.
Transport	Bus 109 serves Fiddien Bridge. Buses 31, 35, 37, 38, 41, 42, 44, 45, 202, 203, 205 and 225 serve Mosta.

The Fiddien Valley, Qlejgħa Valley and Ta' l-Isperanza Valley are essentially the same long valley. With a source near the highest parts of Malta around Dingli, and an exit to the sea at Salina Bay, this long valley was always a reliable source of water. The late 19th-century Chadwick Lakes were constructed in the middle of the valley to impound some of the water, and the mid-20th century Fiddien Reservoir impounds even more water. It is possible to walk all the way down through the valley from Fiddien Bridge, near Rabat, to the centre of Mosta, taking in a variety of scenes through the valley system.

Bus 109 runs from Rabat to **Fiddien Bridge**. Immediately beside the road is a large notice, and a rugged track leaves the road, reaching an overgrown picnic site beside an overgrown riverbed in the **Fiddien Valley**. Walk a little further to reach a children's play area at the next bridge, which is the double-arched **Għemieri Bridge**. ◂

An information board at this point explains about the flora and fauna of the valley. Rushes and reeds are abundant alongside the riverbed, but frogs and snakes are difficult to spot.

Go under the bridge and follow a path further downstream, crossing the riverbed a couple of times where necessary to reach a single-arched bridge. On the way, note the difference between the old drystone embankments above the riverbed and the cages full of boulders used in the restoration of the banks. Go under the bridge

An arch spans the Fiddien Valley

and cross the riverbed again. The way ahead is choked, so use a path leading up and along a terrace.

Walk back down to a wider path close to the river further downstream. This area would be very muddy when wet, passing great tangled masses of reeds. Continue along a narrow concrete road to join and follow another patchy concrete road further down the valley.

The **Chadwick Lakes** are no more than a series of small, dammed pools; in dry weather they may be waterless and are in any case heavily silted and vegetated. There is pleasantly mixed woodland below one dam, then the road crosses the valley and passes a couple of tall eucalyptus trees at another dam. Keep to the road and study the potholed riverbed alongside for a while. Pass a number of bridges and the Saliba Borehole, following the quiet road to a junction with a busy dual carriageway at **Il-Qattara**.

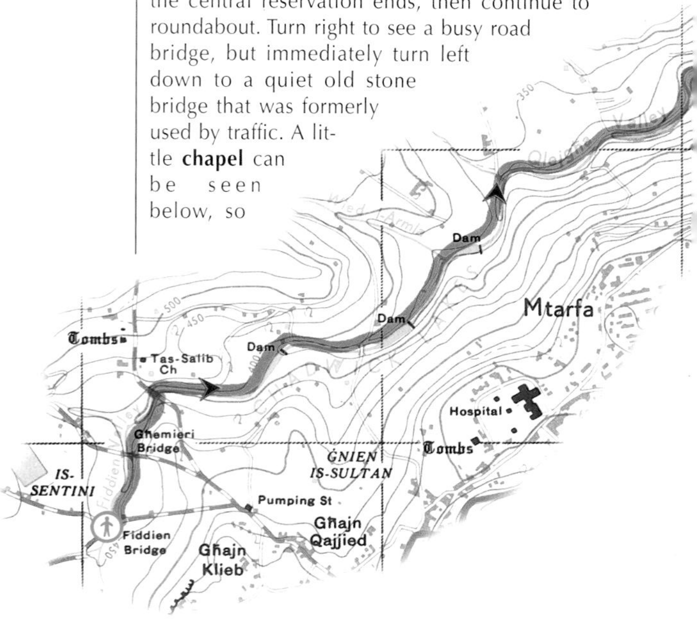

Turn left and follow the busy road, crossing it where the central reservation ends, then continue to roundabout. Turn right to see a busy road bridge, but immediately turn left down to a quiet old stone bridge that was formerly used by traffic. A little **chapel** can be seen below, so cross the bridge and walk down steps to reach it. A few more rough-hewn steps lead back down to the riverbed, where it's possible to walk beneath the triple-arched bridge.

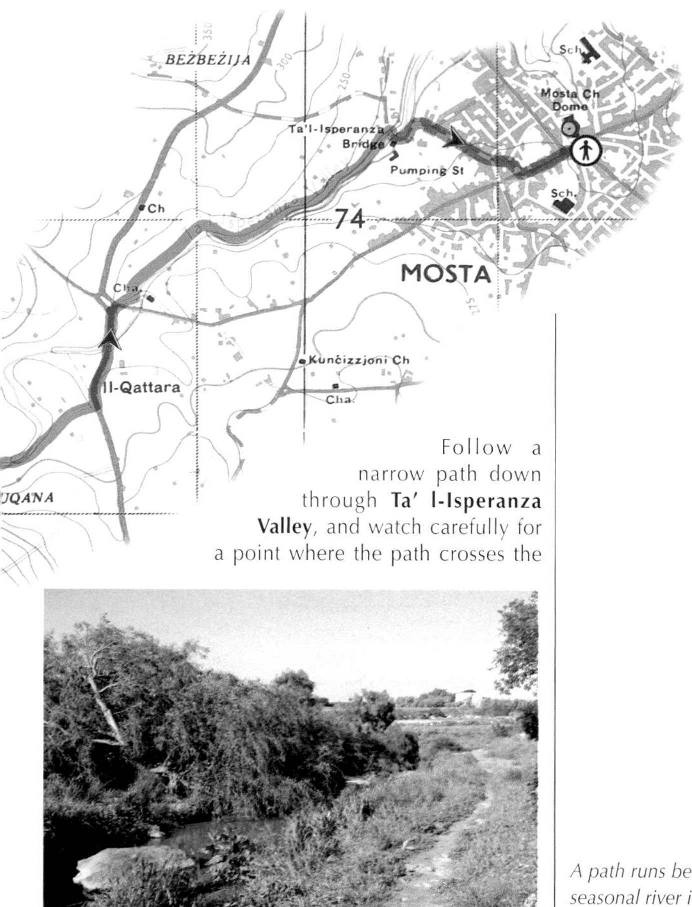

Follow a narrow path down through **Ta' l-Isperanza Valley**, and watch carefully for a point where the path crosses the

A path runs beside a seasonal river in the Ta' l-Isperanza valley

valley on a patch of smooth limestone. This happens just before a deep, rocky gorge opens up, so be sure to cross beforehand. Next, watch carefully as the path runs along the top of the gorge and then works its way back into the valley to run along the riverbed. The path is quite plain at times, but less obvious in places. It's clearer later, then flanked by walls as it passes left of a concrete dam in a wooded area. ◂

Steps can be used to explore below the dam, but if taken, climb back afterwards and follow the path a little further to a road.

Turn right to cross **Ta' l-Isperanza Bridge**, which spans the gorge. Take a look at the domed Speranza Chapel beside the bridge; stone steps can be used to reach a grotto beneath the structure, but climb back to the road afterwards. ◂ Follow the widest road away from the bridge and straight into **Mosta**. At the end of Triq l-Isperanza, turn left along Triq il-Kbira to reach the Mosta Dome in the middle of town, where there are plenty of places offering food and drink, as well as frequent bus services to Valletta, Sliema and Buġibba.

According to a local story, the chapel was founded in the mid-18th century after a woman was miraculously saved from falling into the hands of a raiding party.

Huge numbers of tourists visit the **Mosta Dome**, or 'Rotunda', or Church of St Mary, which is one of Malta's greatest landmarks. The interior is particularly ornate, with a great sense of space created beneath the unsupported dome, which was raised between 1833 and 1860. Walk through the Sacristy to visit a small museum, where the 'Mosta Miracle' is explained. On 9 June 1942, three bombs were dropped on the dome. Two of them were deflected without exploding, while the third punched a hole in the dome and entered the church, but failed to explode! A replica of the offending bomb can be seen, along with thousands of postcards showing the bomb and telling the story.

WALK 20

Rabat and Dingli

Start	Busugrilla, Rabat (451 714)
Finish	Bus stops, Rabat (461 715)
Distance	10km (6¼ miles)
Time	3hr
Terrain	Quiet country roads and tracks, with a couple of short paths
Maps	1:25,000 Malta sheet
Refreshments	A few shops, bars and restaurants at Dingli. Plenty of shops, bars and restaurants at Rabat.
Transport	Buses 50, 51, 52, 53, 109, 201, 202, 203, 205 and X3 serve Rabat and turn at the roundabout at Busugrilla. Buses 52, 201 and 202 serve Dingli.

This route makes a circuit round some of the higher parts of Malta, between Rabat and Dingli. You leave town to reach the Annunciation Chapel and St Catherine's Chapel, then cross a quiet and attractive agricultural valley to climb steadily towards Dingli. On leaving the village, the route runs along a quiet road for a while, joining a busier road to return to Rabat. Any spare time could be spent enjoying the town trail described in Walk 24, taking in several features of interest around Mdina and Rabat.

Use any bus making a loop around the suburbs of Rabat to reach a roundabout at **Busugrilla**. Follow the road signposted for Baħrija and Fiddien, heading downhill towards a roadside pumping station. Turn left up a narrow road before reaching the pumping station, as signposted for Tas-Salvatur, and climb past houses and farms.

A huddle of houses is reached at **Nigred**, where the tarmac road gives way to a concrete road on one corner, then the concrete gives way to broken tarmac at another corner. Smooth tarmac is reached at a junction with Triq il-Ġarġir. Turn right here, pass Qamma Farm and walk downhill, then keep left at a road junction at a small rock

map continues on page 142

cutting. The road is narrow and might bear puddles on the way to the Annunciation Chapel at **Tal-Lunzjata**.

Pass the chapel and turn left, following a road uphill. This appears to be heading all the way back to Rabat, but before reaching the edge of town, turn sharp right along a wider road signposted 'Sta Katarina'. Follow it past a hardstone quarry, then head downhill past **St Catherine's Chapel**. A bendy road drops into the valley of the **Wied Liemu**, crossing a streambed at the bottom. Keep straight ahead at a junction of concrete roads, climbing a tarmac road. Leave this by turning left along a track which runs through fields, turning left and right, then swings right and climbs as a concrete track.

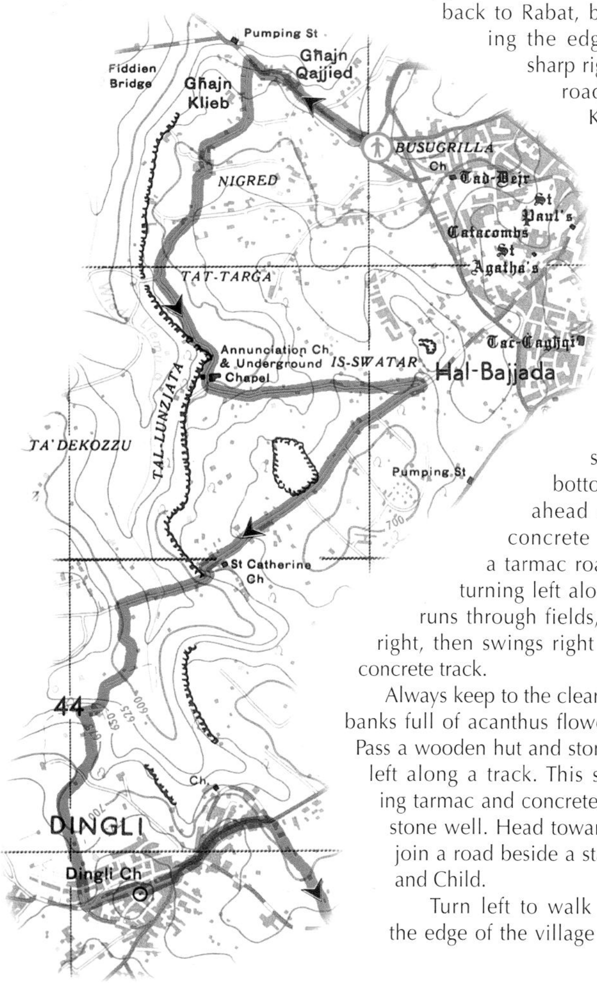

Always keep to the clearest line, admiring banks full of acanthus flowers in the spring. Pass a wooden hut and stone huts, then turn left along a track. This swings left, joining tarmac and concrete tracks, passing a stone well. Head towards buildings and join a road beside a statue of the Virgin and Child.

Turn left to walk along a road at the edge of the village of **Dingli**. Reach

The twin towers of Dingli Church obscure its even taller central dome

a road junction and walk up a flight of steps between housing blocks. Keep walking straight ahead to reach a mini-roundabout and turn left along Triq il-Knisja, passing **Dingli church**. Walk down from the church to find bars and the main bus stops in the village. Turn left to follow the main road, Triq il-Kbira, through the centre of the village.

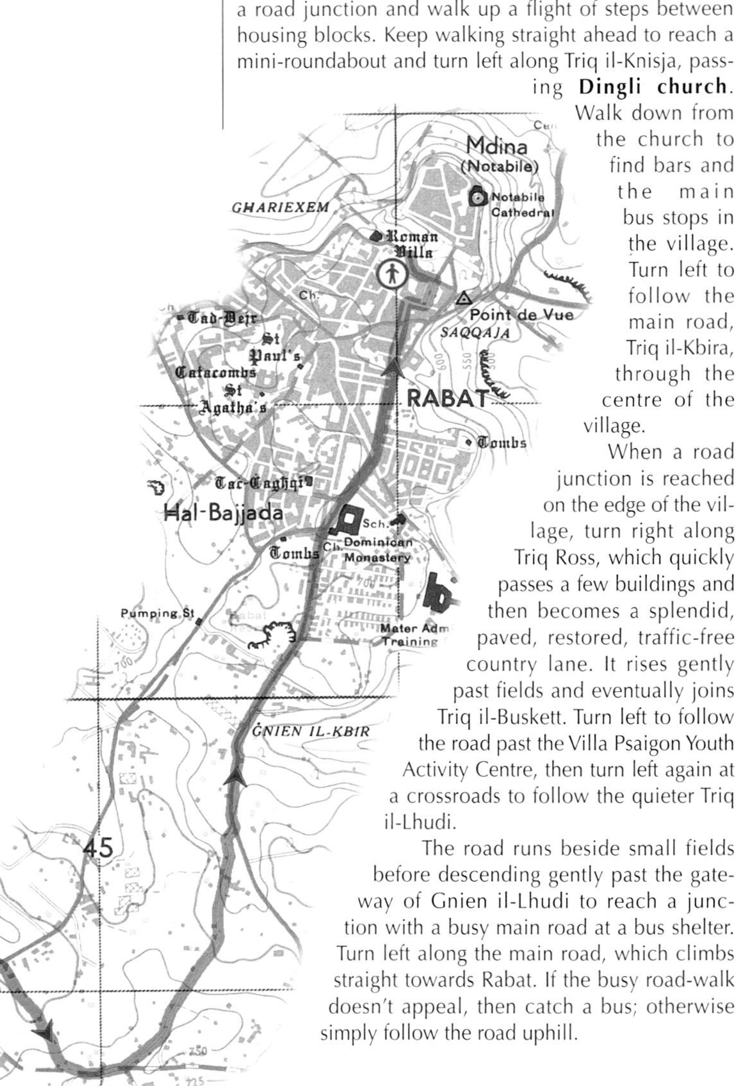

When a road junction is reached on the edge of the village, turn right along Triq Ross, which quickly passes a few buildings and then becomes a splendid, paved, restored, traffic-free country lane. It rises gently past fields and eventually joins Triq il-Buskett. Turn left to follow the road past the Villa Psaigon Youth Activity Centre, then turn left again at a crossroads to follow the quieter Triq il-Lhudi.

The road runs beside small fields before descending gently past the gateway of Gnien il-Lhudi to reach a junction with a busy main road at a bus shelter. Turn left along the main road, which climbs straight towards Rabat. If the busy road-walk doesn't appeal, then catch a bus; otherwise simply follow the road uphill.

The cloisters of St Dominic's are worth visiting on the way into Rabat

Eventually, pass Ta' Klariċċ Restaurant on the outskirts of **Rabat**, passing the big church of St Dominic's, whose cloister is worth viewing. Walk straight along Triq Ġorġ Borg Olivier, noting the old mansion of Villa Luginsland on the right. ▶

This was built in the late 19th century for the Imperial German Consul Baron Maximilian Von Tucher.

Fork left along Triq San Franġisk, passing the Franciscan Convent and Malta National Archives. Follow Triq l-Isptar, which narrows and appears to become a dead-end. However, turn right along the narrow Triq Santu Wistin and left along the attractive Vjal Santu Wistin. Another left turn leads to the main bus stops in town. From here it's easy to continue exploring with reference to Walk 24.

WALK 21

Siġġiewi and Buskett

Start/Finish	Siġġiewi church (493 681)
Distance	17km (10½ miles)
Time	5hr
Terrain	Quiet country roads, with a few tracks and short paths
Maps	1:25,000 Malta sheet
Refreshments	Shops, bars and restaurants at Siġġiewi. Bar-restaurant near the Buskett Gardens and the possibility of an ice-cream van inside the gardens.
Transport	Buses 62, 109, 201 and 209 serve Siġġiewi. Bus 201 runs near the Inquisitor's Palace. Bus 202 serves Buskett.

The countryside between Siġġiewi and Dingli is full of interest. On the outskirts of Siġġiewi, the Limestone Heritage Park and Gardens offers a splendid introduction to the bedrock of the Maltese islands, and a visit is recommended. Leaving town, country chapels and roadside shrines are passed, and there are views of the Inquisitor's Palace and Verdala Palace. Ancient features include a Roman quarry, Bronze-Age 'cart ruts' and a series of caves once used as burial sites and dwellings. The tree-shaded Buskett Gardens are very popular with local people, and the walk could be finished there, which is roughly the halfway point. A series of roads, tracks and paths lead back to Siġġiewi.

Start at **Siġġiewi church** and walk down from the statue in the Pjazza San Nikola to reach the Siġġiewi bypass. The best option is to follow Triq il-Qajjied and Triq Nikola Saura. If time can be spared, cross the bypass, turn left along it, then turn right to reach the **Limestone Heritage Park and Gardens**, which is located in a former softstone, or Globigerina Limestone quarry.

A JOURNEY IN STONE

A multi-lingual audio-visual presentation sets the scene, then you can make a tour around a number of exhibits on the quarry floor that demonstrate stone-cutting from the days when everything was done with hand tools, to the later modern mechanised stone-cutters. Blocks generally measured 28x28x56cm, forming an ideal building material, and specimen building styles can be studied. The softstone could also be carved into the most intricate shapes for ornamental use. There was very little waste, and even chippings were collected in baskets.

Mule transport gave way to army surplus Dodge trucks after the Second World War. Fossils in the lowest beds include shark's teeth, bivalves and sea urchins. Exhausted quarries were often used for citrus cultivation, and the site includes a citrus grove, gardens, farm animals and a restaurant. The entire site can be hired for events: tel 2146 4931, limestoneheritage.com.

If the Limestone Heritage isn't visited, leave Siġġiewi, cross the bypass and turn right along it. Go straight past a large roundabout and soon continue straight past a smaller roundabout. Continue along a narrow road that

The walk starts at the imposing church in the middle of Siġġiewi

Just before the main road, turning left leads to the ornate Tal-Providenza chapel, which is crowned with fine statues. If visited, return to the main road to continue.

becomes even narrower. Turn right at a junction, walk until a main road is reached, and turn right to follow it. ◂

The main road bends gradually left, then right. Watch out for a narrow tarmac road on the left and follow it very gently uphill towards a prominent cross seen ahead on the skyline. The road passes fields and a few houses, and all turns to right and left should be avoided. The surface is concrete for a while,

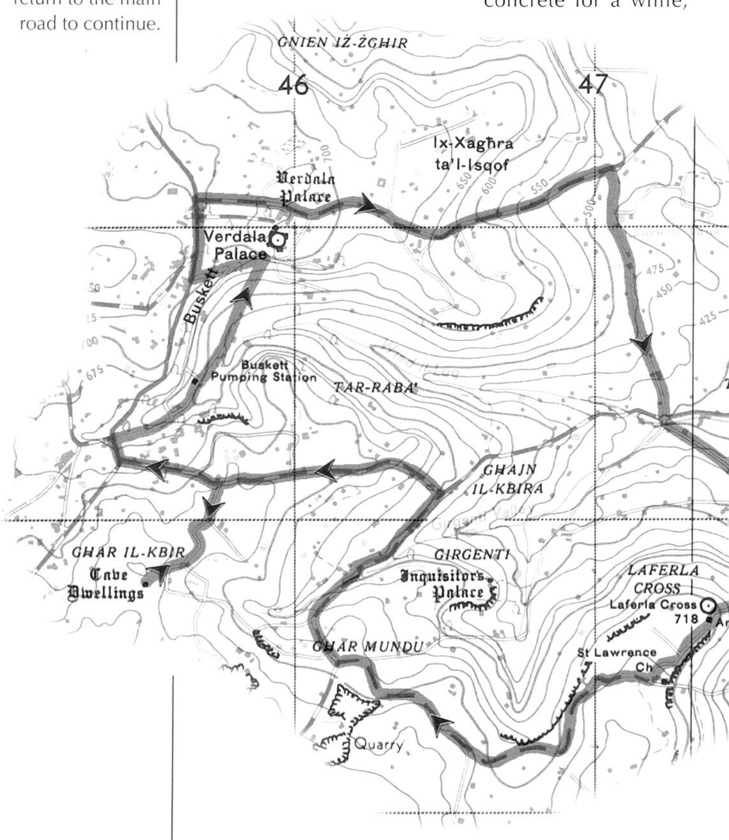

then there's a junction. Turn left to walk up to a crossroads, then turn right up another road to reach another crossroads. There's an old house here and a statue of an angel ministering to Christ.

Turn left, as marked for the 'Laferla Cross Footpath'. This is actually a very narrow road that climbs past a couple more statues before becoming a rough, stone-paved path leading up to the **Annunciation Chapel**, originally founded in 1420. Wooden steps lead up to the **Laferla Cross**, but also note the cave cut underneath the structure. ▶ The altitude here is 219m (718ft); fine views extend around Malta from Dingli and Rabat to Mosta and the urban sprawl around Valletta. The industrial Freeport area is in the far distance.

The cross was erected in 1900, fell in 1946 and was re-erected in 1963.

Follow a concrete track from the Annunciation Chapel to the nearby **St Lawrence Chapel**, then turn right along a tarmac road. This winds about through rocky terrain and overlooks the Girgenti Valley and its cultivation terraces. Pass close to the Ta' Zuta **quarry**, then turn left and right at road

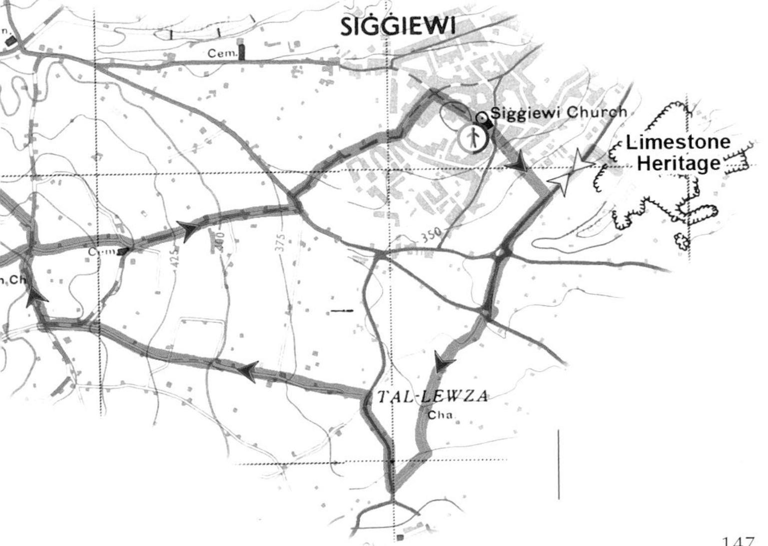

By tradition, travellers should check the candle in the shrine, and if it's about to burn out, replace it with another from the stock available.

junctions. Walk downhill and watch out for a roadside shrine on the left between two tall trees. ◂

Walk down the road, which can be busy with quarry trucks. There's a stone arch to the right, and later a layby offers a view across the Girgenti Valley to the **Inquisitor's Palace**, dating from 1625 and now used as the prime minister's residence.

This was quarried by the Romans, and plenty of old square cuts can be seen.

When a big road sign is reached at **Għajn il-Kbira**, turn left up a narrow road. Keep left at a junction, then look across the open limestone area to the right. ◂ Continue along the road and it becomes flanked by walls. Turn left at a gateway marked for Clapham Junction, where a big sign also reads 'Għar il-Kbir and Cart Ruts'.

Some of the caves are inter-connected and are surprisingly light inside. The caves were used as burial places and dwellings, and were last inhabited in the 19th century.

Follow a road uphill a short way, then branch right along a track. Look out for the ancient, deep lines of 'cart ruts' scored left and right. Follow the track further to reach a large hole in the ground, **Għar il-Kbir**, where a series of small caves can be explored. ◂

Retrace steps all the way back down to the motor road and turn left. Walk down the road and swing right at the bottom to reach the former Buskett Grape and Wine Station. A left turn at this point leads past a bus stop to the Cahteau Buskett and its restaurant, if food and drink are required. To continue the walk, however, turn right at the old Wine Station as signposted for Buskett.

Follow the road and head down to the left, aiming to stay low in the well-wooded valley to enter the **Buskett Gardens**. There are plenty of pines, a few olives, palms and cypresses, as well as a number of fruit trees and shrubs. Follow a path that passes toilets and the Buskett Water Booster, with the Verdala Palace seen straight ahead uphill. Follow the track as it gradually steepens and climbs towards the palace, although there's no access to the building from this side. Turn left before reaching the palace's barred gates, walking along a terrace and up a few steps to reach a road bend.

Verdala Palace was built in 1586 for Grand Master Hugues Loubenx de Verdalle. It was a summer

The Verdala Palace can be glimpsed while passing Buskett

residence and hunting lodge, with much of the hunting done using falcons. The Buskett Gardens were used as a hunting area in the 16th century, and were planted in their current form in the 17th century, although the pine trees date from the 19th century. On 28 and 29 June each year – the Feast of SS Peter and Paul – the Buskett Gardens are crowded with local people, complete with music, dancing, food, drink and an agricultural exhibition.

Walk up the road, in the shade of pine trees, turning right at the top to pass a fine gateway leading into the palace. Turn right along a road, with barely a glimpse of the palace beyond its tall wall and surrounding pine forest. However, there's a little chapel to the right and a view of Rabat away to the left.

Follow the road downhill, and the shade afforded by pines alongside the road eventually runs out. There's a stretch of road without trees or buildings alongside, and the road appears to be heading straight for distant Valletta. Turn right at a road junction with pine trees alongside. Follow the narrow tarmac road past a small reservoir called the **Laurenti Tank** and keep walking straight ahead until a main road is reached at **Ta' Brija**.

Cross the main road, avoid another tarmac road on the left, then take the next turning left. This quickly becomes a rather overgrown path rising gently between fields. Follow the path up to a couple of buildings, and it becomes a track that is easier underfoot. Follow the track up to a road and keep walking straight ahead from a pillar inscribed 'GR'. Keep right at what looks like a mini-roundabout built around a manhole. The road leads back to the old building and statue where the sign for the 'Laferla Cross Footpath' was seen earlier in the day.

Turn left down a very narrow road and follow it down to a road junction beside an old **cemetery** and poultry works. Turn left down a busier road, aiming for the church in the middle of Siġġiewi in the distance. Go through a staggered crossroads marked by a pillar bearing a 'Holy Souls' sculpture in a ball of fire. A narrow country road gives way to the broad Triq il-Fawwara on the outskirts of **Siġġiewi**. Note an old mill on the left at a roundabout, but walk straight ahead and turn left along Triq San Ġwann.

Reach a tiny square with a small tree in it at the Farrugia Bar, then turn right along Triq il-Parroċċa. This leads straight to **Siġġiewi church**, which has been considerably extended over the years. Keep right to reach the centre of town and bus stops.

WALK 22

Siġġiewi to Qormi

Start	Siġġiewi church (493 681)
Finish	Pinto's Lodge, Qormi (529 705)
Distance	9.5km (6 miles)
Time	3hr
Terrain	Quiet roads and tracks, with some paths that may be narrow and overgrown.
Maps	1:25,000 Malta sheet
Refreshments	Shops, bars and restaurants at Siġġiewi. Shops, bars and restaurants off-route at Żebbuġ and at the end in Qormi.
Transport	Buses 62, 109, 201 and 209 serve Siġġiewi. Buses 61, 62, 109 and 209 serve Żebbuġ. Buses 61, 62 and 209 serve Qormi. Dozens of buses serve the nearby Marsa Park & Ride station.

The head of the Girgenti Valley is seen during Walk 21 around the higher parts of Malta near Dingli. Proceeding downhill, the valley becomes the Wied il-Ħesri, Wied Qirda and Wied il-Kbir, eventually draining into the Grand Harbour. A walk down through the valley is quite varied, and often seems remote from the nearby towns of Siġġiewi, Żebbuġ and Qormi. One part of the valley is close to the busy airport, yet this is also the deepest and wildest part. At the bottom end, where the valley broadens, the Marsa Sports Club and its many sporting facilities occupy the land.

Start at the statue on the Pjazza San Nikola, facing **Siġġiewi church**, and keep to the left of it as signposted for Rabat, Żebbuġ and Qormi. Walk along Triq il-Parroċċa and continue along Triq il-Mitħna. At a crossroads, follow Triq il-Qamar, which is signposted for Rabat. ▶ Follow the road, Triq Blat il-Qamar, straight ahead and out of Siġġiewi, passing a **cemetery** and a small roadside pillar memorial. Turn right along a narrow road, which leads straight down into the **Wied il-Ħesri**, rapidly becoming a track through the valley.

Turn right here to short-cut to the Siġġiewi Sports Complex, keeping right of it to follow a road and a grassy track into the Wied il-Ħesri.

A colourful section of the Wied il-Ħesri on the outskirts of Siġġiewi

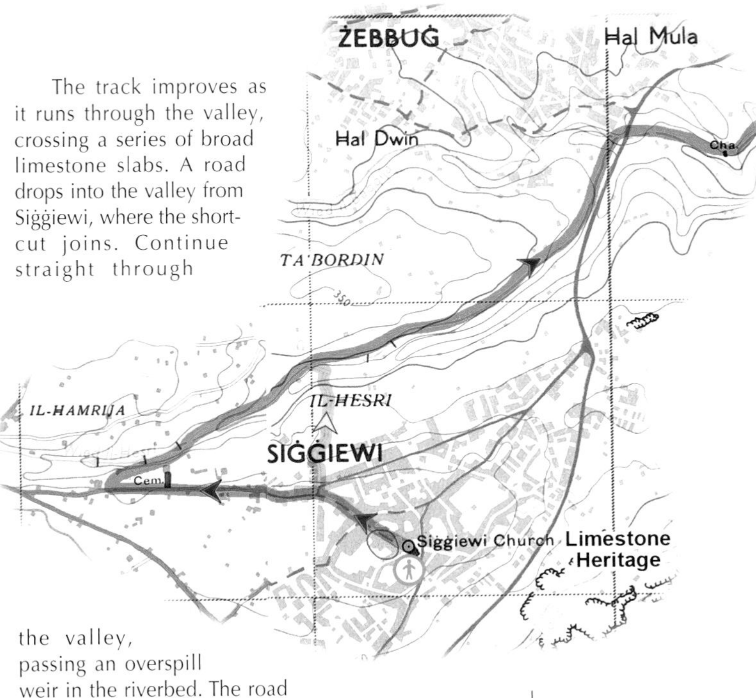

The track improves as it runs through the valley, crossing a series of broad limestone slabs. A road drops into the valley from Siġġiewi, where the short-cut joins. Continue straight through the valley, passing an overspill weir in the riverbed. The road crosses the riverbed, then becomes concrete. Follow it back across the riverbed and uphill a little.

Eventually, the road turns right and appears to leave the valley to reach a farm called St Philip. Don't climb up to the farm, but follow a clear track that eventually runs back into the valley. There's later a busy road up to the right and a bridge is reached on the outskirts of **Żebbuġ**. ▸

Triq is-Siġġiewi can be followed into Żebbuġ to reach shops, bars and restaurants. There are also bus services both in town and on the main road.

A raised concrete path leads under the busy main road bridge, where the Wied il-Ħesri and Wied il-Baqqija combine to form the **Wied Qirda**. There's another road bridge a short way downstream: don't cross it, but note the short verse about Wied Qirda carved in stone alongside.

Follow the quiet road alongside the riverbed, drifting away slightly to pass an old **chapel**. Continue along

the road, avoiding another road that crosses the valley from a big concrete overspill. Eventually, the road crosses a bridge over the riverbed at Tazzi Farmhouse and becomes a rougher track. It rises slightly onto a terrace and passes below a fireworks factory. Later, the track splits into two and both lines climb steeply to the right.

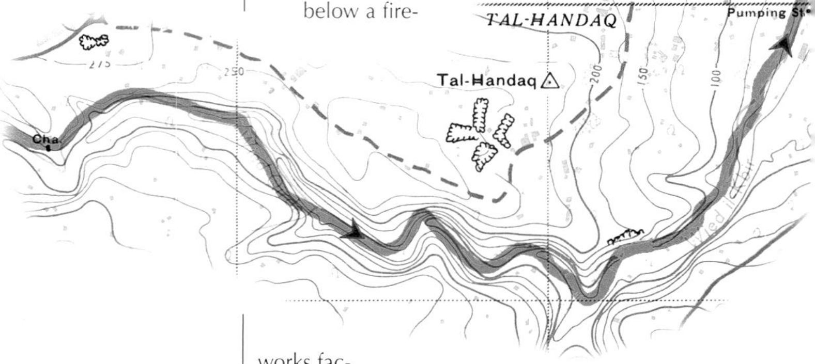

At this point, look carefully to spot a narrow path running onwards across the bushy valley side. There are a couple of alternatives, but aim to pick a way down a short, steep slope to reach the dry riverbed. The valley sides ahead are steep and rocky; they're sometimes terraced but also feature sheer cliffs. Walk along the cobbles in the riverbed and look out for a portal carved into the cliff face on the right, while turning around a bend in the valley.

Continue along a rugged track that improves as it passes further into the rocky gorge. Pass a couple of fruit farms at a confluence, where the Wied Qirda becomes the **Wied il-Kbir**. Follow a road downstream, passing small industrial units. ◄ Pass the Gejxa Farmhouse and the St Sebastian fireworks factory. Eventually reach a junction with a very busy main road at **Għammieri** on the outskirts of Qormi.

Look up to the left to spot intriguing, overgrown stone steps cut into the cliff face.

Cross the main road with care, or use a nearby pedestrian crossing. There are two bridges close together at this point, but the older stone-arched bridge is now defunct. Continue along a narrow road beside the riverbed, which gives way to a track leading to another road. Cross over the road and follow another road straight ahead. This passes the former Löwenbräu brewery site, to the left, and the extensive **Marsa Sports Centre** to the right but largely out of sight.

Walk to the end of the road to reach Marsa Park & Ride, where a bus station offers an early finish with a wealth of bus services. Just behind the bus station is the Malta Racing Club, where two-wheeled horse-drawn gigs are often seen being prepared for races. ▶

On race days, expect this area to be very busy!

To walk a little further, follow the road between the bus station and Lidl supermarket. Turn left along a busy road to reach a large, flowery roundabout centred on a statue of the 18th-century Grand Master Manoel Pinto de Fonseca. A nearby pedestrian crossing gives access to a tree-shaded park-cum-walkway. Follow this towards **Qormi**, turning right at the end of the park to reach a modern, domed church. Look around the square, Misraħ il-Granmastru, to find the preserved remains of Pinto's Lodge. Buses can be caught from the nearby road.

An imposing, modern, domed church is passed at the end in Qormi

WALK 23

The Wignacourt Aqueduct

Start	San Anton Gardens (503 726)
Finish	Casa Leoni, Santa Venera (529 719)
Distance	3.5km (2 miles)
Time	1hr
Terrain	Easy road-walking in built-up areas.
Maps	1:25,000 Malta sheet
Refreshments	Bars are available near the start and finish of the walk.
Transport	Bus 54 serves San Anton Gardens, and buses 51, 52 and 53 run close. Buses 42, 51, 52, 53, 55 and 123 pass through Santa Venera and Ħamrun.

Each of the Grand Masters of the Knights of St John left their mark on Malta. Alof de Wignacourt was Grand Master from 1601 to 1622, and he brought water to Valletta by means of a remarkable aqueduct. Springs were tapped around Mdina and channelled underground to Attard. A Bolognese engineer called Bontadino de Bontadini constructed a series of stone arches to carry the aqueduct over undulating ground from Attard to Ħamrun. Cisterns were dug at Valletta to store the water before further distribution. Only a couple of miles of the aqueduct arches remain, mostly alongside a busy road, but it makes an interesting historical linear feature to follow.

By all means start this walk with a thorough exploration of the tree-shaded **San Anton Gardens**, which lie beside the San Anton Palace. Across the road from the San Anton Gardens is the exclusive Corinthia Palace Hotel, which is highly favoured by those who visit the President of Malta.

The **San Anton Palace** was built as the country residence of Grand Master Antoine de Paule in the 17th century. It served as the British governor's residence, and is now used by the president of Malta. The gardens can be visited for free throughout the day, while access to the palace courtyard is available only at certain times.

Walk along the road, Triq Birkirkara, as if heading for the village of **Attard**. The road runs through a gap in a stout stone wall, and lying to the left is a small planted area called Il-Ġardina Emvin Cremona. A suburban road beside the garden is called Qrib San Anton; turn left to follow it, and the Wignacourt Aqueduct lies out of sight, buried beneath the long planted strip beside the road.

Later, watch out to spot what appears to be a stone cistern at ground level. Don't worry if this is missed, but continue walking along Triq Peter Paul Rubens. This quiet road features a good stretch of sunken stone arches and leads to a busy main road on the outskirts of **Ħal Balzan**.

The aqueduct is no more than a low limestone wall as it reaches the main road. Simply continue alongside the main road, on the left-hand side, to pass a busy road junction and a bus stop. Follow a tree-shaded path between the main road and a quieter parallel road, noticing that the stone slabs underfoot lie on top of the old aqueduct.

Pass the embassies of Libya and Kuwait as the aqueduct is carried onto a series of fine stone arches. The aqueduct bends slightly to the left as it passes a stone cross beside another busy road junction on the outskirts of **Birkirkara**.

Stay beside the main road, as the aqueduct goes behind the Mrieħel Estate apartments before entering a fenced area to which there is no access. However,

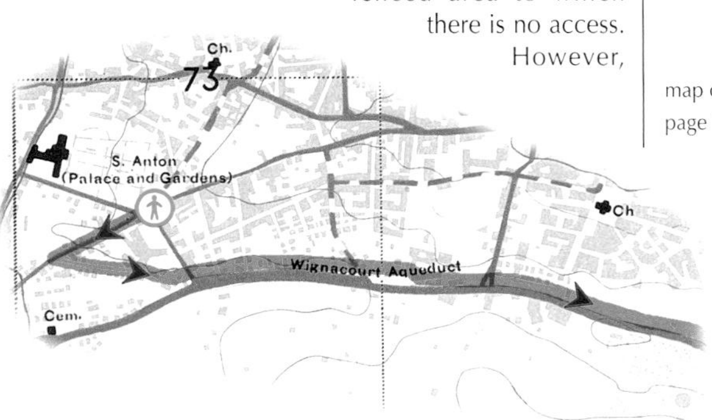

map continues on page 158

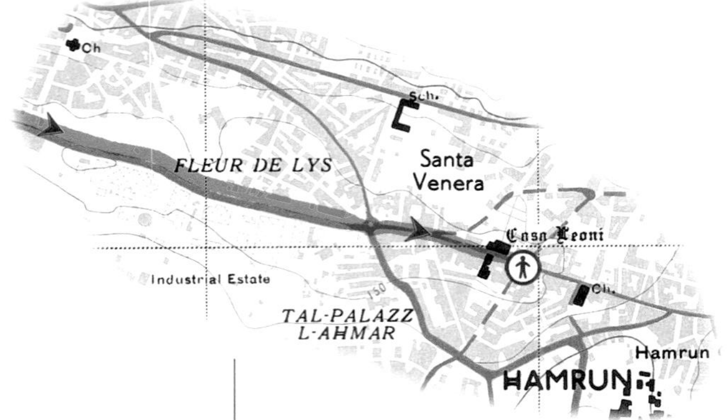

Note how four of the arches accommodate road traffic at this point, although trucks are barred from passing through.

further along, the aqueduct is seen riding high on very tall arches at a junction between the main road and Triq l-Imrieħel. ◂ Keep walking alongside the arches, and if a break is needed from the traffic on the main road, just step through the arches and follow a quieter road on the other side.

As the ground rises gently, the arches become lower, then the aqueduct is simply encased in a stone wall before it drops all the way to ground level. At a bus shelter, a house sits on top of the old watercourse, so step onto the main road briefly to pass it.

Continue along a path shaded by Aleppo pines, bearing in mind that the aqueduct is still present, albeit buried underground. On the other side of the main road is the Farsons Brewery, then shortly afterwards, at another bus stop, the aqueduct rises from the ground onto a line of arches again. These are particularly lofty while passing the Devon biscuit factory. ◂

Note how the aqueduct bends slightly to right and left.

Later, along Triq Notabile, the aqueduct is supported on a ridge of limestone. Obviously, the ground level has been lowered since the structure was built. A busy roundabout between Birkirkara and **Santa Venera** suddenly severs the aqueduct; note how narrow the cross-section of the channel is on top of the arches. ◂

The Fleur-de-Lys arch, built in 1615, was demolished by the British in 1943. The replica on the roundabout was built in 2015.

While passing the roundabout, note the splendid building on the left, which is the Conservatorio Vincenzo Bugeja. The aqueduct runs along the right-hand side of the main road, and bends slightly right as it passes St

Roads run through the Wignacourt Aqueduct at Triq l-Imriehel

Joseph's Church. (People living alongside the road park their cars under almost every one of the arches for a stretch.) Pass a snack bar and local council office, then look across the road to spot **Casa Leoni** with its stone lions, with toilets nearby. The aqueduct ends abruptly at a portal where Santa Venera gives way to **Ħamrun**. Catch a bus from a nearby stop, or walk down through the town for a little longer.

WALK 24

Mdina and Rabat Heritage Trail

Start/Finish	Bus stops, Rabat (460 715)
Distance	3km (2 miles)
Time	(walking time) 2hr
Terrain	City streets and steps, as well as optional underground catacombs
Maps	1:25,000 Malta sheet. Town maps available from the TIC.
Refreshments	Plenty of shops, bars and restaurants around Mdina and Rabat.
Transport	Buses 50, 51, 52, 53, 109, 201, 202, 203, 205 and X3 serve Rabat.

Long before Valletta was constructed, the fortified city of Mdina was the main settlement on Malta, and was known as the Citta Notabile (Noble City). Its earliest fortifications date to 1000BC. Located far inland on one of the highest parts of the island, at almost 200m (650ft), this site was easily defended in times of strife. It became the seat of Malta's government, the Universita. The Knights of St John, however, were not keen to uphold Mdina's defences and proposed to abandon the city in 1644, but were forced to strengthen the place when the citizens objected. In 1693 Mdina was badly damaged by an earthquake, and although the cathedral was rebuilt, there was again talk of abandoning the city. In the 18th century there was considerable rebuilding and remodelling. The population spilled from the confines of the city wall and neighbouring Rabat assumed its current form.

This route looks inside the fortified city of Mdina, where there are several attractions, then wanders through Rabat mainly to visit a series of ancient catacombs. If the catacombs are of particular interest, please check the current opening times to avoid disappointment, and if necessary, restructure the route by visiting the catacombs first.

Start at the bus stops at **Rabat** and walk along paths shaded by trees to reach **Mdina**, noting how the huge defensive ditch has been converted into a pleasant park. Go through the **Main Gate** to enter the walled city. Just

The ornate Main Gate leading into the ancient citadel of Mdina

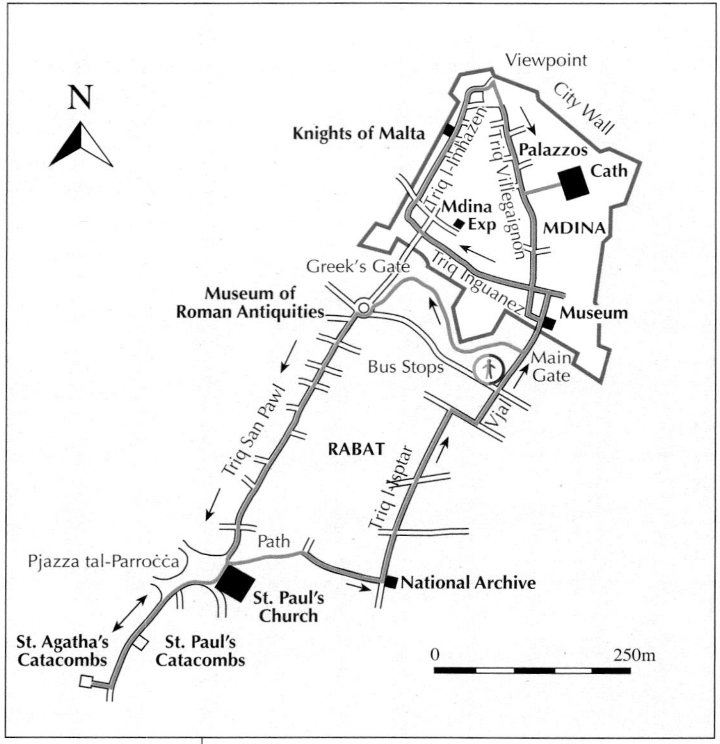

The building was formerly the palace of the Grand Masters of the Order of St John, but also served as a sanatorium.

inside, on the right, are the Mdina Dungeons, billed as a 'Dark Walk' attraction, and a courtyard leads to the **National Museum of Natural History** (tel 2145 5951, heritagemalta.org). ◂

Turn left to find St Agatha's Chapel on a corner; this was built in 1410, destroyed by the 1693 earthquake, then rebuilt in 1695. Go along the narrow **Triq Inguanez** opposite, and on the left is the Bacchus Restaurant, whose building dates from 1660 and was built between the first-century Roman walls and 10th-century Arab walls of Mdina, originally to house gunpowder magazines.

At the end of the narrow street, have a look at the **Greek's Gate** on the left, but turn right to continue along **Triq l-Imħażen** (Magazine Street). Another gate on the left looks out across the valley to the neighbouring hilltop settlement of Mtarfa, while the **Mdina Experience** is signposted to the right along the kinked Triq Mesquita, in Pjazza Mesquita. ▶ Further along Magazine Street there's a little chapel on the corner of Triq San Pietru (St Peter Street).

The audio-visual show offers a good grounding for explorations of the walled city (tel 2145 4322, **themdinaexperience.com**).

Just beyond the chapel, built into the city wall, is the **Knights of Malta** – an 'Epic Adventure Experience' (tel 2145 1342, theknightsofmalta.com). This is a walk-through visitor attraction in another former gunpowder magazine. Continue round to the Pjazza tas-Sur (Bastion Square), where there's a fine **viewpoint** on the city wall, taking in Mtarfa, Mosta and the urban sprawl around Valletta to the airport. There are a couple of good restaurants here too.

Walk straight into the middle of the old city by following **Triq Villegaignon**, next to the Casa Mdina, passing a number of **palazzos**, or palaces. To the left is the Palazzo Falson, also known as the Norman House. The Palazzo Constanzo is nearby – a 17th-century Baroque palace now serving as a restaurant – while Palazzo Santa Sophia is on the right. The street suddenly opens up at the broad Pjazza San Pawl (St Paul's Square), facing **St Paul's Cathedral**.

Tradition maintains that Publius, governor of Malta, was converted by St Paul on **this spot**, and a church has stood there from the fourth century. The church was enlarged in 1090 and 1490, but had to be rebuilt following the earthquake of 1693.

Continuing along Triq Villegaignon, Tales of the Silent City (tel 2145 3530) is an audio-visual presentation on the right, while on the left is St Peter's Monastery, housing Benedictine nuns. Turn left when you pass St Agatha's Chapel on the corner again, then either turn right to leave Mdina or take a short stroll straight ahead to

Deep underground in ancient rock tombs at St. Paul's Catacombs

see a fine little square at Misraħ il-Kunsill, where a building housing a *trattoria* is dated 1530, and was formerly the Herald's Loggia.

After walking back through the **Main Gate**, turn right and weave along paths through gardens of gnarled Aleppo pines, palms and shrubs. Turn around St Paul's Bastion to reach an outwork viewpoint overlooking the valley and nearby Mtarfa. Double back among the trees, aiming for a roundabout at a road junction. To the right of the roundabout is the **Museum of Roman Antiquities** and Roman Townhouse, also referred to as the Roman Villa (tel 2145 4125, heritagemalta.org).

Follow **Triq San Pawl** straight into **Rabat** from the gift shop called the Roman Villa Centre. Head straight to the **Pjazza tal-Parroċċa** in the middle of Rabat to visit **St Paul's Church** and its underground grotto.

The **grotto** was cut by hand around 100BC, and it's said that St Paul lived there following his shipwreck in AD60. It was essentially a Roman prison, where Paul converted a number of people during his three-month stay on the island. There are 16th-century frescoes, a couple of interesting statues and a silver model of a galley. The Wignacourt Museum lies beside the church, and beneath it are ancient catacombs and more recent wartime tunnels used as air raid shelters (tel 2749 4905, www.wignacourtmuseum.com).

Cross the Pjazza tal-Parroċċa and follow Triq San Kataldu as signposted for St Paul's and St Agatha's Catacombs. Keep left and right as signposted to find **St Paul's Catacombs** on the left. You can wander at will underground, examining the intricate system of passageways and burial niches. Walk further along Triq Sant' Agata, then turn right along a paved, tree-lined path to find **St Agatha's Catacombs**.

St Agatha is a patron saint of Malta. She was a third-century Sicilian Christian who fled to Malta, but was captured and returned to Sicily to suffer martyrdom. She is said to have stayed for a while in these catacombs. Visitors are guided through the catacombs and are shown a series of frescoes (tel 2145 4503, stagathamalta.com/catacombs.html).

Walk back along the street, which features lace-making places, to return to St Paul's Church in the centre of town. Face the front of the church, then go through a gateway on the left. A paved **path** called Iz-Zuntier is marked as private, but is used as a through-route when the gates are unlocked. In the middle of the path, take a look at a stone pillar inscribed in eight languages with quotes from the Acts of the Apostles, chapter 28, verses 1, 2, 10 and 11. ◂

These verses record St Paul's time in Malta.

Leave the enclosure and turn right along Triq Cosmana Navarra. This leads to the old Franciscan Convent and Santo Spirito Hospital, now the **National Archive**. Turn left to follow Triq l-Isptar, which narrows and appears to become a dead-end. However, turn right along the narrow Triq Santu Wistin and left along the attractive Vjal Santu Wistin. Another left turn leads back to the bus stops where explorations started.

GOZO

Salt pans and the bald-headed hill of Qolla l-Bajda at Qbajjar Bay (Walk 28)

GOZO

A Gozo Channel Line ferry leaves Mġarr Harbour

Gozo is much quieter than Malta, and although many towns are quite built up, there's still plenty of countryside to explore, as well as a remarkable cliff coastline. Start by exploring the citadel and enjoy a view over the whole island. Most of the walks can be linked to offer a complete tour around the coast, as well as a walk over a handful of fine little hills. By walking all the way round coastline of Gozo, some of the best scenery on the Maltese islands can be enjoyed. Regular Gozo Channel Line ferries operate from early until late, daily, between Malta and Gozo (tel 2210 9000, www.gozochannel.com).

WALK 25

Victoria Heritage Trail

Start/Finish	Bus Station, Victoria (316 892)
Distance	3km (2 miles)
Time	(walking time) 2hr
Terrain	Busy streets, quiet streets and flights of steps
Maps	1:25,000 Gozo sheet. Town maps available from the TIC.
Refreshments	Plenty of shops, bars, restaurants and cafés around Victoria, and one snack bar at the citadel.
Transport	All bus services on Gozo lead to Victoria/Rabat.

Victoria, or Rabat, is centrally located on Gozo and is the island capital. Rising above the town is the older citadel, now partly in ruins; in years gone by, most of the population of Gozo would have retreated here in times of strife. Anyone with a morning or afternoon to spare would enjoy a stroll through Victoria, taking in a couple of churches and other features. The citadel area is crammed full of interesting buildings, while its defensive walls offer splendid views of almost the whole island. Aim to spend most of your time in the citadel, where the cathedral and four small museums can be explored, along with poky alleyways and desolate areas of ruined buildings.

Leave the **bus station** in Victoria and follow the road gently uphill to the **Pjazza San Franġisk**. The church of San Franġisk is well to the left of a fountain, but walk straight across the square for a glimpse inside the **Department of Trade**. ▸ Follow the road signposted 'Citadel', which is the **Triq Vajrinġa**. Almost immediately, on the left, is the 'crib made in wax', which can be inspected for free when open in the winter months – although a donation is welcome.

The building was an old hospital that opened in 1792, founded by Grand Master Manoel de Vilhena.

When the **library** (which also houses a primary school) is reached, turn right along Triq l-Iskola, which is signposted for St George's Basilica. Continue along **Triq il-Karita** to reach St George's Basilica, or Bażilika San Ġorġ. As you enter the **Pjazza San Ġorġ**, bear diagonally

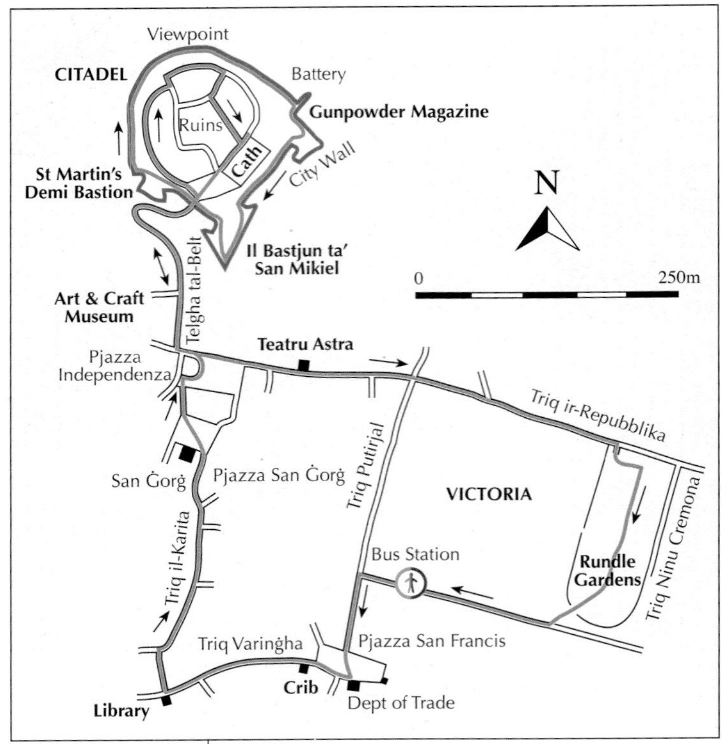

left and leave by following a narrow street called **Triq San Gużepp**. This leads to a circular building housing toilets and the tourist information centre on the **Pjazza Independenza**.

The square is sometimes full of market stalls, and the busy Triq ir-Repubblika runs alongside it. Cross the busy road and climb two dozen steps uphill alongside **Telgħa tal-Belt**. 'Gozo 360°' is an audio-visual introduction to Gozo on the right (tel 2155 9955, www.gozo360.com.mt). The road leads up to an enormous arch giving access to the **Citadel**.

The Cathedral dominates the citadel, as seen from Victoria

Standing on the Pjazza Katidral, the **cathedral** stands on top of an impressive flight of 30 steps, while the Court of Justice is to the left.

> Unlike most ecclesiastical buildings around the Maltese islands, the **cathedral** has no dome, but inside is a fine *trompe l'oeil* supported on four sides by biblical women. The perspective of the trompe l'oeil is upset when seen from other angles. The Cathedral Museum can be accessed by a separate entrance on Triq il-Fosos (tel 2155 4101, **www.gozocathedral.org**).

To explore the citadel walls, climb steps to reach Triq il-Kwartier San Martin – the Old Prison – and step up onto **St Martin's Demi Bastion**. ▶ Keep climbing steps to work your way around the walls and out onto a high **viewpoint** to enjoy splendid views around Gozo. Look into the citadel and notice that the upper streets are in ruins.

St Martin's Citadel Bar offers snacks and drinks.

Walk down flights of steps to reach the **Gunpowder Magazine**. The walk around the walls continues up and

Tall palms trees form an avenue on the way through the Rundle Gardens

down steps, passing cannons on the way to **Il Bastjun ta' San Mikiel**. Follow the parapet over the main gate to enjoy a fine view of the Pjazza Katidral and return to St Martin's Demi Bastion.

Next, to explore the poky alleyways, walk up the narrow street signposted for the **Gozo Nature Museum** (tel 2156 4188, heritagemalta.org), which is Triq il-Kwartier San Martin. Include a visit to the museum, or pass it and follow the old paved street up past ruined buildings. Turn right, then left at a junction, and right again for a good plan view of the ruins. This course leads briefly back to the wall, but turn right and walk down through an arch, along **Triq il-Kwartier San Ġwann**. Note the little chapel of St Joseph's (or San Ġużepp il-Qadim) and the 17th-century Palazz ta' l-Isqof Cagliares just beyond the arch, but turn left down Triq Bernardo deOpuo beforehand.

This alley leads down to the Folklore Museum (tel 2156 2034, heritagemalta.org), and the Cathedral Museum is found by making a left turn at the bottom. However, to continue the tour, turn right and walk down towards the main gate beyond the Pjazza Katidral again. Turn left just before reaching the gate, walking through another arch, to find the **Museum of Archaeology** (tel 2155 6144, heritagemalta.org). There are toilets nearby. Leave the citadel by walking through the main gate, via Triq Bieb l-Imdina.

Walk back down to the busy **Triq ir-Republikka** and turn left, passing the **Teatru Astra** and Bishop's Palace. ▶ Either turn right for the bus station to finish, or walk further down Triq ir-Republikka and turn right into the tree-shaded **Rundle Gardens**. Admire the tall trees, savour the coolness of the shade, then leave via a rear exit and turn right to return to the bus station.

The island of Gozo is a separate diocese to Malta, so has its own bishop.

WALK 26

Mġarr to Sannat

Start	Harbour, Mġarr (367 870)
Finish	Santa Margerita, Sannat (318 873)
Distance	9km (5½ miles)
Time	2hr 30min
Terrain	Rugged at first, with care needed in windy weather. A rocky path is followed by a series of easier paths and tracks.
Maps	1:25,000 Gozo sheet
Refreshments	Bars and restaurants around the harbour at Mġarr. Small restaurant at the head of Mġarr ix-Xini, and a bar-restaurant off-route near the mouth of the inlet. Several bars and restaurants around Sannat.
Transport	Gozo Channel Line ferries serve Mġarr from Ċirkewwa on Malta. Buses 301, 303 and 322 serve Mġarr. Bus 305 serves Sannat.

Walkers who wish to explore the cliff coastline of Gozo could start anywhere, but Mġarr is where the ferries berth and it makes a good starting point. The hustle and bustle of the ferryport is left behind in mere minutes, leaving walkers to pick their way across a boulder-strewn landslip slope. Note that when high winds send waves breaking onto the base of a crumbling clay cliff near Mellieħa Point, it's best to avoid the coast. Fortunately, another path climbs high above the cliff. The rest of the route uses good paths and tracks, taking in the beautiful rocky inlet of Mġarr ix-Xini and the high, cliff-fringed plateau of Ta' Ċenċ, noted for its wealth of wild flowers.

There are bars, restaurants, toilets and an ATM in and around the ferryport. Take note of the small ferries to Comino, for future reference.

Start where the buses and taxis meet the ferry at **Mġarr** harbour. ◀ Cross the ferry access road, pass left of a restaurant and walk up a concrete road into a car park. A track leaves the car park, soon giving way to a coastal path.

There are two or three intertwined options as the clay slopes are gradually creeping down towards the sea, and walkers keep treading new lines. Dodge huge boulders and squeeze past tamarisk, spurge and occasional prickly pears. A junction is reached before a bare clay cliff, where there are two options.

> **If the sea is calm**, walk round the base of the crumbling **Tafal Cliffs** to reach a huddle of boathouses on the low rocky outcrop of **Mellieħa Point.** Continue along a low, smooth rock platform to reach more huts, but note the signs warning of the danger of rock-fall.

If the sea is rough, and beating against the cliffs, then climb towards Fort Chambray. Turn left when a turning space is reached at the end of a track and follow a path down to the coast, completely avoiding the cliffs and rocky point.

Pass the bay of **Xatt l-Aħmar** and look at the salt pans carved into the rock. Continue walking along a concrete track, reaching a parking space and seats where a notice explains about three commercial vessels that were deliberately scuttled offshore and are visited by divers.

Fine fossils are embedded in the rock below, where the Lower Coralline Limestone gives way to Globigerina Limestone.

Follow a gravel track onwards, which becomes a fine cliff path. Step down to the left as marked by a red arrow beside a manhole cover. Drop to a lower cliff path near the headland of **Ras il-Ħobż**, overlooking more salt pans. ▶ The path drifts gently uphill, often hand-carved into the bedrock, to reach **Mġarr ix-Xini Tower**.

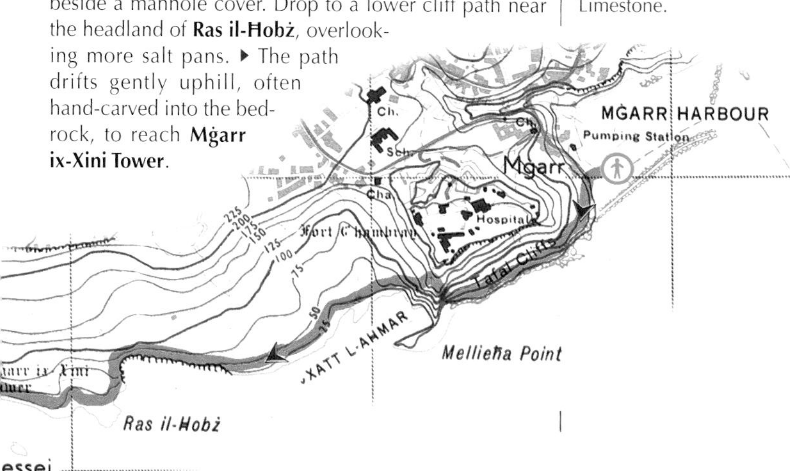

A 17th-century tower guards a fine rocky inlet at Mġarr ix-Xini

The **tower** was built by the Knights of St John in the 17th century. It was rescued from ruin, completely restored and re-opened in 2009. It can be visited whenever someone from Wirt Għawdex is in attendance (www.wirtghawdex.org).

Follow a path away from the tower, again often hand-carved into the bedrock, rising gently along a rocky brow overlooking **Mġarr ix-Xini**.

Mġarr ix-Xini (Port of the Galleys) is a splendid **natural harbour**. The shallower parts of the inlet are popular with divers. The Turk Dragut Reis, who stormed Gozo in 1551, used this inlet to invade, then carried most of the island's inhabitants into slavery.

A cabin operates as a bar-restaurant specialising in fish dishes.

Enjoy the views and marvel at the bushy spurges that seem rooted in solid rock, but take care to spot the line of descent to the head of the inlet. Crude rock steps give way to a set of neatly carved rock steps, leading to a little beach at the head of the inlet. ◂

Follow the concrete road up from the beach, reaching a picnic site on a bend. Walk further up the road, looking left to spot a small stone wall with a gap beside it. The wall blocks an old track, preventing it being used by vehicles, but the way is open to walkers. The track later turns right, leads to a house and becomes a road running up the **Wied Sabbar** valley. ▸ When the road suddenly bends right, leave it to follow a stony track on the left, blocked against vehicles by a wall. Follow the track further into the Wied Sabbar and turn left to cross a stout stone causeway bearing a narrow path for walkers.

A turning on the left leads off-route down to a bar-restaurant.

Swing right and follow the path roughly parallel to the coast, albeit some distance from the cliffs. The path later swings left onto a dead-end headland, so watch for another path climbing to the right up some old terraces. Swing left onto a track, which itself later swings right to avoid rocky outcrops ahead. After being drawn back into the Wied Sabbar, a path leads up to a small shone-arched bridge.

Cross the bridge and almost immediately turn left along another track. If time is running short, this track leads straight to Sannat; otherwise, turn sharp left at the next junction to follow yet another track further uphill and closer to the cliffs near **Ta' Ċenċ**. To see the cliffs, wait until the track begins to drift inland to the right, then step to the left to locate the cliff-line. A sheer drop of

map continues on page 178

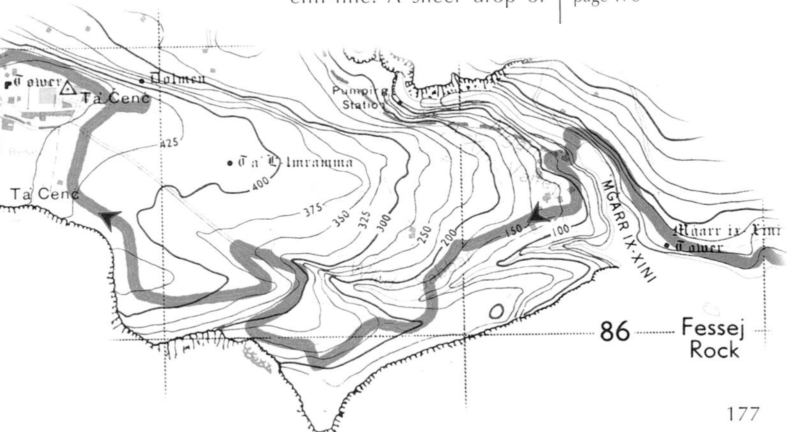

Ancient dolmen and a view towards the dome of St John's Church in Xewkija

120m (400ft) comes as quite a shock, so tread with care! Unfortunately, a stout wall in the distance bars further access to the cliffs, so follow the track to a junction with a broad dirt road. ◄

By turning right along the dirt road, then looking to the left, a small dolmen might be spotted. Look across the Wied Ħanżira Valley to Xewkija, where the domed church of St John's is the largest on Gozo.

Turn left to follow a dirt road, passing the gates of the Ta' Ċenċ Reservoirs, while the exclusive Hotel Ta' Ċenċ is largely hidden from view. Simply follow the road straight down through **Sannat**, avoiding turnings to the left. There are bus stops, but it's worth walking down to the middle of the village to reach the church of Santa Margerita. ◄ There are bars and restaurants, if a bus isn't due for a while. Even so, the centre of Victoria is only 2km (1¼ miles) distant.

Fine statues stand in front of the church, replacing a weatherworn set that now stand in a corner.

WALK 27

Sannat to San Lawrenz

Start	Santa Margerita, Sannat (318 873)
Finish	San Lawrenz (283 905)
Distance	13 to 16.5km (8 to 10¼ miles)
Time	4–5hr
Terrain	Good tracks and cliff paths for the first half. Roads can be used to avoid a steep, rocky climb from Xlendi. Tracks and cliff paths lead to Dwejra Bay and San Lawrenz.
Maps	1:25,000 Gozo sheet
Refreshments	Bars and restaurants at Sannat, Xlendi, Dwejra Bay and San Lawrenz.
Transport	Bus 305 serves Sannat. Bus 306 serves Xlendi. Bus 311 serves Dwejra Bay and San Lawrenz.

The cliffs between Sannat, Xlendi and Dwejra Bay sometimes rise in excess of 120–150m (400–500ft). Great cliff scenery and historical interest abound on this walk. Good paths and tracks lead away from Sannat, reaching a splendid lookout tower. Leaving Xlendi requires careful thought: either use a steep and rocky scramble on old, worn steps, or divert inland to find a longer way round by road. The route continues to Dwejra Bay, which is both scenic and interesting, so allow time for exploring. Apart from an interesting lookout tower, the cliffs on either side of the bay seem to embrace the stark outline of Fungus Rock. The Azure Window and Inland Sea are two geological curiosities worthy of appreciation, and short boat trips are available to explore them. The route runs up to the village of San Lawrenz at the end of the day.

Face the church of Santa Margerita in **Sannat**, then keep to the right of it and pass behind it. Follow Triq Dun Xand Aquilina, later keeping right as signposted for the Saguna Cliffs. Go through a staggered crossroads, also signposted for the cliffs, reaching a road-end picnic site. Follow a track, but when it turns right, keep straight ahead up a narrow path. This suddenly reaches a cliff edge around

135m (450ft). Look left to the remarkable cliffs beyond **Iċ-Ċnus**, but turn right to follow a cliff path onwards.

Pass a number of shooters' huts and enjoy stunning views around **Tal-Bardan**, although the path runs rather close to a crumbling edge, so it needs care. Follow the path downhill and it joins a concrete track, which in turn joins a stone-paved road. Turn left to follow the road as it winds and undulates, with splendid cliff views. The road suddenly gives way to a path at **Bajjada**, where the cliff edge should be avoided.

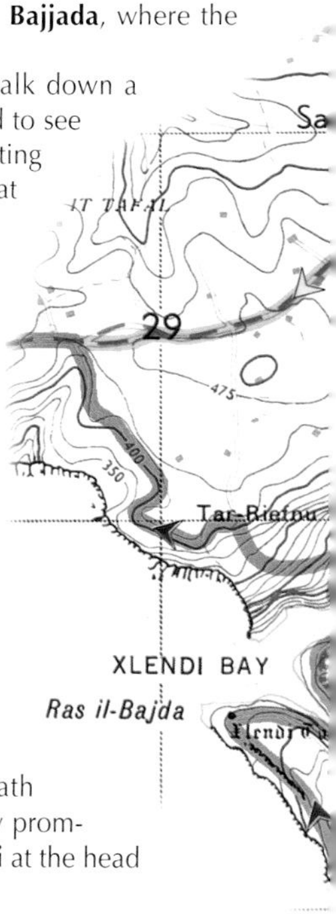

Move inland slightly and walk down a few crude rock steps. Look ahead to see Xlendi Bay and Xlendi Tower, spotting a number of paths heading in that direction. A winding path shifts between terraces and passes a small rocky bay. ◄ Either keep to the cliff edge or keep to the nearest obvious path, heading for the well-preserved 17th-century **Xlendi Tower** on the headland of **Ras il-Bajda**.

Look out for a rock arch on the far side of the bay.

It looks possible to walk straight from the tower to the bustling village of Xlendi, but the deep and rocky inlet of Wied tal-Kantra is tucked out of sight. Although this forces walkers to detour inland, rugged steps lead down to a fine stone-arched footbridge. The path on the other side leads to an easy promenade heading straight into **Xlendi** at the head of the bay. ◄

There are plenty of bars and restaurants, as well as bus services to Victoria for anyone wishing to finish early.

There are two options to continue. The first option is a direct route, which involves a very steep, rocky, scrubby scramble up a flight of old, worn, carved rock steps. Some walkers would find this unnerving. The only way to avoid it is by taking a detour far inland by road, which although longer, is safer and easier.

Direct scramble

Pass in front of the Boathouse and Stone Crab restaurants, then climb an obvious flight of 76 rock steps built against the cliffs. Turn right at the top, following an old path carved across a rocky slope but partly obscured by scrub. After going down three rock steps,

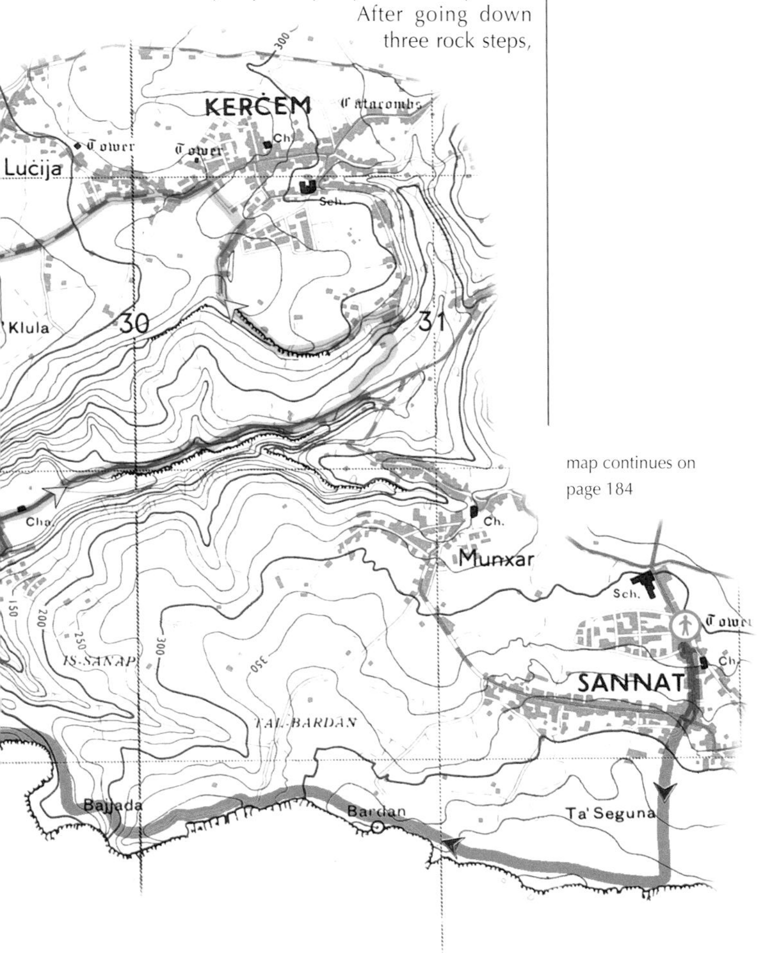

map continues on page 184

A 17th-century tower guarding Xlendi Bay with cliffs rising beyond

turn left and watch carefully to find a flight of old, worn rock steps. These are steep and awkward, and should not be used when wet. Care is needed throughout the ascent, along with a head for heights and a willingness to use hands in places.

Watch for a series of cairns to continue up towards a rubble wall. Bare rock gives way to a path through scrub, passing the end of a wall. There's no further access inland, so turn left later, passing a shooter's hut to follow a grassy terrace. Later still, turn right inland, heading towards a stone-block building. Follow a path towards another shooter's hut to join a track, which becomes concrete and leads to a junction with a tarmac road. Turn left to follow the road onwards.

Inland road route

Head straight inland from Xlendi along Triq Ir-Rabat. Pass the Underground Flour Mill and a church. Use a concrete strip beside the road, overlooking the **Xlendi Valley** while rising from the village. Pass a café/bar and later descend gently past a restaurant, reaching a road junction on the right. However, turn left and walk up a narrow concrete road, which becomes steep and bendy as it climbs past houses.

Turn left along Triq Għajn Tuta and follow the road gently uphill until a junction is reached on the built-up edge of **Kerċem**. Turn left along Triq il-Kalandbrijiet and left again at a crossroads along Triq L-Avukat Anton Callea. Enter **Santa Luċija** and turn left along Triq Qasam San Pawl. Follow the road out into the countryside, as signposted for Għadira ta' Sarraflu, avoiding all other roads and tracks to right and left. The road later forks either side of an 'island' and the direct route joins from the left.

The road is quite wide as it runs onwards, reaching clumps of tamarisk growing around the Roman Lake. A narrow concrete road branches off to the left; follow it gradually downhill until it suddenly turns right uphill. Continue straight ahead along a rugged track, which later

Don't follow a path running parallel, along a terrace below the overhang.

climbs gently. It gives way to a path along the top of an overhanging layer of rock. ◂

The path later turns right uphill, reaching the foot of a rocky hill-top. Turn left through a gap between the rock and a stone wall. There's a fine view ahead of Dwejra Bay, Fungus Rock, the Azure Window and Inland Sea.

Pick a way down a path, staying on the most obvious whenever junctions are reached. There may be a marked

Sunset tinges the Azure Window on Dwejra Bay

diversion away from one of the shooter's huts dotted around the slopes. The path reaches a valley floor at the head of **Dwejra Bay** and the rocky islet of **Fungus Rock** (or Il-Ġebla tal-Ġeneral) stands guard. ▶

Pick a way around Dwejra Bay and head down onto a shattered spine of limestone projecting seawards. This leads close to Fungus Rock, where crumbling rock steps can be seen, that were cut to allow the precious 'fungus' to be gathered. It's worth picking a way along the rocky coast, rather than looking for easier paths and tracks, to discover a wealth of fossils; the most notable are the 'sand dollars', which are a round, flat form of sea urchin.

The 'fungus' is a rare parasitic plant called Cynomorium coccineus. It was highly prized by the Knights of St John, who believed it had a wide range of medical applications.

Visitors often mill around **Dwerja Bay**, where the Dwejra Tower – a National Trust of Malta property – and the Kappella Sant' Anna, along with a couple of bar-restaurants and toilets, sit at the road-end. The Inland Sea lies in a rocky hollow and is connected to the rest of the Mediterranean by a narrow cave leading through the cliffs. The Azure Window can be viewed beyond the chapel, but stay off the high rock arch, which is close to collapse. There are boat trips from the Inland Sea to the Azure Window and back. Spend as much time as possible marvelling at the landforms around Dwejra: an area so special that it's been proposed for World Heritage Site status.

If a bus is due, then by all means catch it; otherwise walk uphill and inland to San Lawrenz. Most people would follow the road, but there's another way. Look at the rocky slopes above the chapel to find a path carved into the rock. This is equipped with rock steps in places, and it gradually climbs high above the Inland Sea. ◄

Clumps of yellow-flowered Maltese Everlasting, or Helichrysum melitense, grow in abundance, and this is the only place in the world where it grows in the wild!

The path runs into a quarry road, so turn right to follow it uphill. The road becomes the Triq Wied Merill, and a left turn along Triq ta' Ċangura leads to the domed church in the middle of **San Lawrenz**. A shop and a restaurant are located around the Pjazza San Lawrenz and there are buses to Victoria.

WALK 28

San Lawrenz to Marsalforn

Start	San Lawrenz (283 905)
Finish	Marsalforn (334 922)
Distance	11.5 to 12.5km (7 to 7¾ miles)
Time	3hr 30min–4hr
Terrain	Road-walking at first, giving way to coastal tracks and cliff paths, ending back on roads.
Maps	1:25,000 Gozo sheet
Refreshments	Shop, bar and restaurant in San Lawrenz. Shop in San Pietru. Bars and restaurants at Qbajjar Bay and more in Marsalforn.
Transport	Bus 311 serves San Lawrenz. Bus 310 serves Qbajjar Bay and Marsalforn.

Walkers trying to trek all the way round the coast of Gozo might find access barred around San Dimitri Point, although paths and tracks do exist. It's better to follow winding village roads from San Lawrenz to San Dimitri Chapel, then walk down to the coast. A clear and easy coastal track and road can be followed, but the scenery is greatly enhanced by walking closer to the cliffs – although this is more difficult underfoot and needs care. A couple of long, narrow inlets can be explored, and there are fine rock arches to admire. Towards the end of the walk, on the way to Qbajjar and Marsalforn, hundreds of salt pans have been carved into the rock. Most are disused, but a few of them are worked in the summer months.

Leave **San Lawrenz** by taking the road signposted for Għarb, running to the left of the church. This runs out of the village to the junction of Triq il-Wileġ and Triq San Pietru. Turn right for **San Pietru**, then turn left in the village at a junction beside Gozo Prestige Holidays. Fork left at another junction, walking down past the Villaġġ Ta' Sbejħa holiday complex. Walk down the road, Triq Mongur, then turn left at a junction along a narrow road called Triq Birbuba. Note Il-Mitħna, an old mill, on the way through **Birbuba**, as well as a countryside view from a roadside playground.

Follow quiet, narrow country roads beyond the village, forking right at a junction and looking ahead to spot the solitary **San Dimitri Chapel**. It lies off-route to the right, but can easily be included in the day's walk; otherwise continue along the road towards the coast. When a concrete corner

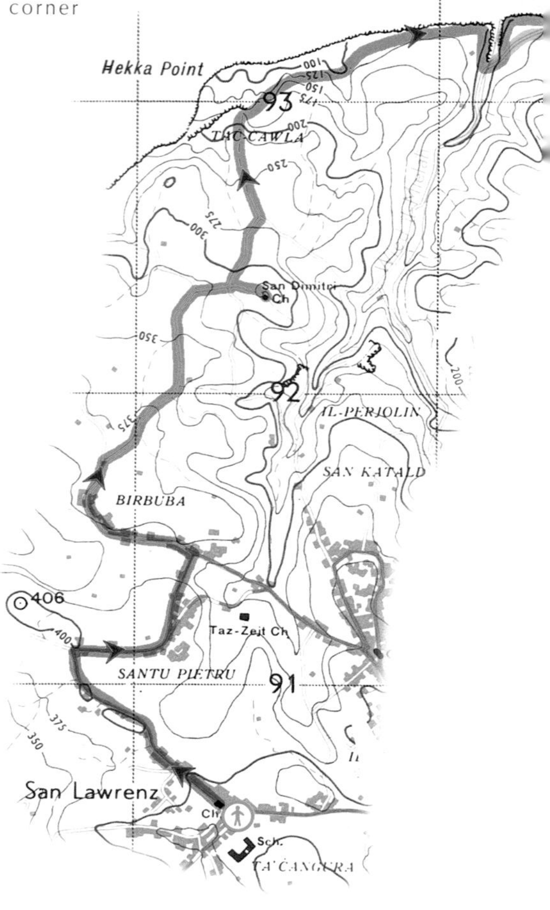

map continues on page 191

is reached, walk down a rugged track worn to bedrock, which itself peters out at a huddle of large boulders at **Taċ-Ċawla**. Pick a way downhill to reach bare rock before a cliff edge at **Hekka Point**. ▸

The cliffs are Lower Coralline Limestone, but the cliff tops are soft and strangely sculpted softstone, or Globigerina Limestone.

Either follow the cliff line or follow a track, passing around a small rocky inlet. Stay on the track to reach a larger rocky inlet at the foot of **Wied il-Mielaħ**. An information board stands at the point where the inlet is bridged by a concrete road. ▸ Either follow a dirt road onwards, or leave it and walk across bare rock to the

A path with over 50 steps enters a rocky ravine, allowing close-up views of a splendid rock arch.

A fine rock arch can be seen at the mouth of the Wied il-Mielaħ

Stone steps lead to a small pebble beach at the head of a rocky inlet

mouth of the inlet, where the rock arch can be admired. A rocky ledge offers good views of the cliffs beyond, but it also narrows alarmingly, and it might be better to follow the dirt road beyond **Pinu Point**.

Again, either follow the dirt road for easy walking, or follow the rugged cliff top around **Forna Point**. ▶ An easy walk along a softstone ledge leads around the point, but it peters out and a higher shooters' path has to be used instead. Drop to a lower terrace and walk out to a rocky point to inspect the mouth of another rocky inlet at **Għar il-Qamħ**.

There are good views over the cliff edges, which often have big caves beaten out of their bases.

Head inland alongside the inlet, picking a way along a rocky ledge that offers fine views along its length. There's a cave and pebble beach at its head, but no way down from this side. Keep walking along the ledge, finding a vague path that's been hammered out of the rock, leading further inland into the **Għasri Valley**. At one point, the rocky ravine is so narrow that a simple stride is all that's needed to get to the other side at **Ta' Nikol**. The riverbed could also be crossed at the same point the dirt road crosses.

Turn left along the dirt road, then continue along a path to reach the top of a flight of steps. ▶ Again, either stay on the dirt road (which later becomes concrete) for easy walking, or walk along the cliff tops to return to the mouth of the inlet. There are hundreds of salt pans carved into the rock around **Nagħaġ il-Baħar** and **Reqqa Point**.

Some 95 stone steps lead to a beach, but it's necessary to climb back up them to continue.

map continues on page 192

Eventually, the concrete road has to be followed around

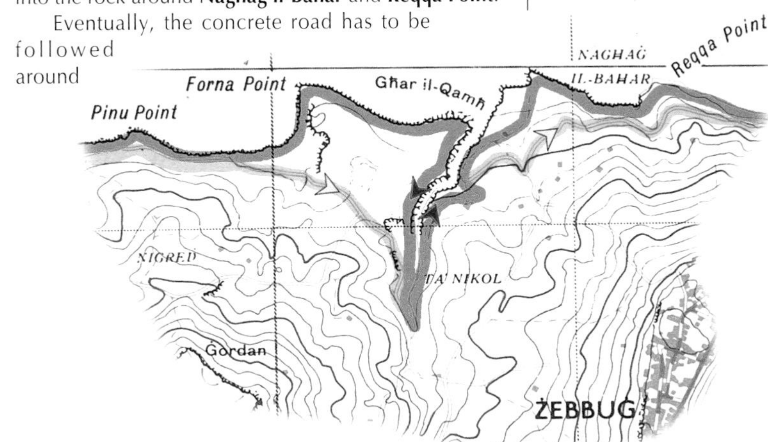

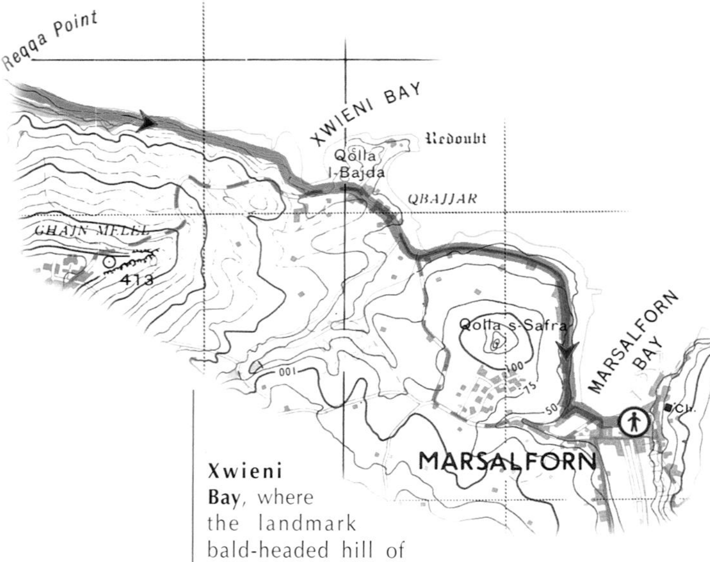

Xwieni Bay, where the landmark bald-headed hill of **Qolla l-Bajda** rises on the other side. **Qbajjar Bay** has a number of bars and restaurants, and there are occasional buses to Marsalforn and Victoria.

The walk from Qbajjar to Marsalforn is easy enough, using the Qbajjar Promenade at first. This is shaded with plenty of tamarisk bushes. The road can be avoided by using seaside walkways linking a couple of beach bars, but these aren't practical if the sea is washing across them. The seafront at **Marsalforn** is full of bars and restaurants, while the bus stop is just a short step inland beside a river that often has a dry bed. There's a good range of accommodation around town, mostly in the form of apartments, but there are hotels and guesthouses too.

WALK 29

Marsalforn to Ramla Bay

Start	Marsalforn (334 922)
Finish	Bus stop, Ramla Bay (356 908)
Distance	6km (3¾ miles)
Time	(walking time) 2hr
Terrain	Roads and tracks, steep at times, with a rugged path used on the final descent.
Maps	1:25,000 Gozo sheet
Refreshments	Plenty of shops, bars and restaurants at Marsalforn and Xagħra. A couple of beach cafés at Ramla Bay.
Transport	Bus 310 serves Marsalforn. Buses 307 and 322 serve Xagħra. Buses 302 and 322 serve Ramla Bay.

Previous editions of this guidebook included a very rugged coastal walk from Marsalforn to Ramla Bay. This part of the coast suffers from rock-falls and mudslides and was always difficult. It remains very messy, although some walkers still rise to the challenge of covering it. An easier and more pleasant way to link the resort and the popular bay is available by heading inland: an interesting valley and a steep climb lead to Xagħra, which has some interesting features, and as this is a short walk there's plenty of time available for additional explorations. Roads lead out of town and down to the Calypso Cave, where a path continues down to Ramla Bay and its sandy beach.

Start at the main bus stop in **Marsalforn**, which is close to where a riverbed (usually dry) slices through town. Don't cross the bridge spanning the riverbed, but walk straight inland instead. A narrow strip of land has been made into a small park, then a road bridge is reached. Again, don't cross the bridge, but follow a track which becomes a path as it continues along the well-wooded riverbank.

Pass a dam, then later turn left where a track crosses a ford to reach a road on the other side of the riverbed. Turn right to continue upstream, quickly reaching a turning

A riverside track, flanked by trees, leaves Marsalforn

area at a sort of ncrete track onwards, as indicated by a red-and-white marker. Note that the concrete fills an old riverbed, and not only can it carry water after rain, but some stretches become very slippery. There are fields on either side, growing all manner of produce.

If this junction is missed, the track running ahead climbs steeply and ends abruptly, in which case come back downhill and turn left at the junction.

Keep left on the concrete track where another track heads off to the right. Walk straight through a complex junction of concrete tracks at **Ta' l-Għezien**, where there's an information board. The track remains low in the valley and bends right and left, over and over, as it continues past fields, tracing the old riverbed.

Watch for a junction with another narrow concrete track, and turn right to follow it uphill. ◂ The track climbs steeply, turns right and levels out, then turns left and climbs steeply, reaching a level tarmac road among houses around 105m (350ft) at **Ta' Bullara**. Turn left to follow the road, Triq il-Bullara, gently uphill.

Watch for 'Ninu's Cave' on the right, which is worth a visit for a small donation. A householder, digging a well for water, broke into a remarkable grotto-like cave.

Later turn left again to follow Triq Jannar towards the centre of **Xagħra**. ◂ At the end of the road, turn right alongside the church, turning left and left again through the Pjazza il-Vittorja to pass around the building. There are bars, as well as a bank with an ATM.

The **Ġgantija Temples** (tel 2155 3194, **heritage-malta.org**) lie off-route on the southern side of Xagħra, and are well worth visiting. (See the photo in 'Discovery and History' in the Introduction.)

map continues on page 196

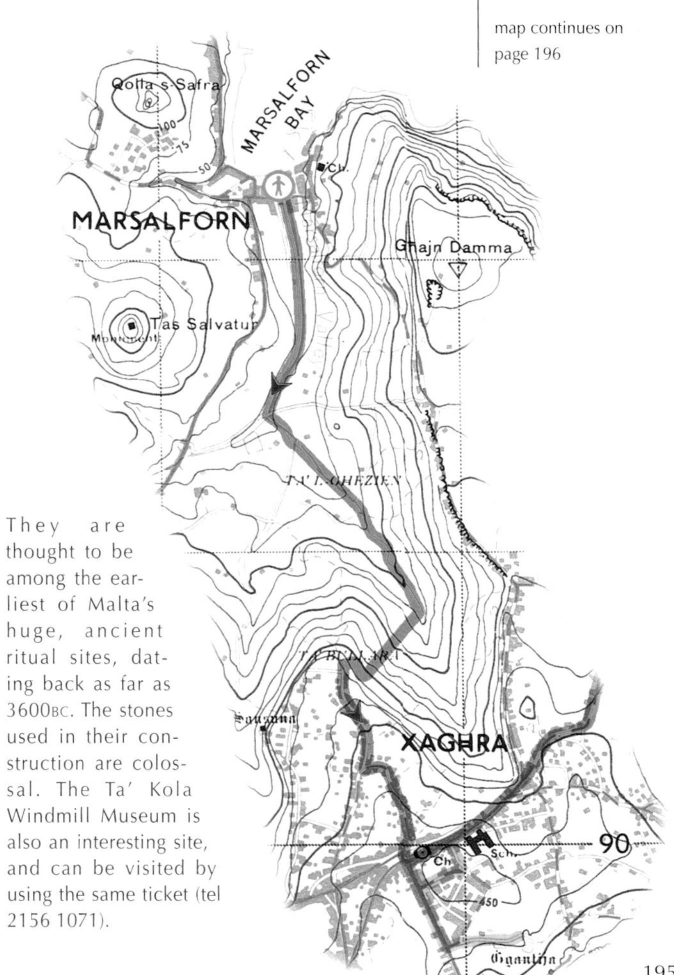

They are thought to be among the earliest of Malta's huge, ancient ritual sites, dating back as far as 3600BC. The stones used in their construction are colossal. The Ta' Kola Windmill Museum is also an interesting site, and can be visited by using the same ticket (tel 2156 1071).

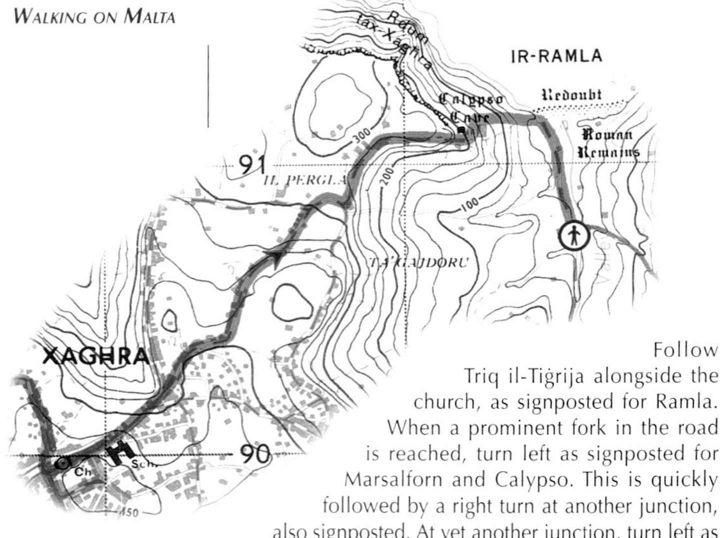

Follow Triq il-Tiġrija alongside the church, as signposted for Ramla. When a prominent fork in the road is reached, turn left as signposted for Marsalforn and Calypso. This is quickly followed by a right turn at another junction, also signposted. At yet another junction, turn left as signposted for Calypso and Ramla. As the road descends from Xagħra, simply watch for 'Calypso' signposts at all other junctions. Eventually, a car park is reached where there are toilets, a gift shop and possibly a snack van.

The famous **Calypso Cave** is reached by going up a few steps, through a doorway, and along wooden decking to a splendid viewpoint. The 'cave' is little more than a few large, jammed boulders beneath the viewpoint. Legend maintains that Odysseus was held here for seven years by the wiles of the nymph Calypso, but there are many other caves around the Mediterranean that make similar claims.

The entire slope is slowly slipping, breaking both the road and the buildings.

Continue down the concrete road, which serves abandoned buildings. ◂ Fork left between large stone blocks to follow a rising path. This avoids the buildings and reaches an open slope. The path winds downhill and can be rather muddy after wet weather. Pass through bushes at the bottom to reach **Ramla Bay**, where there are a couple of restaurants, toilets and a car park.

Ramla Bay has the largest sandy beach and sand dunes in the Maltese islands

The **sandy bay** is the best in the Maltese islands, where vegetated sand dunes form the largest habitat of its type in the islands. Just a short way inland, beside a stream, is a small huddle of uncommon 'chaste trees'. However, the bay was also a weak point that allowed the French to invade and occupy Gozo in 1798. A Ranger Station is operated by the Gaia Foundation, offering information about the natural history of the bay.

It's possible to link directly with Walk 30 here, but if finishing this particular walk, then bear in mind that buses don't actually serve the road-end. To catch a bus, follow the road inland to the first junction and turn left. Bus stops stand on either side of the road.

WALK 30

Ramla Bay to Qala

Start	Bus stop, Ramla Bay (356 908)
Finish	Church, Qala (379 885)
Distance	10km (6¼ miles) with a 2km (1¼-mile) extension
Time	3hr 15min
Terrain	Mostly country roads, with short, steep and rugged paths
Maps	1:25,000 Gozo sheet
Refreshments	A couple of restaurants at Ramla Bay. Possibility of a snack cabin at San Blas Bay. A couple of bars and restaurants at Qala.
Transport	Buses 302 and 322 serve Ramla Bay. Bus 303 serves Qala.

The coastline around the north-eastern part of Gozo is very rugged and is easily visited only in a few places. This walk climbs steeply inland to avoid rugged headlands, and descends steeply to visit certain bays and coves. This happens over and over again, but if a shorter walk is required, it's possible to catch a bus early near Nadur. There are interesting features along the way, and a detour can be made to a new 'family park' and the Sopu Tower on the Qortin headland. Some fine paths and tracks are followed through spectacular scenery, but there are also a number of quiet country roads. A large quarry finally forces a detour uphill into Qala, where bus services can be found.

Bus services don't go all the way to **Ramla Bay**, so a short road-walk is necessary to reach the sandy beach. Turn right along the beach until the sand meets rock, then come ashore and pick a way along a rugged path. Aim for the end of the rugged headland, but on approaching it, watch carefully to spot a path that climbs straight inland, uphill. Follow it, and don't worry that there seems to be a small cliff at the top of the slope, as the path finds a way up it and onto the top, at over 75m (250ft).

map continues on page 202

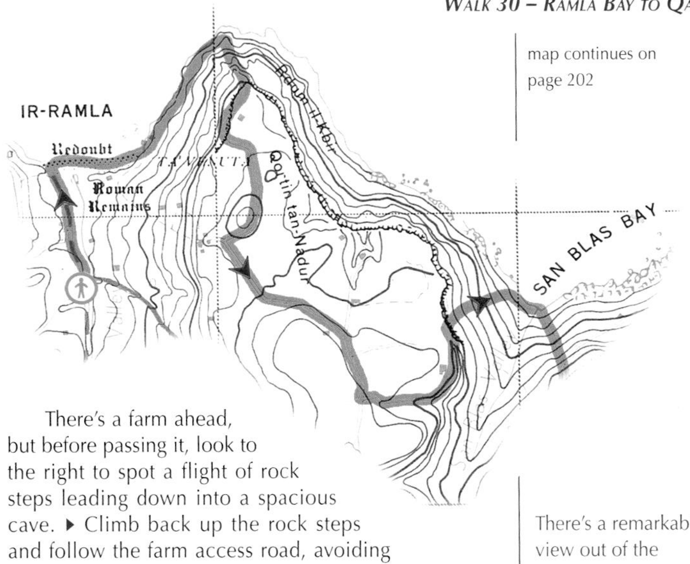

There's a farm ahead, but before passing it, look to the right to spot a flight of rock steps leading down into a spacious cave. ▸ Climb back up the rock steps and follow the farm access road, avoiding two turnings on the left as it heads inland through **Qortin tan-Nadur**. Turn left at another junction, and keep right at a junction where there's a monument to the 50th anniversary of Malta's independence.

There's a remarkable view out of the cave, back across Ramla Bay.

When a crossroads and picnic site is reached, alongside an unsightly rubbish skip, turn left and follow a road downhill. This passes the Gun Blast shooting range, which is very noisy when it's in use. The road bends left along the upper part of the **San Blas Valley**, rising a little and then descending further.

Just before the road bottoms out, turn right down a concrete path. When this ends, walk straight down a vague, overgrown path, passing cane windbreaks that protect fruit and vegetable plots. It can be muddy after rain at the foot of the slope. Turn right along a beach of golden sand in **San Blas Bay**, reaching a huddle of huts, one of which might be offering basic refreshments.

Vehicles can't come down to the bay, although there's a narrow concrete access road. The only visitors are those who are prepared to climb this road when they

Ramla Bay has the largest sandy beach and dunes in the islands

leave, and it's very steep and tiring. The concrete gives way to tarmac at a small parking space, and the climb continues. Citrus groves shelter behind cane windbreaks, and the road eventually reaches buildings and a shaded garden at Weraq, which is the northernmost part of **Nadur**. ▶

The 304 bus turns around at this point and can be used to cut this walk short.

Extension to Sopu Tower

To take this 30min detour, turn left to follow the road signposted for Sopu Tower. Pass lots of tangled scrub on the way to a military site called Qortin Camp. Turn right down a broad concrete road between a greenhouse and the camp. When the road ends, keep right along a track, which rises and is later worn to bedrock. When the **Sopu Tower** is seen ahead, walk down a rocky path to reach it and enjoy rugged coastal views. ▶ Afterwards retrace steps to Weraq.

The tower dates from 1667 and was restored by the National Trust of Malta. The area has been redeveloped as a 'family park' with thousands of trees and shrubs being planted.

From the bus stop at Weraq, follow the road as if walking straight to **Nadur**, but turn left at the first junction, up a short road called Triq Għajn Berta. Face an old building called Tal Bukkaċċ and turn left again. The road quickly

The Sopu Tower is the centrepiece of a 'family park' near Weraq

leads away from the built-up edge of town, dropping into a valley. Watch out for a concrete track branching off to the right at an information notice; this track quickly becomes grassy and leads into another little valley.

Turn left after a notice about the Mistra Rocks, to find a narrow path routed along the margin between enclosed plots and the higher slopes of rock and tangled *maquis*. Follow the path faithfully down beneath a cliff face and through a jumble of enormous boulders. When a track is joined, follow it uphill and it becomes concrete, reaching a road in the **Daħlet Qorrot Valley**. Turn left and walk down the road, enjoying fine views back towards the jumbled boulders of the Mistra Rocks. The road stands on

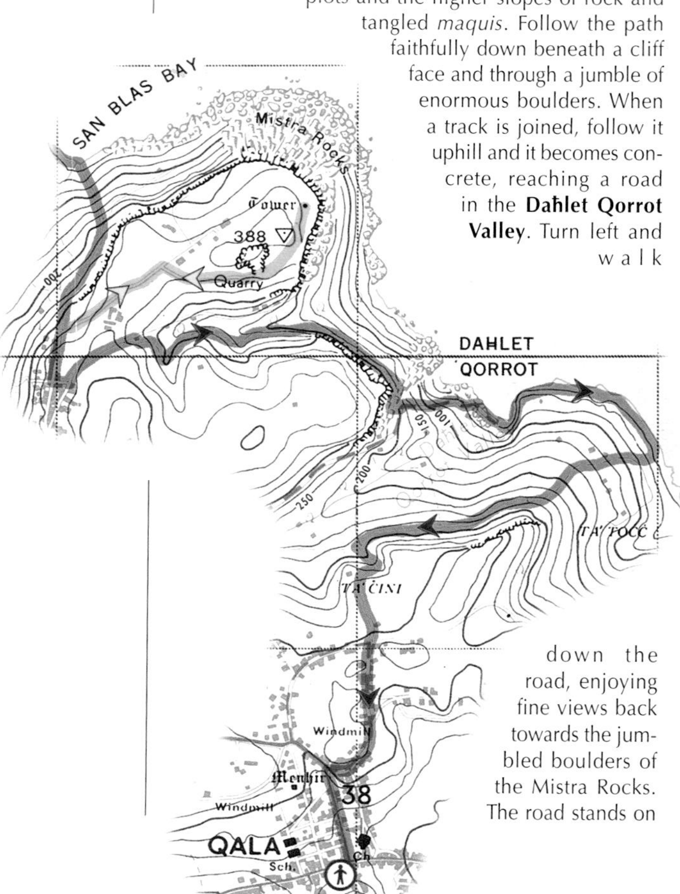

Bouldery slopes at Daħlet Qorrot, looking back to the Sopu Tower

stout stone supports as it drops to a little bay at **Daħlet Qorrot**. ▸

Rows of huts have been built into the softstone layer all around the bay, and there are toilets.

A flight of 36 steps lead up onto the softstone terrace at the end of the bay. Follow this onwards, then climb a little higher and stay on the seaward side of any rubble walls. Watch for a narrow track on the right, climbing between rubble walls, heading inland at **Ta' Toċċ**. ▸ The track is concrete later and leads past a mixture of cultivated and abandoned plots. Limestone crags rise high above, then the rough road levels out at **Ta' Ċini** and there are good views back across the Daħlet Qorrot Valley.

Trying to follow the coast onwards leads to a large quarry which is best avoided altogether.

When a junction is reached with a wider concrete road, turn left further uphill. The road winds up to a crossroads, and keeping straight ahead leads into **Qala**. ▸ The road is Triq il-Mitħna, and it includes a brief glimpse of an old windmill, which is now part of a boutique hotel. The road bends right and later reaches a complex junction. Turn left down Triq **San Ġużepp**, which leads down to the centre of the village at the Pjazza San Ġużepp, where a fine church can be admired and a couple of bars and restaurants are available.

Turning left leads straight into Walk 31.

WALK 31

Qala to Mġarr

Start	Church, Qala (379 885)
Finish	Harbour, Mġarr (367 870)
Distance	9km (5½ miles)
Time	3hr
Terrain	Roads and tracks at first, linked by a rather narrow and fiddly path. A narrow cliff path is used towards the end.
Maps	1:25,000 Gozo sheet
Refreshments	A couple of bars and restaurants at Qala. Snack bar at Ħondoq ir-Rummien. Bars and restaurants at Mġarr harbour.
Transport	Bus 303 serves Qala. Buses 301, 303 and 322 serve Mġarr harbour. Gozo Channel Line ferries link with Ċirkewwa on Malta.

The last stretch of the coastal walk around Gozo involves turning round the easternmost end of the island. Leaving Qala, the first part is along roads, and one of these roads can be very dusty when quarry trucks are rumbling along it. However, this is followed by a pleasant walk along tracks and paths with fine views across the Comino Channel to Comino and Malta. A detour inland, almost back to Qala, is rather fiddly to locate. True coastal walking and a splendid cliff path feature later in the day. The walk from Ħondoq ir-Rummien to Mġarr is exceptionally scenic and dramatic in places. If contemplating a visit to Comino, then the island can be studied closely from this walk, before checking the availability of ferries from Mġarr.

Start in **Qala** at the Pjazza San Ġużepp. Face the church and follow the road to the left, on the same side as the bus stop. Walk straight uphill along Triq San Ġużepp. Towards the top, turn right along Triq il-Mitħna. The road swings left and includes a brief glimpse of an old windmill, which is now part of a boutique hotel. Keep left as the road leaves the village, to avoid being drawn along Triq il-Wileg, which can be busy with quarry trucks.

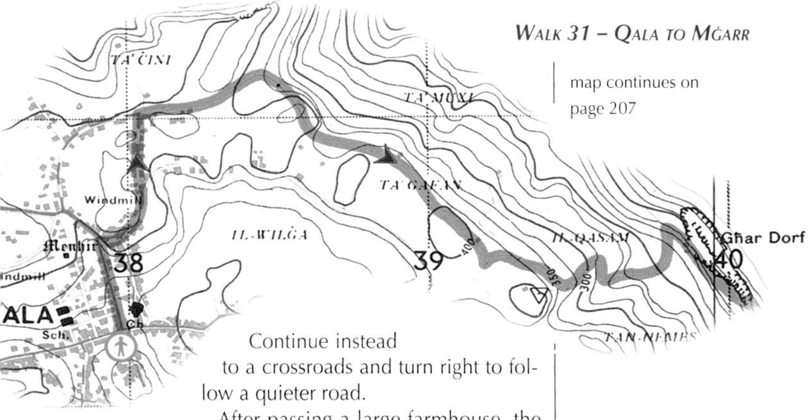

map continues on page 207

Continue instead to a crossroads and turn right to follow a quieter road.

After passing a large farmhouse, the road surface becomes rather patchy. There are three dips and three crests along this empty road, with views down the cultivated slopes of **Ta' Gafan** to the sea. When a junction is reached, turn left downhill, bearing in mind that this road can be very dusty when quarry trucks are using it. Follow the road as it winds downhill towards the quarry at **Għar Dorf**. Note a more direct line that short-cuts one bend, although the course of the old road is now rather overgrown.

Turn right along a track before reaching the quarry, passing above the actual quarry face. When the track ends, pick a way along the rocky coast towards an old **redoubt** overlooking the South Comino Channel. ▶ Pass seawards of it, then watch carefully for the way ahead. Don't follow the path running closest to the coast, and don't follow the access track inland from the redoubt. Instead, spot a path between these two lines and continue walking until a narrow, rocky inlet is reached, with the rocky stack of **Ġebel tal-Ħalfa** beyond.

The St Anthony Battery, built in 1734, is a National Trust for Malta property (**dinlarthelwa.org**).

Turn right inland, and watch carefully to spot a narrow, stony and sometimes overgrown path, which winds uphill. It twists and turns, but later makes a distinct turn to the left to join and follow a stout, straight, stone wall. The path beside the wall is rocky, then when the far corner of the wall is reached, turn right to join a track and follow it straight ahead. When a junction of tracks is reached, turn left to follow a track that becomes a road, leading to a junction near a chapel and **cemetery** on the outskirts of a built-up area. ◂

Following the road inland leads to a drinks machine, and if followed further, it leads back to Qala.

Turn left to follow the road, Triq Ħondoq ir-Rummien, away from the chapel and buildings. It leads down to another chapel, which has a fine viewpoint terrace overlooking the coast, Comino and Malta. A bendy stretch of the road leads down to a tiny beach, snack bar, toilets and a former desalination plant at **Ħondoq ir-Rummien**. This is a fine little place to take a

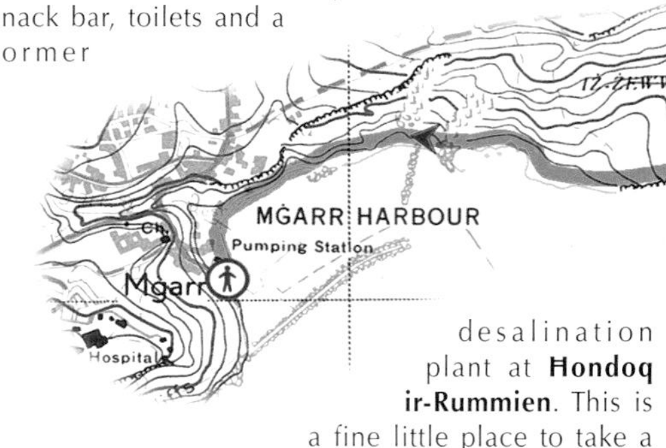

Looking along the splendid cliff line towards the Taċ-Ċawl Rocks

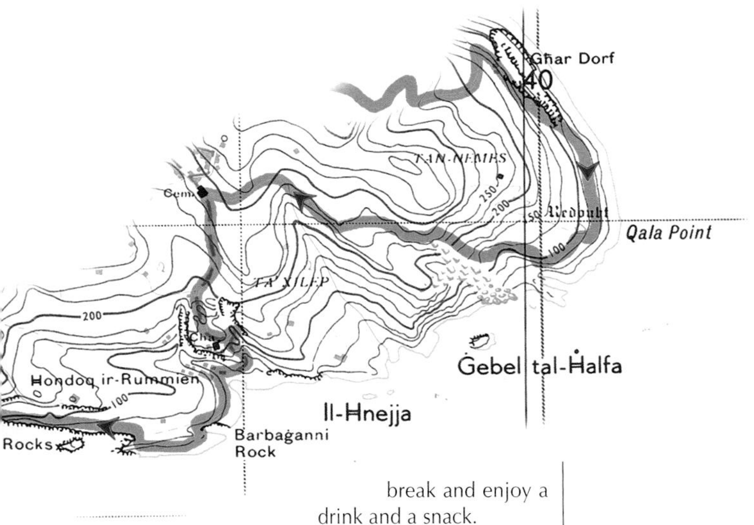

break and enjoy a drink and a snack.

Walk off the road-end and continue along the low, rocky coast along a broad, rugged path. Pass above a fine little rocky inlet at **Barbaġanni Rock**. Later, pass close to the rugged stacks of the **Taċ-Ċawl Rocks**, which are close to the cliff edge where the rock is quite bare. Follow a narrow cliff path, which is often no more than a narrow ledge cut into the cliff. It needs a little care and a sure foot. Roughly contour across the rugged slope then step down through a gap in a defensive wall. This was built of softstone, so it has weathered very badly and is crumbling away.

Stay close to the sea and follow a path through a chaotic heap of boulders to reach a road-end. The road leads past toilets and a couple of memorials as it makes its way around the harbour at **Mġarr**. It becomes increasingly busy, with a number of bars and restaurants offering food and drink. Buses and taxis meet the ferries, and people wander around admiring the colourful fishing boats. There are bus stops and toilets on the far side of the harbour, where the Gozo Channel Line ferries berth.

WALK 32

Għarb to Marsalforn

Start	Għarb (288 911)
Finish	Marsalforn (334 922)
Distance	12km (7½ miles)
Time	4hr
Terrain	Mostly along quiet country roads and farm tracks, with one muddy path.
Maps	1:25,000 Gozo sheet
Refreshments	Bars and restaurants are available in Għarb. Bar at Żebbuġ. Plenty of shops, bars and restaurants at Marsalforn.
Transport	Bus 312 serves Għarb. Bus 308 serves Ta' Pinu. Bus 309 serves Żebbuġ. Buses 310 and 322 serve Marsalforn.

Looking out from the walls of the Citadel in Victoria, hills are seen rising north and west of the town. Although the hills are really quite small, and the whole of Gozo is at a lesser elevation than neighbouring Malta, they are quite shapely and stand out well from the cultivated landscape. The flat summits are formed of hard Upper Coralline Limestone capping crumbling slopes of Blue Clay. The lower ground between the hills is based on the soft Globigerina Limestone. From the walker's point of view, the landscape of north-west Gozo offers the chance to indulge in a little gentle hillwalking, from Għarb to Żebbuġ and Marsalforn.

The Għarb Folklore Museum is to the right in an 18th-century house containing 28 rooms and a bewildering collection of bygone objects.

Start in the middle of **Għarb**, facing the church, and note the Human Sundial embedded in the ground. ◂ Keep to the right of the church to walk through the little Pjazza Taż-Żjara tal-Madonna, then continue along Triq Frenċ ta' L-Għarb – named after Frenċ Mercieca (1892–1967), a local healer commemorated by a shrine in a small garage where he used to practice.

Pass the Salvina Restaurant and Bar to reach Pjazza Gerano. Turn right down Triq ta' Sdieri, signposted for Ta' Pinu, to leave the village and cross a valley. The road partly represents the original profile of the valley, but it now has cliffs on either side where the soft Globigerina Limestone has been quarried. Follow the road uphill and turn right for **Ta' Pinu** and its fine pilgrimage church.

> The **neo-Romanesque church** at Ta' Pinu was completed in 1931, and the interior is light and elegantly carved. It stands on the site of a small chapel where an old woman heard the Virgin speaking in 1883, and the site has been a centre of pilgrimage ever since. Pope John Paul II visited in 1990, and the car park is often filled with coaches.

Across the road from the church are toilets and a drinks machine. Just alongside is a track, lined with statues representing scenes from the Way of the Cross, leading onto a hill. ▶ After wriggling uphill, the track spirals round the summit and leads into a circular amphitheatre centred on an altar. The highest point on the hill is 183m (600ft) – only a little lower than the highest point on Gozo, which is the nearby hill of Ta' Dbieġi at 190m (625ft).

During Lent the hill may be busy with people deep in prayer.

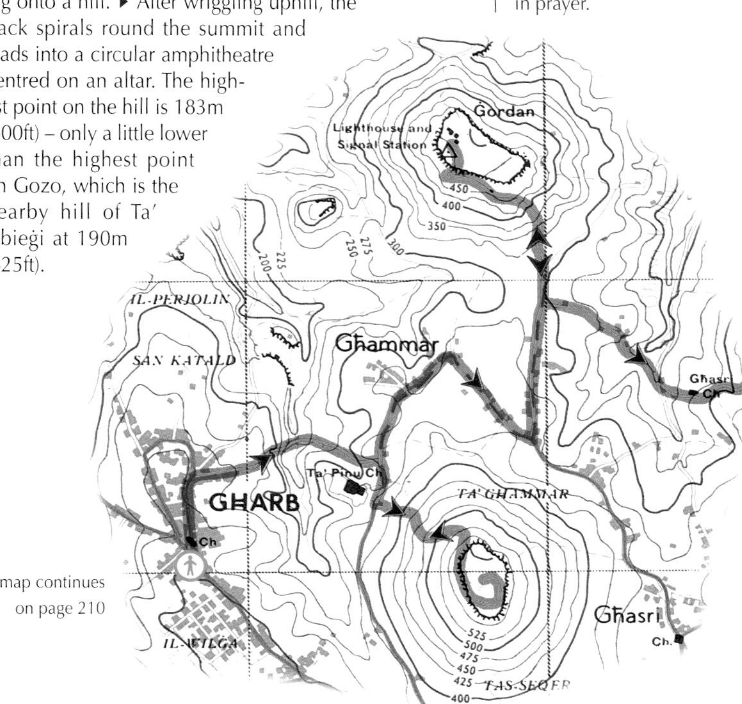

map continues on page 210

A shaft of sunlight illuminates the church at Ta' Pinu

map continues on page 212

Follow the track back down to **Ta' Pinu** and turn right along the road. Pass a junction and head straight along Triq Għammar. Turn right in the village of **Għammar** as signposted for Fanal ta' Ġordan. A left turn is later signposted the same way, and the road, Triq il-Fanal, passes the Villaġġ Tal Fanal accommodation complex. Leave the village and keep left at the next couple of junctions to be led up a concrete road onto the summit of **Ġordan**. Surprisingly, there's a 19th-century lighthouse on top of the hill, around 150m (500ft), and fine views are available around the island.

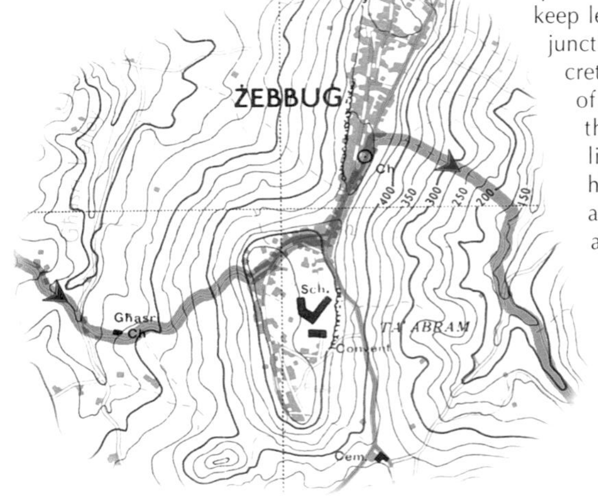

Walk back down the concrete track, towards the village, but turn left down Triq it-Tamar. Pass the **Għasri Chapel**, then climb to

Stations of the Cross above Ta' Pinu with a view across to Ġordan

the left up a patchy road called Triq tal-Kanun. The hillside is defended with stone terracing and prickly pears, while the battered road climbs steeply and steadily all the way. Turn left at a junction at some houses at the top of the road, to follow Triq tal-Kanun. Turn left again at a junction marked by a telephone kiosk. Walk down Triq il-Kappillan Dun Franġisk Vella, then turn left at the bottom, passing a small museum to walk to the church in the hilltop village of **Żebbuġ**.

Pass to the right of the church to follow a road, but watch on the right for the short Triq ta' Milied. This quickly gives way to a steep concrete track, which narrows to a path. When the concrete ends, continue down a narrow path between low tumbled walls and fields. Join a concrete road and follow it further downhill, turning right at a junction at the bottom. There might be running water in the **Wied tal-Qleigħa** as it's followed gently up to a junction with a broader concrete road.

Turn right along the broad concrete road, then almost immediately turn left up a narrow concrete road. The surface is broken and strewn with grit and gravel, but simply walk up to a junction with another track. Turn left and follow this

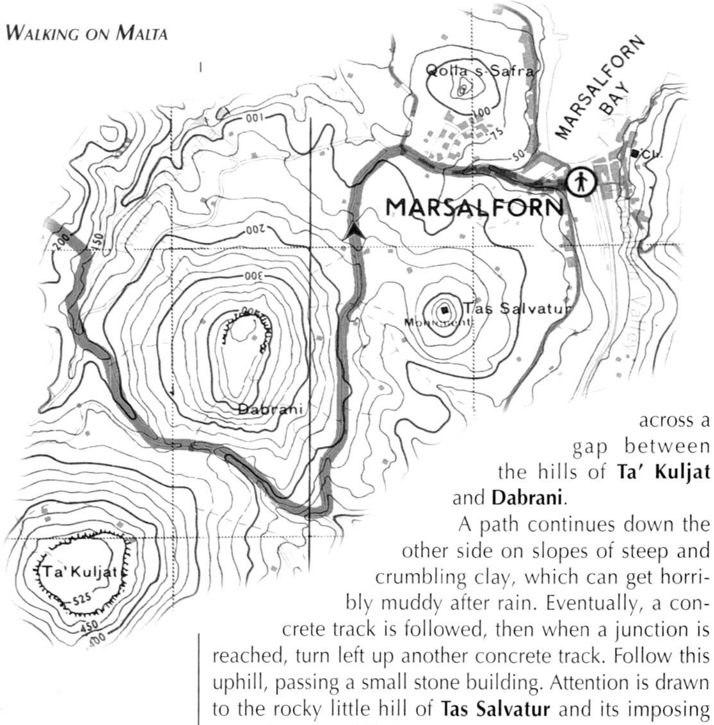

across a gap between the hills of **Ta' Kuljat** and **Dabrani**.

A path continues down the other side on slopes of steep and crumbling clay, which can get horribly muddy after rain. Eventually, a concrete track is followed, then when a junction is reached, turn left up another concrete track. Follow this uphill, passing a small stone building. Attention is drawn to the rocky little hill of **Tas Salvatur** and its imposing summit statue of Christ.

Follow the track onwards, then continue down a road from the large Villa Florita. Turn right at a junction of tarmac roads to enter **Marsalforn** and simply follow the road straight down a canyon-like street of apartment blocks. The road leads to the main bus stop, which is near a riverbed that slices through the town. If there's time to spare, there are plenty of bars and restaurants to visit, and the little harbour is worth exploring.

COMINO

Rugged headlands and islets flank the Blue Lagoon, with Gozo seen beyond

COMINO

A bouldery coastline near Mġarr, looking across to the island of Comino

Comino is sandwiched between Malta and Gozo and is served by ferries from either island. Some ferries run every hour, and there are also day cruises that allow visitors ashore for a few hours. To make the most of Comino, try to arrive on an early ferry and start walking before the crowds descend. The usual landing point is the Blue Lagoon, which is a remarkable place when you have it all to yourself, but it becomes quite hectic with visitors later in the day. Most walkers stay on the dirt roads, so it's possible to have some cliff-walks to yourself. The expensive Comino Hotel offers accommodation, but there's also a basic campsite available. Staying overnight allows visitors to enjoy the solitude of early morning and early evening.

WALK 33

Circuit of Comino

Start/Finish	The Blue Lagoon, Comino (391 859)
Distance	8km (5 miles)
Time	3hr
Terrain	Some good tracks and paths are used, but some of the cliff-walking is quite rugged and needs care.
Maps	1:25,000 Gozo sheet
Refreshments	In addition to the Comino Hotel bar and restaurant, a couple of snacks vans usually set up at the Blue Lagoon.
Transport	Ferries run to Comino from Ċirkewwa and Ramla Bay on Malta, and from Mġarr on Gozo. There are several operators, and schedules vary widely. Sailings may be infrequent in winter and cancelled altogether when the sea is rough.

The walk around Comino attempts to hug the cliff coastline, although there's no access near the Comino Hotel. Coastal walking isn't practical in a few other places too. Walkers who find the cliffs too rugged to follow may switch to dirt roads around the island as an alternative. The south coast includes visits to the Santa Marija Battery and the impressive Comino Tower. Although there are splendid views of the Blue Lagoon at the start and finish, check whether the ferry to and from Comino also includes a short tour around the lagoon, cliffs and caves, which are well worth seeing at close quarters.

Unless you're staying at the Comino Hotel, or using the campsite, start walking from the ferry landing at the **Blue Lagoon**. The earlier you can get there, the more likely you'll be to have the place to yourself. The tiny island of Cominotto lies across the shallow lagoon, as well as a couple of other attractive islets and rocks.

Follow the dirt road away from the ferry landing and pass a building, but quickly switch to a narrow path that's been trodden around the low cliff coast. There's a sparse covering of scrub, a rugged headland and a couple of

Rugged headlands and bays on the way back to the Blue Lagoon

rocky inlets at **Għar Għana**. A bay is reached where a water pipeline comes ashore; head inland as the fence surrounding the Comino Hotel bars further coastal access.

Turn left along the dirt road to reach a junction. The Comino Hotel is down to the left, if its bar or restaurant is required. If a visit isn't being made, then avoid the turning and continue along the dirt road to reach another junction. Turn left and walk down a dusty road flanked by Aleppo pines to reach the **Annunciation Chapel**. A police station and the bungalows of Comino Minor are further down the road, but turn right before reaching them. Bushy tamarisk grows by the beach at the head of **Santa Marija Bay**, and there are a few uncommon 'chaste trees' too. ◂

The very basic island campsite is located here.

Follow a rather vague stony path around the bay to reach a shattered headland at **Għemieri**. Walk with care, as the rock is uneven underfoot and there are hidden caves and overhangs. Scout around the cliffs, looking for interesting little caves and rock arches. Turn around and aim to pick a way along the north-eastern cliff line of Comino, gradually climbing higher and keeping a look-out for more caves. ◂

Diving operators find this part of the island irresistible, but if you want to peep over the cliff edges to see them, bear in mind that there are plenty of unseen overhangs.

INLAND SHORT-CUT

If the rugged cliff-walk proves too difficult, then return to the head of the bay and follow an obvious track short-cutting straight inland. It climbs gradually, reaching a large, derelict former **pig farm**. Keep to the right-hand side of all the buildings.

The cliff-walk continues to gain height. It's best to drift inland from the cliffs, although without the benefit of a trodden path. Walk on the bare limestone and stony patches, rather than on the delicate scrub, and there is later a length of rubble wall just off the rugged crest of the hill. The highest point on Comino is here, at only 75m (247ft), but it might as well be

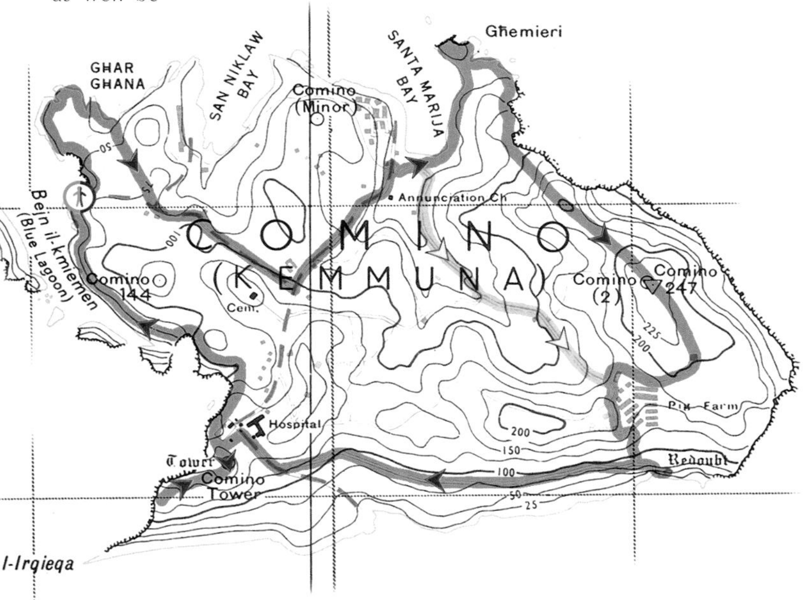

the top of the world as views stretch away to both Malta and Gozo.

Later, a vague vehicle track runs beside the rubble wall, reaching an enclosed compound. This is served by a clearer track, which can be followed down and around the large, derelict, former **pig farm**. Turn left at a junction of tracks, where the alternative short-cut across the island is joined.

Turn right at a junction of tracks, then almost immediately turn left to pick up and follow a winding path down towards the coast. A prominent **redoubt** lies to the left and is well worth visiting.

This is the **Santa Marija Battery**, a National Trust for Malta property. It was built in 1715 but abandoned by 1750. It's been restored and features a fine set of cannons pointing out to the South Comino Channel. It's also worth walking a little further beyond to see the sheer cliffs at the eastern end of the island.

Boat trips regularly explore the cliffs and caves below the Comino Tower

Follow a clear track away from the battery, crossing stony, rocky scrub with a few Aleppo pines in view

at a higher level. There's another track down to the left later, but keep climbing straight towards a prominent tower. Turn left towards it once an empty building is reached – formerly an isolation hospital. Climb a flight of stone steps and cross a drawbridge to enjoy views from **Comino Tower**. ▸

This is also known as the Torri ta' Santa Marija, and it was built in 1618. It has been restored and is a National Trust for Malta property (**dinlarthelwa.org**).

It's worth walking out towards the nearby rocky headland of **Ras l-Irqieqa**, just to get a good view of more caves and rocky stacks arranged between the headland and the Blue Lagoon. Retrace steps afterwards, then to complete the circuit of the island, aim to stay close to the cliffs all the way back to the Blue Lagoon, bearing in mind that the cliffs may be undercut or fissured and there's a huge hole along the way, where the sea sloshes around in the bottom.

One rugged headland is almost a separate island, clinging to Comino by a narrow neck of land. Note how it has a hole punched through from one side to the other. The next little island has one, two or three holes punched through it – the number increasing each time you look! The last little island in line is Cominotto, sheltering the far side of the **Blue Lagoon**, and it too has a hole punched through it.

If your walk started early in the morning, it might be finished in time for lunch, and there might be snack vans operating. It's likely that the Blue Lagoon will become much busier as the day progresses, and some of the ferry services might also be making additional runs to nearby caves. Small cruise boats might also arrive, so that the landing stage becomes jammed with vessels. Be sure to remember which boat brought you to Comino, and what time you're supposed to leave!

A view across Marsascala Bay showing a rocky shore and saltpans (Walk 2)

APPENDIX A

Route summary table

No	Title	Start	Finish	Distance	Time	Page
1	Valletta Heritage Trail	City Gate, Valletta	City Gate, Valletta	5km (3 miles)	2hr	38
2	Rinella to Marsaskala	Fort Rinella	Marsaskala	7km (4½ miles)	2hr	44
3	Marsaskala to Birżebbuġa	Marsaskala	Pretty Bay, Birżebbuġa	18.5km (11½ miles)	5hr 30min	48
4	Birżebbuġa to Gudja	Birżebbuġa	Gudja	5km (3 miles)	1hr 30min	55
5	Żurrieq to Siġġiewi	Żurrieq church	Siġġiewi church	14km (8¾ miles)	4hr	58
6	Siġġiewi to Dingli	Siġġiewi church	Dingli	10km (6 miles)	3hr	64
7	Dingli to Mġarr	Dingli	Mġarr church	19km (11¾ miles)	6–7hr	68
8	Għajn Tuffieħa circuit	Golden Bay	Golden Bay	4km (2½ miles)	1hr 30min	76
9	Mġarr to Għadira	Mġarr church	Għadira Nature Reserve	16km (10 miles)	5hr	79
10	Marfa Ridge circuit	Mellieħa Bay	Mellieħa Bay	16km (10 miles)	5hr	86
11	Mellieħa Bay to Xemxija	Mellieħa Bay	Porto del Sol, Xemxija	8km (5 miles)	2hr 30min	93
12	Selmun circuit	Roundabout south of Mellieħa	Road junction in the Mistra Valley	5km (3 miles)	1hr 30min	97
13	Xemxija Heritage Trail	Porto del Sol, Xemxija	Porto del Sol, Xemxija	2.5km (1½ miles)	1hr 30min	101
14	Bajda Ridge circuit	Porto del Sol, Xemxija	Porto del Sol, Xemxija	10km (6¼ miles)	3hr	105

No	Title	Start	Finish	Distance	Time	Page
15	The Wardija Ridge	Porto del Sol, Xemxija	Wied l-Arkata, near Burmarrad	12.5km (7¾ miles)	3hr 30min	109
16	Falka Gap to Salina	Falka Pumping Station	Coastline Hotel, Salina	11km (7 miles)	3hr 15min	114
17	Baħar iċ-Ċagħaq to St George's Bay	Baħar iċ-Ċagħaq	St George's Bay	6.5km (4 miles)	2hr	120
18	The Victoria Lines	Mġarr church	Baħar iċ-Ċagħaq	22km (13¾ miles)	8hr	124
19	Fiddien to Mosta	Fiddien Bridge	Mosta Dome	6.5km (4 miles)	2hr	134
20	Rabat and Dingli	Busugrilla, Rabat	Bus stops, Rabat	10km (6¼ miles)	3hr	139
21	Siġġiewi and Buskett	Siġġiewi church	Siġġiewi church	17km (10½ miles)	5hr	144
22	Siġġiewi to Qormi	Siġġiewi church	Pinto's Lodge, Qormi	9.5km (6 miles)	3hr	151
23	The Wignacourt Aqueduct	San Anton Gardens	Casa Leoni, Santa Venera	3.5km (2 miles)	1hr	156
24	Mdina and Rabat Heritage Trail	Bus stops, Rabat	Bus stops, Rabat	3km (2 miles)	2hr	160
25	Victoria Heritage Trail	Bus Station, Victoria	Bus Station, Victoria	3km (2 miles)	2hr	169
26	Mġarr to Sannat	Harbour, Mġarr	Santa Margerita, Sannat	9km (5½ miles)	2hr	174
27	Sannat to San Lawrenz	Santa Margerita, Sannat	San Lawrenz	13–16.5km (8–10¼ miles)	4–5hr	179

No	Title	Start	Finish	Distance	Time	Page
28	San Lawrenz to Marsalforn	San Lawrenz	Marsalforn	11.5–12.5km (7–7¾ miles)	3hr 30min–4hr	187
29	Marsalforn to Ramla Bay	Marsalforn	Bus stop, Ramla Bay	6km (3¾ miles)	2hr	193
30	Ramla Bay to Qala	Bus stop, Ramla Bay	Church, Qala	10km (6¼ miles)	3hr 15min	198
31	Qala to Mġarr	Church, Qala	Harbour, Mġarr	9km (5½ miles)	3hr	204
32	Għarb to Marsalforn	Għarb	Marsalforn	12km (7½ miles)	4hr	208
33	Circuit of Comino	The Blue Lagoon, Comino	The Blue Lagoon, Comino	8km (5 miles)	3hr	215

A path descends a flowery slope from Żebbuġ to Wied tal-Qleigħa (Walk 32)

APPENDIX B

Useful contacts

There are no area codes for telephone numbers around the Maltese islands. When calling any of the following numbers from outside the islands, prefix each number with 00356.

Island administration

Government of Malta
www.gov.mt

Malta Environment and Planning Authority (MEPA)
St Francis Ravelin
Floriana
tel 2290 1007
www.mepa.org.mt

Visit Malta
freephone 8007 2230
www.visitmalta.com

Tourist information offices

Malta

Malta International Airport
Arrivals
tel 2369 6073

229 Merchants Street
Valletta
tel 2291 5440

Pinto Wharf
Valletta Waterfront
tel 2122 0633

Inquisitor's Palace
Birgu
tel 2180 0145

Torre Dello Standardo
Mdina
tel 2145 4480

Misrah Iż-Żjara tal-Papa Gwanni Pawlu II
Mellieħa
tel 2152 4666

Local Council Sub Office
St Paul's Bay
tel 2141 9176

Gozo

17 Independence Square
Victoria
tel 2291 5452

Heritage and environmental associations

Gaia Foundation
Naħħalija Road
Għajn Tuffieħa
Malta
tel 2158 4474
www.projectgaia.org

Il-Majjistral Nature and History Park
Visitor Centre
tel 2152 1291
www.mt.majjistral.org

BirdLife Malta
57/28 Triq Abate Rigord
Ta' Xbiex
Malta
tel 2134 7646
www.birdlifemalta.org

Nature Trust
Malta
PO Box 9
Valletta
Malta
tel 2131 3150
www.naturetrustmalta.org

Heritage Malta
Ex Royal Naval Hospital
Triq Marina, Kalkara
Malta
tel 2295 4000
heritagemalta.org

National Trust for Malta (Din l-Art Ħelwa)
113 Melita Street
Valletta
Malta
tel 2122 5952
dinlarthelwa.org

Walking resources

Ramblers Association of Malta
First Floor
University Sports Complex
Msida
Malta
www.ramblersmalta.org

Great Walks in Malta and Gozo
Jonathan Henwood
greatwalksmalta.com

Transport

Public Transport Malta
tel 2122 2000
www.publictransport.com.mt

Gozo Channel Line
tel 2210 9000
www.gozochannel.com

Tall, sheer cliffs are seen most of the way from Sannat to Bajjada (Walk 27)

APPENDIX C

Brief history of Malta

Seven thousand years of human history in the Maltese islands are not easily condensed into a list of key events. This brief history lists only a few such events to illustrate the initial settlement of the islands, followed by centuries of colonization and invasion by a succession of powers. Maltese history is exceedingly complex and is inextricably linked with the history of the many colonizing powers. Anyone with a particular interest in Maltese history could make it a lifetime's study, and any good bookshop on the islands will be able to offer plenty of background reading. There are several museums and visitor centres that illustrate Malta's history.

Prehistoric Malta

5200–4100BC – The Neolithic settlement of the islands, comprising the distinctive Għar Dalam, Grey Skorba and Red Skorba phases. Basic subsistence farming involving periodic clearing of land.

4100–2500BC – Megalithic temple-building, creating what may now be the oldest free-standing stone structures in the world and the huge Ġgantija and Tarxien Temples. A peaceful period that ended suddenly.

2300–800BC – Bronze Age settlement of the islands in at least three waves. A time of increasing conflict, as evidenced in the later defensive settlements. Strange 'cart ruts' date from this period.

Classical Malta

800–480BC – Phoenician rule, which may not have been an actual conquest, but possibly involved using the islands as a trading base. (The 'Eye of Osiris', seen on fishing boats, dates from this time.) There was a little influence from the Greeks during this period.

480–218BC – Carthaginian rule, in which the islands were colonised and a number of temples were constructed. During the First Punic War of 262–242BC, the islands were in the front line.

218BC – Roman rule was established during the Second Punic War, although Carthaginian influences were still evident around the islands.

AD60 – St Paul's Shipwreck (Acts 28:1–10). Paul converted the island governor, Publius, and other inhabitants to Christianity.

AD395–870 – After the division of the Roman Empire, the islands became part of the Byzantine Empire. Around AD450–500 the Vandals and Goths from North Africa held sway, but Byzantine rule was re-established around AD533.

AD870–1090 – Arab conquest and rule. The language and most of the place-names around the islands date from this period. Efficient systems of water-management and new crops were introduced.

Medieval Malta

1091–1194 – Norman rule, or at least a notional conquest by Roger the Norman from Sicily, which had little effect on the Arabic culture of the islands. In fact, a further 'conquest' was needed in 1127. (Malta's red-and-white national flag is said to date from this time.)

1194–1265 – Swabian rule, during which Frederick II reorganised his kingdom and the islands were brought more under his influence. A majority of the population were Muslim, but were later expelled.

1265–1282 – Angevin rule, under which the islanders were poorly treated and heavily taxed. Resentment gave way to rebellion.

1282 – The 'Sicilian Vespers'. A rising against Angevin rule, during which Aragonese forces displaced the Angevin military garrison.

1283–1479 – Aragonese rule, during which period the Kings of Aragon granted the islands in fief to various noblemen, along with the power to raise taxes. The population largely resented this, and the islands were eventually brought under direct rule by the crown. A class of Maltese nobility formed in this period, and religious orders began to move to the islands and build churches.

1479–1530 – With the marriage of Ferdinand of Aragon and Isabella of Castille, the islands were in effect at the fringe of a new Spanish empire. Through the Spanish crown they passed to the Holy Roman Emperor, and through the Emperor to the Knights of St John.

Knights of St John in Malta

The Sovereign and Military Order of the Knights Hospitaller of St John of Jerusalem trace their origins back to the 11th century. They were displaced from Jerusalem and Rhodes before reaching Malta.

1530 – The Knights of St John were not happy to relocate to Malta, nor were the islanders keen to accept their presence. However, they settled on the islands and started repairing fortifications.

1551 – The Turkish corsair Dragut Reis invaded Gozo and took over 1000 islanders into slavery. Fort St Elmo was restructured.

1565 – The Great Siege. Dragut Reis sailed to Malta with 200 vessels and mounted a devastating series of attacks, culminating in a siege that almost broke the Knights of St John. Thousands of lives were lost on both sides, but the greater number was on the Turkish side, including Dragut Reis himself.

1566 – The fortified city of Valletta was founded, named after Grand Master Jean de la Vallette, heroic defender during the Great Siege.

1566–1798 – The Knights of St John spent vast amounts of money rebuilding and strengthening fortifications, as well as restructuring towns and villages, encouraging and developing trade, building churches and palaces, and generally improving infrastructure of the islands. A Turkish force landing in 1641 was quickly repulsed. A severe outbreak of the Plague in 1676 decimated the population. A massive earthquake in 1693 damaged many buildings. During this period, and despite occasional discontent, the islanders enjoyed prosperity, brought to a sudden end in the Napoleonic Wars.

1798–1800 – Napoleon Bonaparte invaded the islands while in transit to Egypt. The Knights of St John were expelled and Maltese nobility was suppressed. When church property was confiscated, the islanders rose in revolt and the French were held siege at Valletta.

1800 – French forces surrendered to the British, who agreed to protect the islands in the name of the King of Two Sicilies.

British rule in Malta

1800–1815 – Various European treaties were concluded, some involving Malta, as the Napoleonic Wars were brought to a close.

1815–1914 – A number of forms of government were tested, with varying degrees of control shared between the islanders and the British. There were periods of prosperity and periods of unrest, but overall the islanders came increasingly under British control. The opening of the Suez Canal in 1869 led to an increase in trade and shipping. In 1903, King Edward VII visited Malta.

1914–1918 – First World War. Although the islands were not at war, they became known as the 'Nurse of the Mediterranean' for their tending of the sick and injured. Immediately after the war, higher prices and higher taxes led to riots against the administration.

1921–1939 – Political parties were formed and parliamentary elections were held. Maltese were responsible for most local issues, while Britain retained responsibility primarily for defence and foreign affairs. During succeeding years the Constitution was variously suspended, restored and revised through years of political turmoil.

1940–1943 – The Second Great Siege. Under British rule, the islands were targeted by the Axis powers in the Second World War, leading to Italian and German bombing raids that were ranked among the worst in the world. In turn, British forces attempted to disrupt Axis supply lines around the Mediterranean and into North Africa. Thousands of military and civilian casualties ensued, along with massive damage to the urban areas and especially the dockyards. King George VI awarded the George Cross to the whole of Malta in recognition of the suffering and bravery of its people. (The George Cross is seen on the top left corner of Malta's flag.)

1943 – King George VI, Winston Churchill and Franklin Roosevelt visited Malta prior to the invasion of Sicily and surrender of Italy.

1945 – Winston Churchill and Franklin Roosevelt met in Malta on their way to take part in the Yalta Conference with Josef Stalin.

1947–1964 – Self-government was restored to Malta and politicians began discussing Malta's future relationship with Britain. Problems of unemployment led to significant emigration, and there were also strikes and social unrest. A referendum on integration with Britain was later followed by a referendum on independence. Britain's involvement with Malta has left the island with a fine command of the English language, red telephone kiosks and post boxes, driving on the left-hand side of the road and beer sold in pint glasses!

Maltese independence

1964 – Malta was granted independence as a sovereign nation in the British Commonwealth with Queen Elizabeth II as head of state.

1965 – Din l-Art Helwa founded to safeguard the natural, historical and cultural environment. Now also known as the National Trust for Malta.

1970 – Malta entered an Association agreement with the European Economic Community, but held back from full EEC membership.

1974 – Malta became a republic with a president as head of state.

1979 – British forces finally left their military bases on Malta.

1989 – USA and USSR met in Malta to formally end the Cold War. Government asked for full membership of the European Community.

1990 – Pope John Paul II visited Malta and some of its churches.

1992 – Queen Elizabeth II visited Malta during the 50th Anniversary of the award of the George Cross to the island.

2003 – A referendum to determine whether Malta should join the European Union was passed by a small majority.

2004 – Malta formally joined the European Union.

2005 – Ramblers Association of Malta established.

2008 – Malta adopted the Euro as its currency and withdrew Maltese Lira from circulation.

2011 – Old ex-British public transport buses withdrawn and replaced by fleets of new buses imported from China.

2015 – A referendum aimed at restricting the shooting of birds in springtime was narrowly defeated.

Looking back across the Għasri Valley to Ġordan and its lighthouse (Walk 32)

APPENDIX D

Topographical glossary

Most Maltese place-names date from the Arab conquest of the islands in the ninth century. As with place-names in many parts of the world, they are often descriptive of landscape features, so a basic understanding of some of the more common names is useful. The names of the islands themselves, however, derive from more ancient sources. 'Malta' comes from *Melita*; 'Gozo' from *Għawdex*; and 'Comino' from *Kemmuna*.

aħrax	rough
baħar	bay
bajja	bay
borġ	tower
casa	house
daħla	creek
ġebel	hill/headland
għajn	fountain/spring
għar	cave
ġnien	garden/orchard
ħal	village
ħarrub	carob tree
kbir	big
knisja	church
kortin	court
Kunċizzjoni	Conception
Lunzjata	Annunciation
marsa	harbour
mdina	citadel
misraħ	square
mitħna	mill
palma	palm
pjazza	square
plajja	beach
pont	bridge
ponta	point
port	port
Prajjet	Anchor Bay
qortin	promontory
rabat	town outside city wall
ramla	sandy bay
ras	point
rdum	cliff
san/sant'/santa/ santu	saint
skola	school
sqaq	alley
telgħa	hill
torri	tower/castle
triq	street
wied	valley
xagħra	plateau
xatt	wharf
żebbuġ	olive
żnuber	pine

DOWNLOAD THE ROUTE IN GPX FORMAT

All the routes in this guide are available for download from:

www.cicerone.co.uk/822/GPX

as GPX files. You should be able to load them into most formats of mobile device, whether GPS or smartphone.

When you go to this link, you will be asked for your email address and where you purchased the guide, and have the option to subscribe to the Cicerone e-newsletter.

www.cicerone.co.uk

NOTES

LISTING OF CICERONE GUIDES

BRITISH ISLES CHALLENGES, COLLECTIONS AND ACTIVITIES

The Book of the Bivvy
The Book of the Bothy
The End to End Trail
The Mountains of England and Wales: 1&2
The National Trails
The Relative Hills of Britain
The Ridges of England, Wales and Ireland
The UK Trailwalker's Handbook
The UK's County Tops
Three Peaks, Ten Tors

UK CYCLING

20 Classic Sportive Rides
South West England
South East England
Border Country Cycle Routes
Cycling in the Cotswolds
Cycling in the Hebrides
Cycling in the Peak District
Cycling in the Yorkshire Dales
Cycling the Pennine Bridleway
Mountain Biking in the Lake District
Mountain Biking in the Yorkshire Dales
Mountain Biking on the North Downs
Mountain Biking on the South Downs
The C2C Cycle Route
The End to End Cycle Route
The Lancashire Cycleway

UK BACKPACKING

Backpacker's Britain
Northern Scotland

SCOTLAND

Ben Nevis and Glen Coe
Great Mountain Days in Scotland
Not the West Highland Way
Scotland's Best Small Mountains
Scotland's Far West
Scotland's Mountain Ridges
Scrambles in Lochaber
The Ayrshire and Arran Coastal Paths
The Border Country
The Cape Wrath Trail
The Great Glen Way
The Hebrides
The Isle of Mull
The Isle of Skye
The Pentland Hills
The Skye Trail
The Southern Upland Way
The Speyside Way
The West Highland Way
Walking Highland Perthshire
Walking in Scotland's Far North
Walking in the Angus Glens
Walking in the Cairngorms
Walking in the Ochils, Campsie Fells and Lomond Hills
Walking in the Southern Uplands
Walking in Torridon
Walking Loch Lomond and the Trossachs
Walking on Arran
Walking on Harris and Lewis
Walking on Jura, Islay and Colonsay
Walking on Rum and the Small Isles
Walking on the Orkney and Shetland Isles
Walking on Uist and Barra
Walking the Corbetts
1 South of the Great Glen
2 North of the Great Glen
Walking the Galloway Hills
Walking the Munros
1 Southern, Central and Western Highlands
2 Northern Highlands and the Cairngorms
Winter Climbs Ben Nevis and Glen Coe
Winter Climbs in the Cairngorms
World Mountain Ranges: Scotland

NORTHERN ENGLAND TRAILS

A Northern Coast to Coast Walk
Hadrian's Wall Path
The Dales Way
The Pennine Way

NORTH EAST ENGLAND, YORKSHIRE DALES AND PENNINES

Great Mountain Days in the Pennines
Historic Walks in North Yorkshire
South Pennine Walks
St Oswald's Way and St Cuthbert's Way
The North York Moors
The Reivers Way
The Teesdale Way
The Yorkshire Dales
North and East
South and West
Walking in County Durham
Walking in Northumberland
Walking in the North Pennines
Walks in Dales Country
Walks in the Yorkshire Dales

NORTH WEST ENGLAND AND THE ISLE OF MAN

Historic Walks in Cheshire
Isle of Man Coastal Path
The Lune Valley and Howgills
The Ribble Way
Walking in Cumbria's Eden Valley
Walking in Lancashire
Walking in the Forest of Bowland and Pendle
Walking on the Isle of Man
Walking on the West Pennine Moors
Walks in Lancashire Witch Country
Walks in Ribble Country
Walks in Silverdale and Arnside
Walks in the Forest of Bowland

LAKE DISTRICT

Great Mountain Days in the Lake District
Lake District Winter Climbs
Lake District: High Level and Fell Walks
Lake District: Low Level and Lake Walks
Lakeland Fellranger
The Central Fells
The Far-Eastern Fells
The Mid-Western Fells
The Near Eastern Fells
The Northern Fells
The North-Western Fells
The Southern Fells
The Western Fells
Rocky Rambler's Wild Walks

Scrambles in the Lake District
North & South
Short Walks in Lakeland
1 South Lakeland
2 North Lakeland
3 West Lakeland
The Cumbria Way

DERBYSHIRE, PEAK DISTRICT AND MIDLANDS

High Peak Walks
Scrambles in the Dark Peak
The Star Family Walks
Walking in Derbyshire
White Peak Walks
The Northern Dales
The Southern Dales

SOUTHERN ENGLAND

Suffolk Coast & Heaths Walks
The Cotswold Way
The Great Stones Way
The Lea Valley Walk
The North Downs Way
The Peddars Way and Norfolk Coast Path
The Ridgeway National Trail
The South Downs Way
The South West Coast Path
The Thames Path
The Two Moors Way
Walking in Cornwall
Walking in Essex
Walking in Kent
Walking in Norfolk
Walking in Sussex
Walking in the Chilterns
Walking in the Cotswolds
Walking in the Isles of Scilly
Walking in the New Forest
Walking in the North Wessex Downs
Walking in the Thames Valley
Walking on Dartmoor
Walking on Guernsey
Walking on Jersey
Walking on the Isle of Wight
Walking the Jurassic Coast
Walks in the South Downs National Park

WALES AND WELSH BORDERS

Glyndwr's Way
Great Mountain Days in Snowdonia
Hillwalking in Snowdonia
Hillwalking in Wales: 1&2
Offa's Dyke Path
Ridges of Snowdonia
Scrambles in Snowdonia
The Ascent of Snowdon
The Ceredigion and Snowdonia Coast Paths
Lleyn Peninsula Coastal Path
Pembrokeshire Coastal Path
The Severn Way
The Shropshire Hills
The Wales Coast Path
The Wye Valley Walk
Walking in Carmarthenshire
Walking in Pembrokeshire
Walking in the Forest of Dean
Walking in the South Wales Valleys
Walking in the Wye Valley
Walking on the Brecon Beacons
Walking on the Gower
Welsh Winter Climbs

INTERNATIONAL CHALLENGES, COLLECTIONS AND ACTIVITIES

Canyoning in the Alps
Europe's High Points
The Via Francigena: 1&2

EUROPEAN CYCLING

Cycle Touring in France
Cycle Touring in Ireland
Cycle Touring in Spain
Cycle Touring in Switzerland
Cycling in the French Alps
Cycling the Canal du Midi
Cycling the River Loire
The Danube Cycleway: 1&2
The Grand Traverse of the Massif Central
The Moselle Cycle Route
The Rhine Cycle Route
The Way of St James

AFRICA

Climbing in the Moroccan Anti-Atlas
Kilimanjaro
Mountaineering in the Moroccan High Atlas
The High Atlas
Trekking in the Atlas Mountains
Walking in the Drakensberg

ALPS – CROSS-BORDER ROUTES

100 Hut Walks in the Alps
Across the Eastern Alps: E5
Alpine Points of View
Alpine Ski Mountaineering
1 Western Alps
2 Central and Eastern Alps
Chamonix to Zermatt
The Tour of the Bernina
Tour of Mont Blanc
Tour of Monte Rosa
Tour of the Matterhorn
Trail Running – Chamonix and the Mont Blanc region
Trekking in the Alps
Trekking in the Silvretta and Rätikon Alps
Walking in the Alps
Walks and Treks in the Maritime Alps

PYRENEES AND FRANCE/SPAIN CROSS-BORDER ROUTES

The GR10 Trail
The GR11 Trail – La Senda
The Mountains of Andorra
The Pyrenean Haute Route
The Pyrenees
The Way of St James: France & Spain
Walks and Climbs in the Pyrenees

AUSTRIA

The Adlerweg
Trekking in Austria's Hohe Tauern
Trekking in the Stubai Alps
Trekking in the Zillertal Alps
Walking in Austria

BELGIUM AND LUXEMBOURG

Walking in the Ardennes

EASTERN EUROPE

The High Tatras
The Mountains of Romania
Walking in Bulgaria's National Parks
Walking in Hungary

FRANCE

Chamonix Mountain Adventures
Ecrins National Park
Mont Blanc Walks
Mountain Adventures in the Maurienne
The Cathar Way
The GR20 Corsica
The GR5 Trail
The Robert Louis Stevenson Trail
Tour of the Oisans: The GR54
Tour of the Queyras

Tour of the Vanoise
Vanoise Ski Touring
Via Ferratas of the French Alps
Walking in Corsica
Walking in Provence – East
Walking in Provence – West
Walking in the Auvergne
Walking in the Cevennes
Walking in the Dordogne
Walking in the Haute Savoie – North & South
Walks in the Cathar Region

GERMANY

Hiking and Biking in the Black Forest
Walking in the Bavarian Alps

HIMALAYA

Annapurna
Bhutan
Everest
The Mount Kailash Trek
Trekking in Ladakh
Trekking in the Himalaya

ICELAND & GREENLAND

Trekking in Greenland
Walking and Trekking in Iceland

IRELAND

The Irish Coast to Coast Walk
The Mountains of Ireland

ITALY

Gran Paradiso
Sibillini National Park
Shorter Walks in the Dolomites
The Way of St Francis
Through the Italian Alps
Trekking in the Apennines
Trekking in the Dolomites
Via Ferratas of the Italian Dolomites: 1&2
Walking in Abruzzo
Walking in Italy's Stelvio National Park
Walking in Sardinia
Walking in Sicily
Walking in the Central Italian Alps
Walking in the Dolomites
Walking in Tuscany
Walking in Umbria
Walking on the Amalfi Coast
Walking the Italian Lakes

MEDITERRANEAN

Jordan – Walks, Treks, Caves, Climbs and Canyons
The High Mountains of Crete
The Mountains of Greece
Treks and Climbs in Wadi Rum
Walking and Trekking on Corfu
Walking on Malta
Western Crete

NORTH AMERICA

British Columbia
The Grand Canyon
The John Muir Trail
The Pacific Crest Trail

SOUTH AMERICA

Aconcagua and the Southern Andes
Hiking and Biking Peru's Inca Trails
Torres del Paine

SCANDINAVIA

Walking in Norway

SLOVENIA, CROATIA AND MONTENEGRO

The Islands of Croatia
The Julian Alps of Slovenia
The Mountains of Montenegro
Trekking in Slovenia
Walking in Slovenia: The Karavanke

SPAIN AND PORTUGAL

Mountain Walking in Southern Catalunya
Spain's Sendero Histórico: The GR1
The Mountains of Nerja
The Northern Caminos
Trekking through Mallorca
Walking in Andalucia
Walking in Madeira
Walking in Mallorca
Walking in Menorca
Walking in the Algarve
Walking in the Cordillera Cantabrica
Walking in the Sierra Nevada
Walking on Gran Canaria
Walking on La Gomera and El Hierro
Walking on La Palma
Walking on Lanzarote and Fuerteventura
Walking on Tenerife
Walking in Costa Blanca
Walking the GR7 in Andalucia
Walks and Climbs in the Picos de Europa

SWITZERLAND

Alpine Pass Route
The Swiss Alps
Tour of the Jungfrau Region
Walking in the Bernese Oberland
Walking in the Valais
Walks in the Engadine

TECHNIQUES

Geocaching in the UK
Indoor Climbing
Lightweight Camping
Map and Compass
Mountain Weather
Outdoor Photography
Polar Exploration
Rock Climbing
Sport Climbing
The Hillwalker's Manual

MINI GUIDES

Alpine Flowers
Avalanche!
Navigating with a GPS
Navigation
Pocket First Aid and Wilderness Medicine
Snow

MOUNTAIN LITERATURE

8000 metres
A Walk in the Clouds
Abode of the Gods
Unjustifiable Risk?

For full information on all our guides, books and eBooks, visit our website: **www.cicerone.co.uk**.

Walking – Trekking – Mountaineering – Climbing – Cycling

Over 40 years, Cicerone have built up an outstanding collection of over 300 guides, inspiring all sorts of amazing adventures.

Every guide comes from extensive exploration and research by our expert authors, all with a passion for their subjects. They are frequently praised, endorsed and used by clubs, instructors and outdoor organisations.

All our titles can now be bought as **e-books**, **ePubs** and **Kindle** files and we also have an online magazine – **Cicerone Extra** – with features to help cyclists, climbers, walkers and trekkers choose their next adventure, at home or abroad.

Our website shows any **new information** we've had in since a book was published. Please do let us know if you find anything has changed, so that we can publish the latest details. On our **website** you'll also find great ideas and lots of detailed information about what's inside every guide and you can buy **individual routes** from many of them online.

twitter

It's easy to keep in touch with what's going on at Cicerone by getting our monthly **free e-newsletter**, which is full of offers, competitions, up-to-date information and topical articles. You can subscribe on our home page and also follow us on **Facebook** and **Twitter** or dip into our **blog**.

Cicerone – the very best guides for exploring the world.

CICERONE

2 Police Square Milnthorpe Cumbria LA7 7PY

Tel: 015395 62069 info@cicerone.co.uk

www.cicerone.co.uk and **www.cicerone-extra.com**